Better Homes and Gardens®

AMERICAN PATCHWORK & QUILTING

BETTER HOMES AND GARDENS® BOOKS

Editor: Gerald M. Knox
Art Director: Ernest Shelton
Managing Editor: David A. Kirchner
Copy and Production Editors: Marsha Jahns, Mary Helen Schiltz, Carl Voss,
    David A. Walsh

Crafts Editor: Nancy Lindemeyer
Senior Crafts Books Editor: Joan Cravens
Associate Crafts Books Editors: Laura Holtorf Collins, Sara Jane Treinen

Associate Art Directors: Linda Ford Vermie, Neoma Alt West, Randall Yontz
Assistant Art Directors: Lynda Haupert, Harijs Priekulis, Tom Wegner
Senior Graphic Designers: Alisann Dixon, Lyne Neymeyer
Graphic Designers: Mike Burns, Sally Cooper, Mike Eagleton, Deb Miner,
    Stan Sams, Darla Whipple-Frain

Vice President, Editorial Director: Doris Eby
Executive Director, Editorial Services: Duane Gregg

Senior Vice President, General Manager: Fred Stines
Director of Publishing: Robert B. Nelson
Vice President, Retail Marketing: Jamie Martin
Vice President, Direct Marketing: Arthur Heydendael

American Patchwork and Quilting
Contributing Editor: Ciba Vaughan
Crafts Editors: Nancy Lindemeyer, Joan Cravens, Laura Holtorf Collins,
    Rebecca Jerdee
Copy and Production Editor: Marsha Jahns
Graphic Designer: Deb Miner
Electronic Text Processor: Cindy McClanahan

Cover project: See page 142.

The lively art
of patchwork has had a unique claim
upon our national affections since
the first settlers arrived on American
shores, eager to piece together
a new life for themselves from the
resources close at hand. And
American patchwork design is as rich
and varied—as interesting and
imaginative—as the people who've
practiced this craft from colonial
times to the present. In AMERICAN
PATCHWORK AND QUILTING
you will be introduced to the best in
traditional patchwork and quilting and
invited to explore many
of the new designs and innovative
techniques that have helped to
keep this time-honored craft a vital
part of the American folk art tradition.

CONTENTS

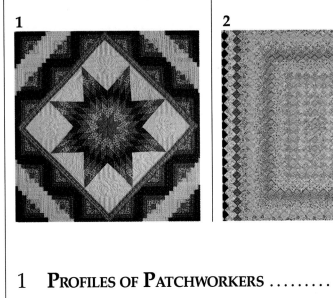

1

2

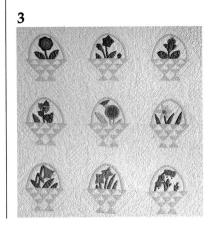

3

7

8

9

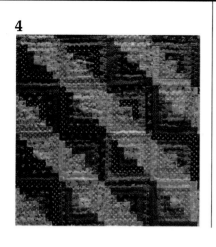

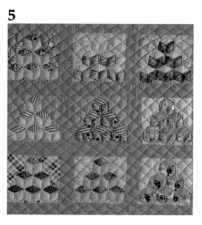

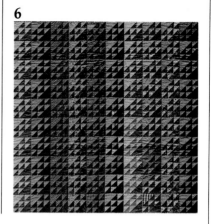

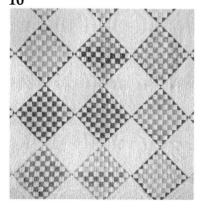

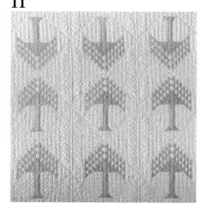

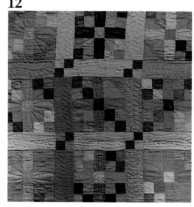

PROFILES
OF PATCHWORKERS

Young and old,
solitary and sociable, trained
artists and self-taught stitchers,
patchwork enthusiasts are a
wonderfully varied lot. For many,
patchwork is a pleasurable
pastime. For a few, cutting and
piecing is a full-time commitment.
On the following pages you'll meet
a sampling of the experts—several
traditionalists and an innovator or
two—who help to keep this
uniquely American needlecraft
alive and flourishing.

PROFILES
OF PATCHWORKERS

Piecework, appliqué, and fine
hand quilting are part of the
stitchery heritage of many lands,
and have flourished separately and
in combination with other textile
arts during every period of history.
Yet the craft of patchwork, with
its traditional emphasis on thrifty
use of fabrics and improvisational
design, remains a distinctly
American folk art that has attracted
enthusiastic practitioners in a
steady stream from colonial days
to the present. Though patchwork
has never been the exclusive
province of women (Presidents
Coolidge and Eisenhower pieced
quilts as boys), the ladies on
the following pages are representative
of patchwork artists today.

"I guess you could say that I'm a fifth generation quilter," says Carolee Knutson of Ames, Iowa. "I didn't actually start quilting myself until about 12 years ago," she confesses. "But I always thought everybody's grandmother made quilts!"

Carolee has since learned that quilting skills are not quite as universal as she once imagined, and that her expertise is in constant demand. Pictured here (standing) with "Gary's Rocking Horse," an appliquéd quilt she designed and stitched for a favorite nephew, Carolee is always ready to share piecing and quilting tips with an interested novice. (For instructions for the quilt, see page 266.)

As with the majority of patchwork enthusiasts today, most of Carolee's stitching and piecing is strictly for family and friends—to beautify her home, celebrate a birth, mark an occasion, or remember a special friend.

A traditionalist at heart, Carolee nevertheless has a knack for invention that is the hallmark of a true patchwork artist. Pictured on pages 6-7 is one of her most spectacular creations, a gift for her son's twenty-first birthday. Called "Randy's Freedom Quilt," it is an imaginative blend of the Blazing Star and Log Cabin patterns, pieced and quilted with exquisite attention to the finer points of design and technique. (For instructions, see page 160.)

Carolee proudly points out that the custom of Freedom Quilts dates to pioneer days, when a young man traditionally received a quilt to mark his coming of age. The quilt usually was pieced and stitched by the single young women among his friends and family, much like the Friendship Quilt or Bride's Quilt presented to a young woman upon her engagement or betrothal.

For Carolee Knutson, planning, cutting, and piecing a patchwork quilt is simply one more way to bring color and comfort into her home and into the lives of the people she loves.

NELLY'S NEEDLERS

A talented and energetic band of volunteer stitchers works together to maintain Virginia's handsome Woodlawn Plantation as a thriving center for the study of needlework.

In 1799, George Washington presented this gracious Georgian-style mansion to his adopted daughter, Nelly Custis Lewis, as a wedding gift. Today, it is part of the National Trust for Historic Preservation.

A talented stitchery designer, Nelly made her interest in needlework an important part of Woodlawn. And her "Needlers" have followed suit. In order to raise money for the preservation of Woodlawn, groups of Needlers re-create stitchery treasures from the Woodlawn collection to be sold at auction each year.

Opposite and *above right,* members of the quilting committee add the final touches to a copy of an Old Maid's Patience Quilt. Great care is taken to match fabrics as closely as possible to the original piece. Like a traditional quilting bee, this is happy work—a time for visiting with friends who share the goal of a thriving Woodlawn.

Below right, the Needlers conduct a workshop for children. The workshops are given each August in a continuing effort to transmit Nelly's love of stitchery to today's youngsters.

To make the quilt, see page 160.

Donna Barnett

A graduate of the Pennsylvania College of Art, fiber artist Donna Barnett often weaves and dyes her own fabrics to get just the right shade for her one-of-a-kind quilts and wall hangings.

The brilliant mix of colors and strong graphic qualities of Donna's designs bear a sure kinship with the Amish quilts of her Lancaster County neighbors. But the special blend of color and pattern that emerges on any piece she stitches is uniquely Donna's own.

Mixing purchased and hand-dyed fabrics with a true colorist's eye, Donna creates spectacular patterns like the Log Cabin wall hanging pictured in the detail photograph, *above left.* To the right, a similar piece seems to glow like a jewel framed against the white wall of the loft above Donna's studio.

Since her home also serves as an informal gallery for her work, Donna's quilts, wall hangings, and other fiber creations are very much in evidence throughout the house. All these elements blend beautifully with the simple country furnishings and folk art objects Donna favors. When she's hard at work, even stacks of fabric and works-in-progress are kept out in the open and cheerfully treated as part of the decor, rather than as something untidy to be tucked away when company comes.

Instructions for the Log Cabin wall hanging are on page 59.

ARLETTE GOSIESKI

Using fabric and thread as a painter uses canvas and oils, this Colorado artist creates patchwork pictures that charm folk art and fine art collectors alike.

Although she trained as a painter, Arlette soon discovered that working in fabric brought some unique satisfactions. "After studying in France and living abroad for many years, I returned home with a new interest in my own country's history and culture," says Arlette. Her fabric paintings depict rural America and the simple pleasures of a by-gone era, drawing inspiration from the work of such grass roots American artists as Grant Wood, Edward Hopper, Grandma Moses, and Currier and Ives.

For insight into the past, Arlette does historical research on costumes and furnishings before beginning a design.

To start work on "Coffeetime," shown here, Arlette first developed a drawing to use as a master pattern. She then snipped pattern pieces from appropriate fabrics, cutting each shape freehand while referring to her sketch, *above*.

Much of the artistry of Arlette's designs lies in her creative use of fabrics and trims. She explains that the grain, texture, and weight of fabric are often as important to the success of a composition as the color of the fabric or the scale

of the pattern. Note Arlette's use of rough wool tweed for the stove doors, a scrap of flowered print for the needlepoint picture, and a porcelain blue print for the spatterware coffeepot.

Once each of the pieces is positioned to her satisfaction, Arlette pins, bastes, and machine-stitches the shapes in place. To complete the picture, the artist embroiders the facial features by hand and adds beads and bits of lace trim for color and texture. (Instructions for "Coffeetime" appear on page 265.)

15

The daughter of an accomplished seamstress, Arlette's interest in fabrics is something of a family tradition. Her maternal grandmother was a seamstress for the Russian aristocracy, and her paternal grandmother, a talented weaver, spun and dyed her own yarns.

True to this heritage, Arlette takes special delight in sharing her interest in the fiber arts with daughters Keelie, *above* with Arlette, and Ellaan.

Arlette's vision of turn-of-the-century America, and her unique ability to communicate that vision in her work, has led to wide demand for her fabric art. Frequently exhibited in galleries across the country, her appliquéd pictures have appeared also as illustrations for stories and articles in national magazines.

Her delightful rendition of an old-fashioned skating party, *opposite,* was commissioned as a cover for *Better Homes and Gardens*® magazine (see inset). The suggestion of

period clothing and accessories, including the curved blades on the skates, is typical of the artist's concern for authentic detail.

Arlette often refers to her paintings as "architecture in fabric." Nowhere is this description more apt than in the meticulously rendered Victorian interior reproduced in her enchanting version of "Grandma's Parlor," *above.* Here in a single picture is a catalog of Victoriana—patterned walls and carpets, overstuffed chairs, sentimental paintings on the walls, dainty antimacassars, family portraits, clusters of knickknacks, and oversize plants—all faithfully captured in fabric.

In less certain hands, all this detail might have been overwhelming. But with Arlette's sure sense of design, it merely provides a cozy setting for the eye of calm in the "storm"—Grandma and her grandchildren snuggled on the settee at the center of the picture.

For tips on creating your own fabric paintings, see the appliquéd portraits and pictures and accompanying instructions beginning on page 252.

CAROL MAGUIRE

Like many of the designers whose work appears in this volume, Carol Maguire came to patchwork with a background in fine arts, but her approach to the subject is uniquely her own.

Growing up in a close-knit Pennsylvania family in which arts and crafts of all kinds were highly prized and energetically practiced, Carol came by her eclectic interests quite naturally. Her father is a talented amateur woodworker, and her mother excels at the needle arts. Carol's training as a painter adds another dimension to the family's pool of talents.

Perhaps because of this early and constant exposure to the arts, both fine and familiar, Carol loves to explore new techniques, to stretch herself both technically and artistically. One result of this willingness to experiment is the technique she's evolved for the quilted patchwork paintings pictured here.

Although she developed the technique as a way to make interesting decorative accents for her own home, Carol now stitches many of her quilted pictures into pillows, totes, quilts, and wall hangings for sale in galleries and boutiques. A sampling of her work appears in the photographs, *opposite* and *below.*

Experimenting with oversize quilting stitches to outline and accent the shapes on her fabric paintings soon led to an interest in more traditional quilt designs. Eventually, Carol decided to try her hand at pieced patchwork.

To this mixing and matching of fabrics, Carol brings the same extraordinary sensitivity to color and pattern that makes her paintings so appealing. One of her favorite patchwork creations—a small quilt stitched for daughter Amanda—is displayed on the rocking chair, *below* (and again on page 99), along with a painted and quilted still-life pillow. Another favorite, combining piecework and appliqué worked in unusual fabrics, is the bedcover shown on page 198.

Opposite, Carol takes a break from working on a painted patchwork wall hanging for a snapshot portrait with Mandy, who's fast developing a passion for color and pattern that rivals her mother's.

For more on Carol's paint-and-quilt patchwork technique, please turn the page.

Tended by a benevolent trio of stitched and stuffed guardian angel dolls, Carol often turns her sunny dining room into a temporary studio when working on a new design *(opposite, above).*

Techniques for creating paint-and-quilt patchwork like Carol's are easy to master. Begin by developing a color sketch of the design and making a master pattern, just as you would if the design were appliquéd. This approach works best if the design has clearly defined patches of color and pattern, as in the pictures, *right.* (Instructions for the design at the top are on page 267.)

Using dressmaker's carbon and a tracing wheel, or an erasable pen, transfer the design to prewashed, unbleached muslin.

For coloring, use full-strength textile paints. Colors can be mixed with each other or lightened with a small amount of clear textile paint medium, if desired. Thinning paints with water might cause colors to run beyond the outlines of the design.

Practice painting on a scrap of fabric to determine how close to pattern lines you can paint without colors bleeding into each other. Paint *up to but not over* pattern lines, and do not put too much paint on the brush at one time.

Allow each color to dry before moving on to the next one. To avoid muddying the colors, clean and dry brushes thoroughly between each use. When all painting is finished and the fabric is completely dry, press the design on the wrong side to set the paint.

To quilt a painted patchwork picture, layer and baste batting and backing fabric to the wrong side of the painted design. Then, using black pearl cotton thread, quilt along the edges of all painted areas with coarse running stitches, following the pattern outline.

To hang, mount the completed picture on artist's stretcher strips, or hem and add a muslin casing along the top edge and suspend the picture from a dowel or curtain rod.

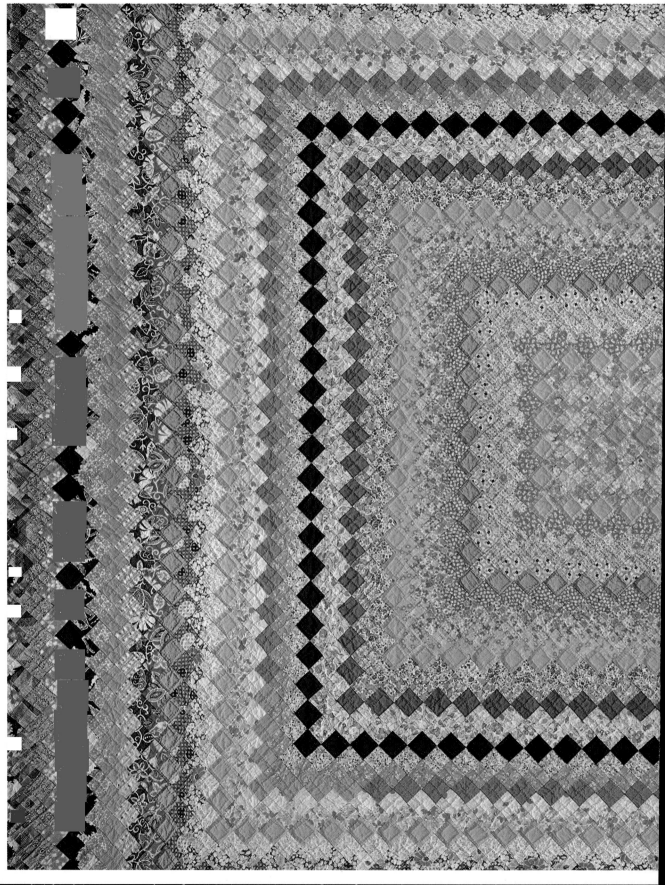

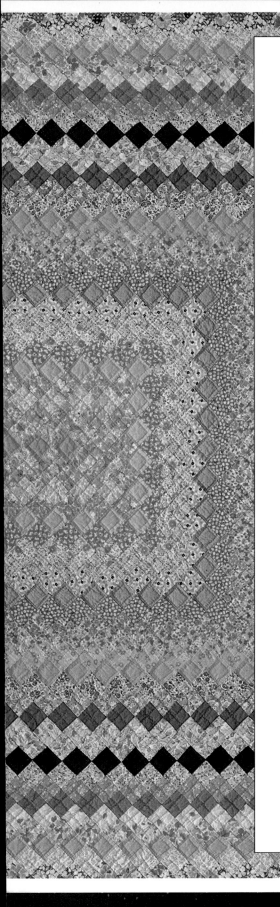

LEARNING TO PIECE WITH SQUARES AND RECTANGLES

Happily
for the novice stitcher, most patchwork patterns are based on the
simplest of shapes: easy-to-handle
squares and rectangles. Master the
elementary cutting and piecing
techniques in this chapter and
you're well on your way to becom-
ing a patchwork pro.

STITCHING ONE-PATCH PLACE MATS

As the basic building block for hundreds of different patterns, the humble square is remarkably versatile yet reassuringly easy to cut and piece.

Because the most intricately pieced or appliquéd patchwork designs usually are based on repetition of square pattern blocks, learning to handle this simple shape is a logical first step toward mastering the art of patchwork.

Because the shape and size of the pattern piece is uniform, one-patch patterns depend upon accurate piecing and skillful use of color for their success. The multicolored squares, laid out in diagonal strips for the place mats, *above,* and for the one-patch quilt on pages 22-23, could have been arranged in many ways, but the basic method of construction remains the same: The squares are stitched into horizontal rows, and the rows are then joined together to complete the pattern.

Absolute precision in measuring, marking, cutting, and piecing is crucial to the success of any pieced project. Use small projects like these one-patch place mats as an opportunity to practice and perfect those skills.

Before you begin cutting and stitching this or any other patchwork project, be sure that all of your cotton and cotton-blend fabrics have been prewashed, preshrunk, and carefully pressed.

1

2

3

4

5

6

❖

1 To ensure that each fabric square used for the project will be exactly the same size, carefully measure and cut square pattern templates from cardboard or plastic lids. Beginning patchworkers will find it helpful to work with *two* templates, as shown: one sized to include ¼-inch seam allowances for marking cutting lines, and a second cut to finished block size for marking stitching lines.

2 Trace squares onto the *wrong* side of each fabric, using the larger (cutting-line) template. Use either a very sharp No. 2 (soft) pencil, a water-erasable pen, or a white wax pencil (good for marking dark fabrics).

Next, center and trace the smaller (stitching-line) template within each large square. Using very sharp scissors, cut out the squares exactly along the cutting lines, and stack and thread all squares of any given fabric on a knotted strand of thread for convenient storage and easy retrieval.

3 To piece one mat top, first stitch eight different squares together horizontally, carefully matching *stitching* lines (*not* the cut edges of fabric squares). Arrange squares as shown on the place mat pictured *opposite,* or create your own design.

Insert pins so they are perpendicular to seam lines, and machine- or hand-stitch the squares together. (Hand stitching allows for more control, but machine stitching is faster.)

Press the seams between each square to one side. Always press toward the darker fabric (refer to the photograph).

4 Complete six rows of eight squares each for each place mat. Stitch the six rows of squares together along long edges, again taking special care to match the stitching lines to ensure accurate piecing. Seams between squares should match perfectly where they meet between rows. Press seams all in one direction, either up or down.

5 To complete the mat, cut batting and backing to size and pin all three layers together.

6 Quilt diagonally across each row of squares and bind raw edges of the mat with purchased bias binding. (See Chapter 10, "Quilting and Finishing Your Patchwork Projects," for additional information.)

PIECING
A FOUR-PATCH
PROJECT

**As these four-patch
projects prove, it's
possible to create
delightfully complex
patterns using just a few
design elements.**

Though simple one-patch patterns are based on patches of a single size and shape, and depend entirely upon choice of fabrics and arrangement of colors for their interest, four-patch patterns introduce an additional design consideration: the possible relationships between pattern pieces of the same shape, but different *sizes*—large and small squares.

The patterns used for the tablecloth and companion chair seats, *above,* are the most elementary variations of the four-patch principle. But pieced as they are in contemporary fabrics, rather than in the more common calicoes, these traditional patterns suddenly seem quite sophisticated.

LEARNING TO PIECE WITH SQUARES AND RECTANGLES

1

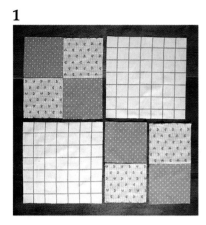

2

3

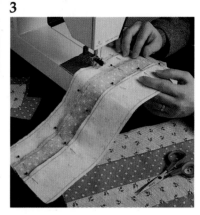

4

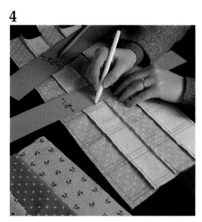

5

6

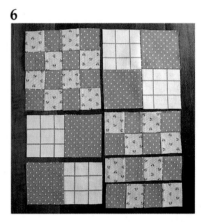

❖

1 The basic structure of the four-patch tablecloth pattern will be apparent from the piecing scheme for a single block pictured here.

First, two small squares of each of two different fabrics are pieced into a single four-patch square.

Next, two of these pieced squares are assembled together with two large squares of a third print fabric to form a larger four-patch square—the basic building block for the tablecloth pattern.

A close study of photograph 6, *above,* shows that the 16-patch variation of the four-patch pattern used for the chair seats is only slightly more complex. It can be pieced in basically the same way: Assemble smaller squares into sets of four, piece these four-patch squares into a 16-patch square, and then sew two 16-patch and two 4-patch squares together to form a complete block.

Hand-piecing four-patch patterns is time-consuming. Fortunately, machine-stitching and strip-piecing techniques can cut assembly time for these and other multiple-patch patterns in half, without sacrificing accuracy or precision.

2 For this method of machine piecing, carefully measure and cut strips of cardboard for use as the pattern templates, rather than the usual squares. Templates should be as wide as the squares are required to be and as long as the fabric width.

Measure and mark cutting and stitching lines, as shown, and cut long strips of each of the two fabrics to be pieced together.

3 For the four-patch blocks, sew one light and one dark strip together lengthwise. For 16-patch

squares, pin and stitch four long strips of fabric together, alternating light and dark strips, as shown in the photograph. Remove the pins and press all the seams in one direction.

4 Next, lay out seamed strips wrong side up. Place the template so it's perpendicular across the seamed strips and mark the next set of cutting and stitching lines.

5 Cut at right angles across the pieced strips, and then pin four of the newly cut strips together again, right sides facing. Reverse every other strip so that alternating squares of fabric meet to form a checkerboard pattern. Make sure the corners meet precisely. Stitch strips together and press all of the seams in one direction.

6 Pictured here is the assembly scheme for one complete block of the four-patch pattern used for the chair seats.

Each of the multiple-patch projects shown here can be assembled using a modified version of the strip-piecing techniques detailed earlier in this chapter.

Patchwork blocks composed of an *odd* number of squares (such as those in the nine-patch wall hanging, *opposite,* or slipcover, *above,* and the 25-patch quilt, *opposite*) have a different visual rhythm than those composed of an *even* number of squares (like the four-patch patterns on the preceding pages). But both types of block patterns are pieced in essentially the same way.

Above the bed, *opposite,* hangs a nine-patch coverlet composed of blocks containing four light- and five dark-colored squares. Occasionally, colors are repeated in more than one block, but rarely in the same combinations. For a multicolored design such as this, in which each block is virtually one of a kind, blocks must be pieced individually.

On the other hand, a nine-patch design in which the same two colors are repeated for each block (such as the slipcover on the boudoir chair, *above*) can be stitched in next to no time, using a variation of the machine strip-piecing method.

For a similar design, you'll need to create two different sets of strips to assemble one series of nine-patch blocks. First, cut three

long, 2½-inch-wide strips of mauve fabric and three matching strips of blue. Stitch these strips together lengthwise as follows: Join one blue strip between two mauve strips (A) and set aside. Then join one mauve strip between two blue strips (B).

Next, cut each of these pieced strips crosswise into 2½-inch-wide strips. Stitch one strip of pattern A between two strips of pattern B to compose each nine-patch block. Pieced nine-patch blocks are then stitched together with solid blue squares to create the patchwork slipcover fabric.

Similarly, an overall repeat pattern such as the 25-patch quilt on the bed, *opposite,* is an ideal candidate for the strip-piecing technique. Again, you will need to piece two different sets of strips— one of three red and two blue strips, and a second of two red and three blue strips—to create the alternate rows of the pattern block.

For specific how-to instructions for the nine-patch slipcover fabric and the 25-patch quilt, see the how-to instructions.

Visually striking, yet delightfully easy to piece, the Sunshine and Shadow quilts pictured here are both elegant variations of the one-patch theme.

Often called Trip Around the World by quilters in other parts of the country, this lovely design has always been known as Sunshine and Shadow among the Pennsylvania Amish, with whom it has been very popular for more than a century.

Sharp pastel colors and tiny prints used for the large square quilt, *opposite,* are typical of Trip designs pieced in the 1930s. The somber hues and solid fabrics used for the rectangular crib quilt, *above,* are more characteristic of the traditional Amish palette.

In both quilts pictured here, squares are pieced on the diagonal to create a diamond effect. For another version of the design, please turn the page.

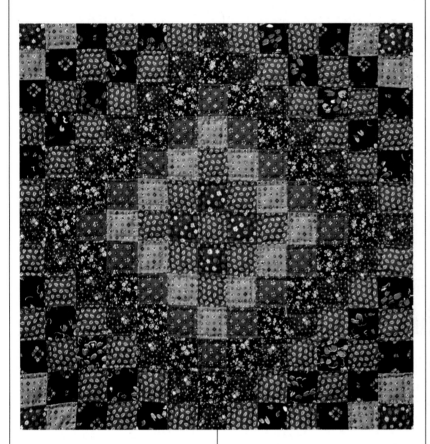

As pictured in the detail above, each 169-patch block of this handsome quilt is actually a miniature version of the traditional Sunshine and Shadow pattern.

Unlike the diagonally pieced designs on the preceding pages, each block of this king-size quilt is pieced so the squares are parallel to the edges of the quilt.

Each block is pieced in horizontal rows, following a graph pattern. Then, in a piecing *tour de force,* completed blocks are pieced together so the edges and corners appear to form a secondary design of entirely different pattern blocks.

Individual pattern blocks, like a full Sunshine and Shadow Quilt, may be made any size you choose. But to achieve the single central square characteristic of this pattern, plan for an uneven number of squares arranged in an uneven number of rows—in this case, 13 rows of 13 squares each for each of the blocks.

The rectangle is another straight-edge figure with almost limitless pattern possibilities, particularly in combination with other shapes. Use the same cutting and stitching techniques for designs with rectangles that you use for patterns of squares.

Opposite are examples of two popular patterns in which rectangles are first pieced into squares and the squares are then pieced into pattern blocks.

The pillow on the couch features the Spirit of St. Louis pattern—a four-patch arrangement in which each square of the design is pieced from a trio of rectangles cut from different wool fabrics. To assemble each pattern block, join four identical squares in pinwheel fashion so that clockwise from the upper right corner of the block, the same color rectangle faces first down, then left, then up, and then right.

Squares pieced from three rectangles also make up the Fine Woven or Roman Stripe pattern that borders the curtains, *opposite left.* In this case, however, the outer rectangles of each square are pieced from the same fabric. The blocks are assembled alternately and in strips for a woven effect.

The Streak of Lightning pattern used for the wool quilt and pillow tops, *above,* also is known as the Stair Steps or Brick Wall pattern. This pattern is patched easily by sewing rectangles end to end into rows. Join the rows horizontally, staggering each strip so that every other row begins and ends with a half-rectangle. For other patterns that combine squares and rectangles, see the pillows pictured on page 23.

ONE-PATCH PLACE MATS
PAGE 24
Finished size is 12½ x 16½ inches

Materials
⅔ yard *each* of backing fabric and fleece
Scraps of eight different fabrics
7 yards of wide bias binding

Instructions
For each mat, cut forty-eight 2½-inch fabric squares; assemble as shown on page 25. Make four.

TRIP-AROUND-THE-WORLD QUILT
PAGE 30
Finished size is 86x86 inches

Materials
1¼ yards of yellow print fabric
⅞ yard *each* of blue and blue print fabrics
¾ yard *each* of yellow, pink print, pink, and green fabrics
½ yard *each* of lavender print and lavender fabrics
⅜ yard *each* of apricot print and apricot fabrics
¼ yard of green print fabric
15 yards of blue bias binding
5 yards of backing fabric
Lightweight batting

Instructions
Cut 3-inch squares as follows: 97 yellow, 200 yellow print, 112 green, 28 green print, 96 pink, 104 pink print, 120 blue, 132 blue print, 56 lavender, 60 lavender print, 48 apricot, and 52 apricot print.

Working diagonally from lower right corner, piece squares into strips, following diagram, *above;* use ¼-inch seams. Join strips to make quilt top.

Piece backing to size. Sandwich batting between top and back; baste and quilt. Trim back and batting to match top; bind edges.

1 Square = 1 Patchwork Square

COLOR KEY
◆ Lavender
◇ Lavender print
◆ Blue
⊗ Blue print
◗ Green
⊖ Green print

◇ Yellow
⊘ Yellow print
⊕ Pink
⊕ Pink print
⊘ Apricot
◇ Apricot print

SUNSHINE AND SHADOW BABY QUILT
PAGE 31
Finished size is 38x50 inches

Materials
3 yards of dark blue cotton
⅝ yard of light blue cotton
¼ yard *each* of red violet, blue violet, red, orange, and brown cotton
⅛ yard *each* of dark green and light yellow fabric
Quilt batting

Instructions
Cut two 3½x22-inch and two 3½x35-inch strips of light blue for inner borders. Cut two 6x28-inch and two 6x39-inch strips of dark blue for outer borders.

Next, cut 1¾-inch squares as follows: 80 light blue, 44 dark blue, 22 blue violet, 34 yellow, 38 green, 46 brown, 50 orange, 54 red, and 60 red violet.

To make templates for border triangles, cut a 1¼-inch square of cardboard in half diagonally; use one triangle as a template, adding ¼-inch seam allowances when cutting out triangles from blue violet fabric.

Beginning in one corner (see diagram, *opposite above*), piece squares into rows. Begin and end each row with a triangle. Join rows to form center of quilt. Sew light and dark blue border strips to center.

Cut backing to size. Sandwich batting between top and backing; baste and quilt. Slip-stitch edge of top to backing.

SUNSHINE AND SHADOW VARIATION
PAGES 32-33
Finished size is 89x105 inches

Materials
1¼ yards *each* of black and beige, and pink print fabrics
1⅓ yards *each* of dark purple and medium-purple prints
1½ yards *each* of dark brown and rust prints; 1 yard of raspberry print; ¾ yard of black print
½ yard of medium-brown print
8 yards of backing fabric
11½ yards of brown bias binding
King-size quilt batting

Instructions
For each block: Cut 2½-inch squares as follows (number for the entire quilt is in parentheses): 20 (268) black and beige, 24 (324) dark purple, 24 (328) medium-purple, 20 (280) dark brown, 12 (168) black, 20 (268) pink, 8 (104) medium-brown, 25 (336) rust, and 16 (212) raspberry.

Following diagram, *below right,* join squares into 13 rows of 13 squares each; use ¼-inch seams. Make 12 blocks. Next, piece the first 5 rows of the full block pattern for each of four half-blocks.

To assemble: Sew pieced blocks into four rows of three whole blocks and one half-block each. Piece backing to size. Sandwich batting between top and backing; baste and quilt. Bind edges.

FOUR-PATCH TABLECLOTH AND CHAIR CUSHIONS
PAGE 26

Materials
1 yard *each* of three fabrics for tablecloth
7 yards of narrow bias binding
3½ yards of backing fabric

Instructions
Using the diagrams for the Four-Patch and Four-Patch Variation, page 38, as a guide, cut and piece blocks for the cloth and cushion.

The tablecloth consists of four-patch blocks pieced from 5-inch squares (finished dimensions) joined to 10-inch-square blocks (finished dimensions). For a similar cloth, piece six rows of six blocks each, following directions on page 27. Bind edges with bias binding.

The cushion consists of blocks constructed from sixteen 2-inch squares joined to blocks assembled from four 4-inch squares. Piece sufficient yardage to cover chair cushions.

NINE-PATCH UPHOLSTERY
PAGE 29

Instructions
Cut 2½-inch squares from each of two fabrics; piece according to the diagram, page 39. Sew pieced blocks to 6½-inch squares of solid-color fabric to make sufficient fabric to cover chair. Upholster or slipcover chair as desired.

TWENTY-FIVE-PATCH QUILT
PAGE 28
Finished size is 68x81 inches

Materials
1⅔ yards *each* of blue-striped and solid-red fabric
2½ yards of blue fabric for sashing and borders
4 yards of backing fabric
Quilt batting

Instructions
Cut 390 red and 360 blue-striped squares, each 2½x2½ inches. Using ¼-inch seams, piece 13 red and 12 blue-striped squares into five rows of five squares each, alternating colors (see photograph). Join rows; make 30 blocks.

(Continued)

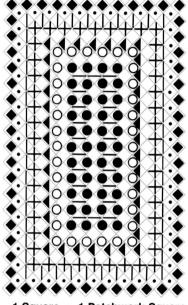

1 Square = 1 Patchwork Square

COLOR KEY
⬨ Blue Violet   ⊕ Brown
◆ Red Violet   ◗ Green
⊘ Red   ◇ Yellow
◇ Light Blue   ⬤ Blue
◊ Orange

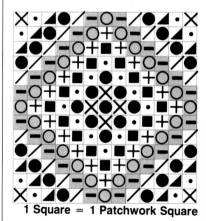

1 Square = 1 Patchwork Square

COLOR KEY
⊞ Black/Beige
◨ Dark Purple
⊟ Medium Purple
◪ Dark Brown
◣ Black
⊡ Pink
⊠ Medium Brown
◕ Rust
◼ Raspberry

(Continued)

From solid-blue fabric, cut 24 strips, each 3½x10½ inches. Sew four strips between five blocks to make a row. Make six rows.

Next, cut seven blue strips, each 3½x62½ inches. Piece these strips between rows and to top and bottom of assembled rows. Sew 3½-inch-wide border strips to both sides of pieced top.

Baste together backing, batting, and top; quilt. Slip-stitch border fabric to back of quilt.

FINE WOVEN PATTERN CURTAIN BORDERS
PAGE 34

Instructions
Note: Fine Woven is an ideal pattern for machine strip-piecing; see page 27.

To piece yardage for curtain borders or other decorating projects (such as a coverlet), sew together long, 1½-inch-wide strips of three different fabrics. Use ¼-inch seams. Press seams; cut pieced strip into 3½-inch lengths.

For contrasting blocks, repeat strip-piecing and cutting procedure, with two strips of one fabric placed on each side of one strip of a second fabric.

Join these pieced blocks in the Fine Woven pattern, *opposite,* making sufficient yardage to complete the project.

SPIRIT OF ST. LOUIS PILLOW
PAGE 34

Instructions
Following basic machine strip-piecing instructions on page 27, sew 1½-inch-wide pieces of three different fabrics into long strips. Cut sixteen 3½-inch-wide blocks from pieced strip and join blocks into the Spirit of St. Louis pattern, *opposite.* Add piping, back square with matching fabric, and stuff with batting or insert pillow form.

STREAK OF LIGHTNING QUILT AND PILLOWS
PAGE 35
Finished size is 78x80 inches

Materials
4½ yards of assorted 60-inch-wide woolens
Quilt batting, backing fabric
Gold pearl cotton floss
Embroidery needle

Instructions
The quilt shown consists of 420 rectangles, each 2½x5 inches, and 30 squares, each 2½x2½ inches (finished dimensions).

Cut pieces, using Streak of Lightning diagram, *opposite,* as a guide and adding ¼-inch seam allowances to all pieces. Stitch 30 rows of 14 rectangles (and one square) each. Adjust number of pieces and rows to achieve desired size. Add 3½-inch-wide borders to all sides of the pieced top.

Sandwich batting between top and backing fabric cut and pieced to size; baste and quilt. Slip-stitch border to backing. If desired, embellish seams with featherstitching, using pearl cotton.

Make pillows to match quilt.

SIMPLE PIECED PILLOWS
PAGE 23

Instructions
From scraps of fabric, piece one or more of the patterns shown in the diagrams, *opposite.*

To simplify pattern-making for these designs, decide first on the size of the smallest block in each pattern (it might be 1 inch square, for example). Sizes of remaining blocks should be in proportion to smallest block. (Pattern pieces are textured to indicate variety and shades of fabrics to use.)

Lay pattern of your choice on pieced fabric; cut out, adding ¼-inch seam allowances. Cut a backing to match. Sew into a pillow.

JUDGING SEAM ALLOWANCES BY EYE

As you gain experience marking and cutting pattern pieces, you may wish to dispense with the double template method described on page 25, and simply trace stitching lines onto fabrics. With practice, you can trust your eye to allow ½ inch between pieces to accommodate the required ¼-inch seam allowances for each piece.

For machine piecing, trace only *cutting* lines on fabric and rely on presser-foot spacing for accurate ¼-inch seams. For hand piecing, however, always mark the *stitching* line on each piece.

4-PATCH

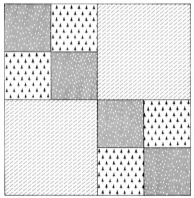

4-PATCH VARIATION

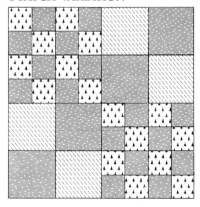

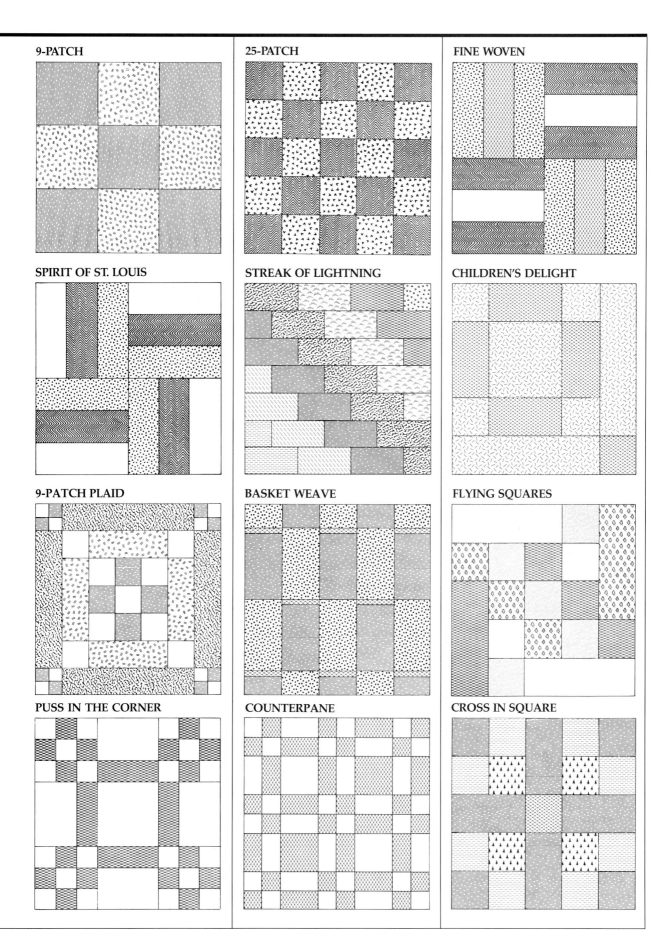

9-PATCH

25-PATCH

FINE WOVEN

SPIRIT OF ST. LOUIS

STREAK OF LIGHTNING

CHILDREN'S DELIGHT

9-PATCH PLAID

BASKET WEAVE

FLYING SQUARES

PUSS IN THE CORNER

COUNTERPANE

CROSS IN SQUARE

PATCHWORK SAMPLER—
A NEW LOOK
AT OLD PATTERNS

Sometimes
naive, often surprisingly
sophisticated, the pieced and
appliquéd patterns on
antique patchwork quilts offer a
rich source of design ideas
for crafters in every medium.

TRADITIONAL PIECEWORK PATTERNS

The harmonious proportions and imaginative interplay of color and pattern so characteristic of a well-designed quilt are worthy standards by which to judge almost any craft. In fact, the very best quilt patterns—those that have been stitched with pleasure and pride by generations of quilters—are a rich source of design ideas for crafters in any medium. This section presents a sampling of favorite quilt patterns, along with suggestions for adapting them to dozens of non-quilt crafts projects.

One of the oldest and most enduringly popular of traditional pieced quilt designs is the lovely Ocean Waves pattern pictured here. In this visually sophisticated design, precisely pieced waves of light and dark triangles seem to sweep across a sea of contrasting color.

This lively pattern probably was first pieced somewhere in the Atlantic coastal states, and then traveled westward with the early settlers. Whatever its origins, by the mid-nineteenth century, the Ocean Waves pattern was a staple of the American quiltmaker's repertoire—even on the vast plains and in mountain reaches where the ocean itself seemed little more than a traveler's tall tale or a half-forgotten dream.

Pictured *at right,* a particularly handsome Ocean Waves quilt (of midwestern origin) provides the pattern inspiration and subtle colorations for a unique collection of picture frames.

Stitched from random scraps in soft shades of brown, beige, light and dark grays, and reds, all of the frames are pieced from the same-size triangles as those used to make the quilt. By varying the number of triangles per row and the number of rows pieced together along each side, you can easily adapt the size and shape of the frame as desired. And an imaginative grouping of custom-designed frames like these will enhance almost any collection—whether it's the batch of cross-stitched quilt motifs pictured here or a colorful selection of family snapshots.

For more patchwork frames and cross-stitch pictures, please turn the page. (Instructions for the Ocean Waves Quilt, matching picture frames, and cross-stitched pictures begin on page 52.)

Small projects, like these made-to-measure frames, are an ideal way to practice your piecing skills and try out fabric combinations before tackling a full-scale quilt.

Use adaptations of the Ocean Waves pattern in the colors of your choice to create a coordinated setting for your framables—a favorite cross-stitched sampler or elegant initial as shown here, or a piece of antique needlework, a small mirror, or even something as whimsical as a special portrait of the family pet.

As long as you're thinking of adaptations, don't limit yourself to fabric frames. You might glue triangles of pretty print papers to a cardboard mat, then protect them with several coats of clear acrylic finish for a decoupage version of the Ocean Waves frame.

For an understated frame, snip the triangles from various wood-grain strips of laminate and glue them in an Ocean Waves arrangement on pieced-to-size frames of lath or plywood.

There are many other techniques to consider for frame adaptations too, such as stenciling, woodburning, and stained glass. Experiment with the design in a craft you've already mastered, or try a technique that is new to you.

**The Wrench pattern quilt
shown opposite might be
called a fabric tribute to
the handy tool for which
the pattern was named.**

Old-time quilt patterns frequently took their names from
the everyday objects that inspired
them—log cabin, morning star,
bow tie, honeycomb, bear tracks,
and birds in flight are just a few
examples.

But patterns and their names
also were strongly influenced by
local customs and events, and the
same pattern is often known by
quite different names in different
parts of the country. For example,
a variation of this same Wrench
pattern is known to quilters
among the Indiana Amish as the
"Hole in the Barn Door" pattern—an equally apt and charmingly colorful description of the
design.

The straightforward piecing of
squares and rectangles in this design creates a block that is every
bit as delightful as the names by
which it is known.

At left, a single 8-inch Wrench
pattern is appliquéd to the bib of a
chef's apron. In the foreground
are a pair of Wrench-pattern
wooden trivets—more kitchen accessories with a decidedly contemporary feel. Denim and plaid
place mats or a set of kitchen appliance covers (toaster, blender,
mixer) boasting Wrench-pattern
appliqués are other interesting
ways to use the pattern.

The Chimney Sweep pattern is another old favorite with intriguing potential for new crafts applications.

Pieced from squares, rectangles, and triangles, the Chimney Sweep design often appeared as an album block on both Friendship and Sampler quilts from the mid-nineteenth century on. The quilter would piece the block, then enter her name, the date, or even a bit of scripture in the center strip, in ink or in fine embroidery stitches.

In the boldly patterned quilt doubling as a tablecloth, *opposite,* cheerful red and blue Chimney Sweep blocks are set on the diagonal, alternating with plain squares of unbleached muslin. Departing from tradition, the unknown needle artist quilted the entire coverlet using contrasting dark blue thread—the better, perhaps, to showcase her exceptionally fine, even stitches.

We used both the piecing pattern and the gridwork of quilting stitches from the original quilt as inspiration for the woodburned and color-tinted tabletop and the cross-stitched shutter inserts, *at right.* Any simple, pieced quilt pattern, based on squares, rectangles, and triangles, can be adapted successfully for similar projects.

The Dresden Plate design was probably named in honor of the Dresden china factory, which was the first in Europe to produce true porcelain in the early 1700s.

One of today's most widely recognized quilt patterns, the Dresden Plate, has been known by several different names over the past 150 years: Friendship Block, Sunflower, and Bride's Quilt pattern, among others.

The pattern is both pieced *and* appliquéd; the petals or spokes are first pieced together, then the completed ring is appliquéd to a background square.

In most examples of the pattern, the petals have either curved or pointed ends, and the center of the plate is either background fabric (as pictured in the example, *above*), or an inserted circle of fabric in a contrasting solid color.

The Dresden Plate Quilt pictured here is unusual because it features a plate with 19 spokes (each different), rather than the 16- or 20-spoke plates more common in this pattern.

We adapted elements of the Dresden Plate design to create the charming child's dress and matching doll costume, *opposite.* The collar of the dress is a duplicate of the plate pattern, minus a few petals so the collar lies flat. The border of the dress is copied directly from the quilt border, in which pie-shape wedges of printed fabric alternate with triangles of lavender, solid-color fabric.

Dresden Plate blocks also make lovely round place mats, pretty pillow fronts, and unusual picture frames. The quilt border can be used to edge sheets and pillowcases or to dress up a purchased linen tablecloth.

OCEAN WAVES QUILT
PAGE 43
Finished size is about 70x76 inches

Materials
1¼ yards of soft red print fabric for center squares
2½ yards *each* of dark and light fabrics in assorted small prints
4¼ yards of white print fabric for backing and borders
8½ yards of bias binding
Batting

Instructions
Each finished block is 12 inches square, and each consists of a 6-inch square set into a pieced border composed of 24 light and 24 dark right-angle triangles. (See the diagram, *above right.*) Each triangle measures 2⅛x2⅛x3 inches.

The quilt top is pieced using 25 full blocks, 12 half-blocks, and four corner quarter-blocks, all set on the diagonal. The length of the quilt is extended by a 3-inch-wide border at top and bottom, and it is bound on all sides with 1-inch-wide bias binding.

To make a similar quilt, cut a 6-inch-square template from cardboard or plastic. Cut 25 squares from red print fabric, adding ¼-inch seam allowances to all pieces.

Next, cut the square template in half diagonally. Cut 12 half-squares from red fabric, adding ¼-inch seam allowances to all pieces. Finally, cut the half-square template in half again, to form a quarter-square template. Cut four of these pieces, adding ¼-inch seam allowances.

For waves, cut a 2⅛x2⅛x3-inch right-angle triangle template. Adding ¼-inch seam allowances, cut 768 light triangles and 768 dark triangles from a variety of print fabrics. (For hints on how to cut and piece right-angle triangles, turn to pages 126-127.)

To piece one block: Following the assembly diagram, *above right,* piece light and dark triangles into rows, joining triangles along the shorter sides. (Use dark triangles

for the shaded portions of the design.) Then piece the rows together to form the border for each side of the block. Press seams toward darker triangles.

Assemble the center square and four borders into a complete block, arranging borders so dark triangles appear to point *toward* the center of the block on top and bottom borders, and *away* from the center of the block on each side, as shown in the diagram.

Next, piece two borders for each of the 12 half-blocks and a single border for each of the four quarter-blocks. *Note:* Six of the half-blocks should be pieced so that the triangles are mirror images of the other six. Two of the quarter-blocks should be pieced as mirror images of the remaining two quarter-blocks.

To assemble the quilt top: Beginning in the upper left corner of the pattern and working diagonally toward the lower right corner, proceed as follows: First, piece the border edge of one of the quarter-blocks to one border edge of a full block. Match the borders so that *all triangles point in the same direction.*

Join a half-block to each side of the full block, again matching borders so that all triangles on either side of the block point in the same direction.

For the second row, sew three blocks together horizontally, with a half-block at each end. Position blocks carefully so that, where borders meet between blocks, all triangles on each border appear to point in the same direction.

For the third row, piece five full blocks together between the two half-blocks; for the fourth row (the center strip of the quilt), piece seven full blocks between the two quarter-blocks. The fifth, sixth, and seventh rows repeat the third, second, and first rows, respectively. Match borders carefully.

To finish: Add 3-inch-wide border strips of light print fabric to top and bottom edges of the quilt. Piece backing to size, then pin and baste backing, batting, and pieced top together and quilt as desired. Bind edges with bias binding.

PATCHWORK PICTURE FRAMES
PAGES 43-45

Materials
Scraps of light and dark print fabrics in colors of your choice
Foam-core board or heavy cardboard for each frame
⅓-½ yard of muslin for each frame
Graph paper, mat knife
Masking tape, white glue

Instructions
Each frame is pieced from the same-size right-angle triangles as those used for the Ocean Waves Quilt described above. Triangles are joined into rows, as for the borders of each pattern block of the quilt, and the rows are then pieced together to form frames of the desired size. *Note:* By using triangles of the size specified, each row of the frame border will be 1½ inches deep.

To make frames: First, sketch a pattern for each frame, using graph paper and following the sizes and patterns pictured on pages 43-45, or devising your own designs. Piece each frame as though it were a quilt block, using muslin for a square or rectangular center of the block. Press all seams toward the outside of the block.

(Continued)

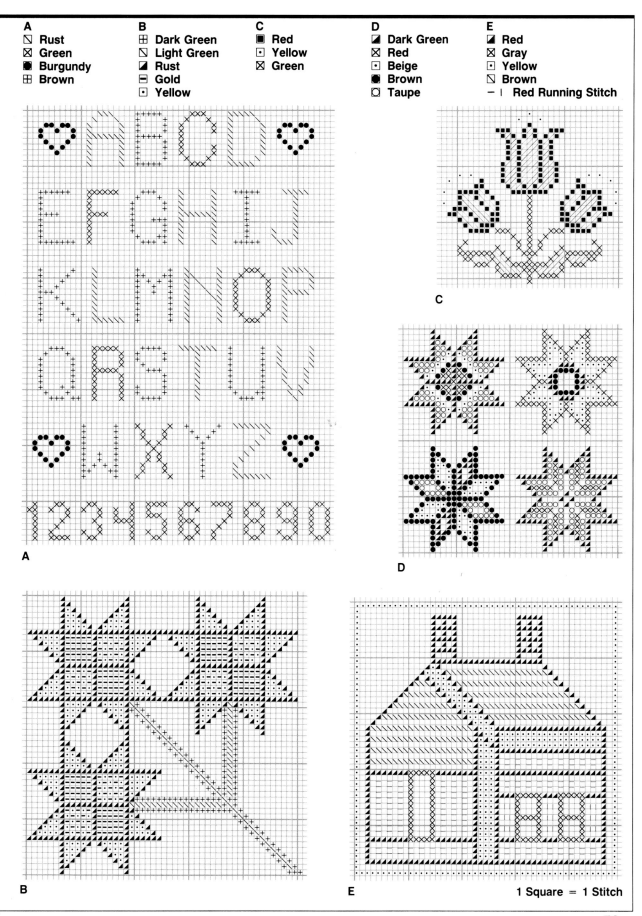

A
- ◺ Rust
- ⊠ Green
- ◉ Burgundy
- ⊞ Brown

B
- ⊞ Dark Green
- ◺ Light Green
- ◪ Rust
- ⊟ Gold
- ⊡ Yellow

C
- ◼ Red
- ⊡ Yellow
- ⊠ Green

D
- ◪ Dark Green
- ⊠ Red
- ⊡ Beige
- ◉ Brown
- ◖ Taupe

E
- ◪ Red
- ⊠ Gray
- ⊡ Yellow
- ◺ Brown
- – ꞁ Red Running Stitch

A

B

C

D

E

1 Square = 1 Stitch

53

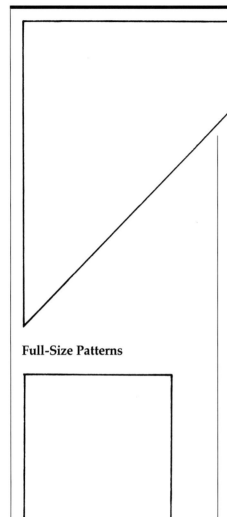

Full-Size Patterns

8" WRENCH

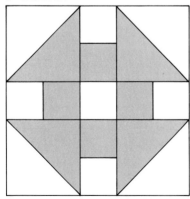

(Continued)

Sew 2-inch-wide muslin strips to each outer edge of the block.

Using a mat knife, cut a foam-core board or cardboard backing for each frame; pad with batting. Use dabs of white glue to hold batting on the front of the frame.

Next, slit the muslin center of the frame from corner to corner, diagonally. Stretch the pieced fabric over padded backing, pulling center muslin and outside strips to the back of the board. Secure with glue and masking tape.

Mount needlework (see directions, following) or some other memento on cardboard; center and secure cardboard to the back of the frame with masking tape.

Cut a second, lighter piece of cardboard slightly smaller than the backing. Cover the cardboard with muslin; whipstitch this piece to the back of the frame to conceal raw edges. Add a small metal ring or a ribbon loop for hanging.

CROSS-STITCH INSERTS FOR PATCHWORK FRAMES
PAGES 43-45

Materials
Even-weave fabric or Aida cloth
Small amounts of embroidery
    floss in colors of your choice
Scraps of cardboard
Needle and embroidery hoop

Instructions
Following charted patterns on page 53, cross-stitch the design of your choice, using two, three, or four strands of embroidery floss.

Press the finished stitchery lightly on the wrong side, using a damp press cloth. Mount on cardboard; frame as described above.

WRENCH PATTERN QUILT
PAGE 47
Finished size is 68x84 inches

Materials
1¼ yards *each* of 10 dark and 10
    light prints (wrench blocks)
4½ yards of white or light back-
    ground fabric (plain squares,
    strips, and borders)
4 yards of backing fabric
Batting

Instructions
The quilt top consists of twenty 8-inch-square pieced blocks and 16 plain (unpieced) blocks joined into strips of nine blocks each. These pieced strips alternate with 8-inch-wide unpieced strips of light fabric to form the quilt top.

To begin, transfer the full-size patterns for square and triangle, *left,* to cardboard or plastic and cut out templates.

From background fabric, cut three 8½x72½-inch strips and sixteen 8½-inch squares for plain blocks (these measurements include ¼-inch seam allowances); set aside. For each pieced block, cut four triangles and five squares from light fabric and four triangles and four squares from dark print fabric. Add ¼-inch seam allowances to all pieces.

To piece one block: Referring to the drawing, *left,* assemble each block as follows: Sew a dark triangle to a light triangle along long edges to form a square. Make three more large squares.

Next, sew a small dark square to a small light square, making a rectangle. Make three more.

Stitch the remaining small light square between two pieced rectangles to form the center strip of the block. Sew a pieced rectangle vertically between two pieced squares to form top row of the block. Repeat with the remaining pieces to form bottom row. Join all three rows to form a complete block. Make 20 blocks.

To assemble the top: Sew five pieced and four plain blocks into a row; make four. Sew 8½x72½-inch strips between rows. Finish with 6-inch-wide border strips of background fabric sewn to the top, bottom, and sides.

To finish: Piece backing fabric to size. Sandwich top, batting, and backing together and baste. Quilt and finish as desired.

❖

WRENCH PATTERN WOODEN TRIVETS
PAGE 46

Materials
Scraps of 1-inch pine or other attractively grained woods
Wood stains in various colors
Wood glue, polyurethane finish
Graph paper

Instructions
Transfer wrench pattern, *opposite*, onto graph paper and enlarge to desired size of trivet. Cut out pattern pieces for square and triangle.

Trace outlines of squares and triangles onto wood, arranging pattern pieces so that wood grain will be displayed to advantage.

Stain pieces as shown, then assemble stained pieces and glue with wood glue. Clamp pieces together until thoroughly dry. Protect completed trivets with several coats of polyurethane.

❖

WRENCH PATTERN APRON
PAGE 46

Materials
Purchased chef's apron or purchased pattern and fabric as required
Scraps of print fabric for appliqués
Fusible webbing, graph paper

Instructions
A 10-inch-square wrench pattern is machine-appliquéd to the bib of the apron, and a row of three 8-inch-square wrenches is stitched

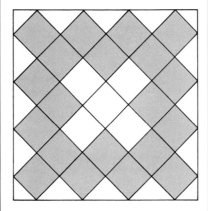

to the pockets along the bottom of the apron. Use graph paper to size the wrench pattern, *opposite*, to fit the bib and pockets of your apron.

For machine appliqués, cut the wrench pattern from a single piece of fabric (rather than piecing it). Cut fusible webbing to match each shape and fuse wrench patterns in place. Machine-satin-stitch around each shape using matching or contrasting thread.

❖

CHIMNEY SWEEP QUILT
PAGE 48
Finished size is about 75x75 inches

Materials
2½ yards of unbleached muslin
1¼ yards of red cotton
2 yards of blue cotton
4¼ yards of unbleached muslin or other backing fabric
Batting

Instructions
The quilt consists of 25 pieced and 16 plain blocks. Blocks are assembled on the diagonal, and the quilt top is pieced out with half- and quarter-blocks cut from muslin.

For pattern pieces, first cut a 1⅝-inch-square template. Trace a second 1⅝-inch square; divide it in half diagonally and then into fourths. Use these patterns for half- and quarter-square templates required for each block. Add ¼-inch seam margins to all pieces before cutting.

Referring to the drawing, *above,* cut 20 red and 5 blue squares, 12 blue half-squares, and 4 blue quarter-squares for each block.

To piece the block: Begin sewing in the upper right corner of the block. Sew a blue corner piece (quarter-square) to a red square (shaded areas on diagram). Sew a blue side-triangle (half-square) to the sides of the same red square.

Continue piecing diagonal rows of squares and triangles until the block is complete. Piece 25 blocks.

To assemble the top: Cut sixteen 9½-inch squares from muslin (this measurement includes ¼-inch seam allowances). Set aside.

Next, draw a 9-inch square on paper and divide it diagonally into half- and quarter-squares, as described above. Use these patterns to make half- and quarter-square templates. Cut 12 large half-square triangles and four quarter-square triangles, adding ¼-inch seam allowances to each piece.

Assemble the top in diagonal rows as for each block, beginning with a pattern block (first row) and alternating pieced and plain squares in each row thereafter.

Border the quilt top with 2½-inch-wide strips of blue fabric and then add a second border of 3½-inch-wide muslin strips.

To finish: Piece backing fabric to size. Baste backing, batting, and pieced top together, then quilt and finish as desired.

❖

WOODBURNED TABLETOP
PAGE 49

Materials
Purchased wooden table with unfinished top
Woodburning tool, yardstick
Red and blue fabric dyes
Artist's brush or small sponge
Graphite paper, polyurethane

Instructions
Enlarge or reduce the Chimney Sweep pattern, *above left*—or any geometric design—to fit the tabletop or any other wooden furniture you wish to decorate.

(Continued)

55

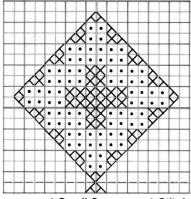

1 Small Square = 1 Stitch

COLOR KEY
⊠ Blue   · Red

(Continued)

Be sure that the wood is free of dirt and finishes. Then transfer the outlines of the patchwork pattern to the wood, using graphite paper. Next, with a yardstick and soft pencil, lightly mark parallel lines of "quilting stitches" with short, evenly spaced dashes, following the pattern lines indicated in the color photograph.

Use the woodburning tool to outline the entire pattern with firm, even strokes. Burn each of the "stitches" with a light touch of the tip of the tool.

To stain the design with a light wash of color, use fabric dyes full strength; apply to each portion of the pattern with a brush or a sponge. Apply one color first, allow dye to dry, and then apply second color. Take care to prevent colors from bleeding over wood-burned outlines. Use more than one coat of dye, if necessary.

When stain is completely dry, protect tabletop with several coats of clear polyurethane, if desired.

CROSS-STITCHED SHUTTER INSERTS
PAGE 49

Materials
Even-weave fabric
Graph paper, colored pencils
Purchased wooden shutters with space for fabric inserts
Red, blue, and brown embroidery floss (or colors of your choice)

Instructions
Following the pattern diagram, *above right,* use colored pencils to transfer the design to graph paper for easy reference.

Considering the size of the insert and the thread-count of the fabric, decide whether stitches should be taken over two, three, or four threads of fabric. Position the design accordingly.

Work the pattern in cross-stitches, using an appropriate number of strands of floss. Fill in the edges of the block pattern with three-quarter crosses.

Using brown embroidery floss, complete inserts with small, evenly spaced backstitches worked in a grid across the fabric, to simulate quilting stitches.

Press completed stitchery on the wrong side, add lining if necessary, and mount in the shutters.

DRESDEN PLATE QUILT
PAGE 51
Finished size is 79x97 inches

Materials
12 yards of white or off-white fabric (background, backing)
Scraps (⅛-¼ yard *each*) of at least 19 different print fabrics
Batting
Graph paper, marking pen
Cardboard or plastic for templates

Instructions
The quilt consists of twenty 17-inch-square pieced and appliquéd blocks arranged in five rows of four blocks each. Each plate design contains 19 wedges or spokes cut from different fabrics.

For each block, sections of the plate are pieced together and then the entire motif is appliquéd to a square of background fabric. Careful cutting and piecing are important to make the appliqué lie flat. It is a good idea to make a sample block before cutting out pieces for the entire quilt.

To make one block: Enlarge the plate pattern, *opposite;* transfer it to tissue paper for use as a master pattern. Without adding seam allowances, trace the pattern for one full-size wedge of the plate design, *opposite,* onto cardboard or plastic and cut out for use as a template.

Adding ¼-inch seam margins, trace and cut out 19 wedges from different prints. Be sure the straight grain of the fabric runs down the center of the wedge, as indicated on the pattern piece.

Join wedges by hand or machine. Sew only from seam line to seam line, leaving ¼ inch unsewn at each end of wedge so the inner and outer edges of the plate can be turned under easily when the design is appliquéd to the background square. Gently press the seams to one side, being careful not to stretch the fabric.

When the plate is assembled, baste a ¼-inch hem along the inner and outer edges of the circle. Then center the plate on a 17½-inch square of background fabric, checking its position against the master pattern. Baste in place.

To appliqué, whipstitch the *inside* edge first, then the outside edge, making sure the plate lies flat. If it does not sit correctly on the block, adjust the seams between the pieces and, if necessary, the template for the wedge.

If the first block is satisfactory, cut 361 more wedges for the remaining blocks. Piece and appliqué them to background squares.

To assemble the quilt top: Stitch four complete blocks into a row, using ¼-inch seams. Make five rows. Sew rows together horizontally; press seams in one direction.

Trace the full-size patterns for the border, *opposite;* cut templates. Adding ¼-inch seam margins, cut 109 white triangles and 117 print border wedges.

Except in the corners of the border, the print fabric wedges and white triangles are pieced alternately. For each corner, piece three border wedges together. Then, with right sides facing,

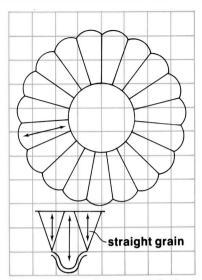

straight grain

1 Square = 2 Inches

stitch the pieced borders to the sides of the quilt top, inserting the corners as required. Press seams toward center of quilt.

To finish: Cut and piece 13 yards of 1-inch-wide bias strips from white fabric and set aside.

Cut and piece backing fabric and batting so they are a bit larger than the top. Baste all layers together. *After* basting, trim batting and backing to match scalloped edges of the quilt top.

Quilt as desired, then bind edges with white bias binding.

❖

DRESDEN PLATE DRESS
PAGE 50

Materials
Purchased pattern for a loose-
fitting, smock-type child's
dress with jewel neckline
Yardage as required for pattern
Scraps of print fabrics for collar
and border
Embroidery floss or pearl cotton

Instructions
The collar of the child's dress is a pieced and lined Dresden Plate from which two spokes have been omitted so the collar lies flat around the neck of the dress. The border of the dress is pieced as the border for the Dresden Plate Quilt, above, is pieced. It is then lined and sewn to the hem of the dress.

(Continued)

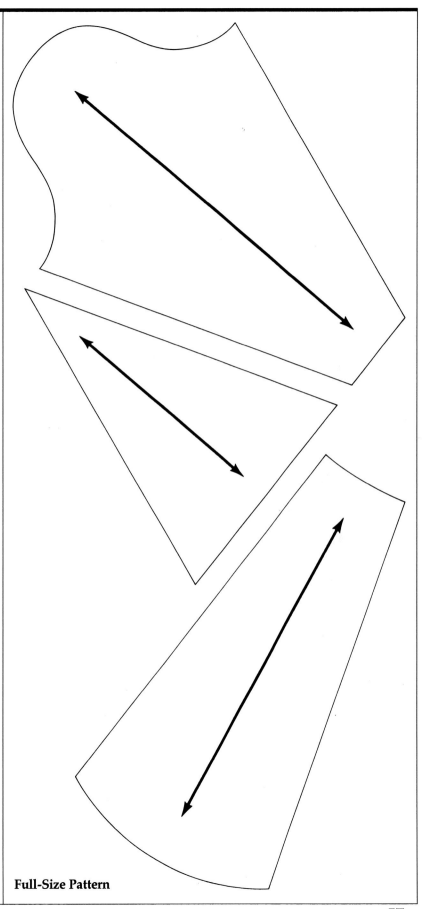

Full-Size Pattern

(Continued)

First, complete the dress according to the pattern instructions, leaving the neckline and hemline unfinished.

For a collar, trace the pattern for a single spoke of the Dresden Plate design on page 57. If necessary, enlarge or reduce the pattern to a size that is in pleasing proportion to the dress pattern you have selected.

Adding seam allowances, cut and piece 17 wedges of the plate as described in the instructions for the quilt on page 56. With right sides together, pin the pieced collar to a matching circle of lining fabric. Machine-stitch the two layers together ¼ inch from the scalloped edges of the collar.

Trim seams, clip curves, turn the collar right side out, and press. Trim the inside curves and clip the edges to fit the neckline of the dress. Match the right side of the collar to the wrong side of the dress; pin in place, baste, and stitch. Turn the collar to the right side of the dress and press.

Next, enlarge or reduce the pattern for the border on page 57 to the desired size. Cut and piece a sufficient length of border to fit gracefully around the lower edge of the dress.

Line the border as described for the collar, using lightweight fabric. Turn right side out and press.

Turn the raw edges of the border and lining to the wrong side, fit the edges of the border over the raw edges of the skirt bottom, and stitch.

Embellish seams of the border pieces with rows of featherstitches worked in complementary shades of embroidery floss or pearl cotton.

Sew the doll's dress in the same manner as the child's, working with pattern pieces scaled to the size of the doll.

FLORAL BASKET QUILT
PAGES 40-41
Finished size is 75x90 inches

Materials
1¼ yards of yellow cotton fabric (for baskets)
10½ yards of muslin (for front and backing)
Fabric scraps (¼ to ½ yard each) in light, medium, and dark reds, blues, purples, greens, and oranges (for flowers, stems, and leaves)
Yellow bias binding
Quilt batting
Plastic lids or cardboard (for templates)

Instructions
The quilt shown consists of 20 basket blocks set on the diagonal (with muslin blocks between) to form five horizontal rows, each with four pattern blocks. A multi-colored sawtooth border (pieced from fabrics used for flowers joined to muslin triangles) set between muslin strips surrounds the blocks. Edges are finished with yellow binding.

To begin: Cut two 44x95-inch lengths of muslin for quilt backing. From each length, cut a strip 3½ inches wide (for outermost border). Set backing and strips aside. From remaining muslin, cut two strips 3½x70½ inches (for outermost border), plus two strips 3½x60½ inches and two 3½x81½ inches (for inner border). Set strips aside.

Next, draw a 10½-inch square on paper; cut it in half diagonally. Use one triangle as a pattern for the half-blocks that are (1) set together with baskets to make complete pattern blocks and (2) set into the ends of the rows along the edges of the quilt. Adding ¼-inch seam allowances all around, cut 34 large triangles—20 for pattern blocks and 14 for edges of the quilt. Set aside.

Cut the remaining paper triangle (see above) in half again, to make a small triangle equal to

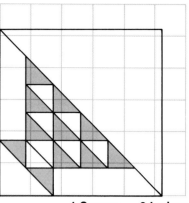

1 Square = 2 Inches

one-fourth the size of the block. Adding ¼-inch seam allowances, cut four quarter-blocks for the four corners of the quilt. Set aside.

To piece pattern blocks: Enlarge basket pattern, *above.* (To make patterns for small triangles, draw a 1¾-inch square. Cut square in half diagonally; trace one triangle onto plastic lids or cardboard for template. For triangle at base of basket, cut a 3½-inch square in half diagonally; trace triangle onto template and cut out.)

Adding ¼-inch seam allowances, cut pieces for 20 baskets from muslin and yellow fabric. Stitch pieces together, referring to pattern and photograph. Note that baskets form half of each 10½-inch-square pattern block.

Flowers in baskets are simple shapes cut from solid-color fabrics and appliquéd onto the large muslin triangles that form the top half of each pattern block.

Enlarge the four flower patterns, *opposite,* and use these patterns to get started on designs for the remaining pattern blocks. (Draft your own patterns or adapt motifs from other quilts, pictures, or other pattern sources. For best results, keep shapes of flowers and leaves simple, as shown on the accompanying diagrams.)

After drafting patterns for flowers and leaves, cut pattern pieces from a variety of solid-color fabrics, adding ¼-inch seam allowances. Turn under seam allowances, baste, and appliqué designs to large muslin triangles.

Then, embellish motifs with simple embroidery stitches using contrasting pearl cotton thread or embroidery floss.

1 Square = 1 Inch

Finally, for basket handle, cut a yellow 1x10-inch bias strip. Turn long edges under ¼ inch; press. Appliqué the basket handle around the flowers on the block (see photograph).

To assemble block, pin together pieced basket and appliquéd triangle; stitch, using ¼-inch seams. Press seams to one side. Make 20 blocks.

To assemble the quilt top: Seam pattern and plain blocks and triangles in eight rows (from upper left to lower right) as follows. *Row 1:* Join long side of quarter-block to upper left side of basket block, then stitch muslin half-blocks (triangles) to lower left and upper right sides of basket block.

Note: Stitch half-blocks in place so long side will fall along perimeter of quilt top before borders are added.

Row 2: Join muslin triangle to basket block, add a muslin block, a basket block, and a second muslin triangle.

Row 3: Stitch two plain blocks between three basket blocks; add muslin triangles to ends. *Row 4:*

Sew three plain blocks between four basket blocks; add muslin triangle to one end (lower left) and muslin quarter-block to other end (upper right).

Row 5: Assemble same as Row 4, except sew half-block to upper right end of row and quarter-block to lower left end.

Rows 6-8: Assemble same as Rows 3-5, except reverse position of triangles at ends.

Next, sew muslin inner border strips to the quilt top, bottom, and sides. Trim the ends of the strips as necessary.

Cut and piece sufficient triangles from colored fabrics and muslin for sawtooth border, using small triangle used for basket as a pattern. Join pieces into squares by stitching a colored triangle to a muslin one along the long edges, then sew squares together into strips long enough for top, bottom, and sides of quilt.

Add muslin outermost border strips to top, bottom, and sides.

Finally, sandwich batting between quilt top and backing. Baste all layers together and quilt as desired. Finish the quilt by binding the edges with yellow bias binding.

WOODEN BASKET
PAGE 41

Materials
1x12-inch clear pine lumber
Small wooden dowels
Nails, glue, woodburner
Acrylic paint, paintbrush
Danish oil or finish of your choice

Instructions
Enlarge pattern, *opposite,* to desired size. (For the basket shown, use a scale of 1 square = 3 inches.) Add a ¾-inch-wide handle.

Using glue and short lengths of dowel to stabilize the pieces, butt-join sufficient 1x12-inch pine for ends of baskets. Trace design onto wood; cut around outline (including handles). Transfer the quilt pattern to the wood using carbon paper. Woodburn the design; paint yellow triangles.

To assemble basket, cut bottom and sides from remaining pine; nail and glue in place. Finish with Danish oil or other finish.

LOG CABIN
WALL HANGING
PAGE 13

Instructions
Using patterns and instructions for Log Cabin blocks (pages 80-93), cut and stitch pieced squares in the design of your choice. To achieve subtle coloration similar to that in Donna Barnett's wall hanging, you may wish to dye your own fabric strips. Use 100% cotton fabrics for dyeing and high-quality commercial dyes; follow manufacturer's directions.

An alternative method of controlling colors (and one with a lot of creative potential) is to combine plain and printed cotton fabrics and overdye some or all of the strips to achieve a variety of subtle color combinations. Test-dye a variety of strips, then choose those that are most appealing for your patchwork projects.

HEARTS AND FLOWERS TO APPLIQUÉ

Among the best-loved of patchwork designs, traditional appliqué patterns adapt with special grace to other craft techniques. Here, and on the following pages, you'll discover dozens of ways to translate your favorite appliqué motifs into an exciting array of projects for your home and family.

Large or small, stitched in simple repeats or intricate patterns, the heart motif turns up with cheerful regularity on quilts of every period and from every corner of the country.

The projects, *right,* take their cue from a heart-bedecked doll quilt on the table. Also suitable as a table mat or wall hanging, this old-fashioned charmer features 30 hearts snipped from plain and fancy cotton fabrics. It's a wonderful project for scrap crafting enthusiasts.

The handsome reverse-appliquéd place mats bring hearts and flowers to the dinner table in grand style. Select a quartet of prints in your favorite colors and stitch them in mix-and-match combinations to create a custom set of mats for your table.

You'll need a jigsaw and a steady hand to fashion a collection of sweetheart candle holders like the pastel beauties pictured here. But scraps of pretty papers, bits of trim, and a lick of glue are all it takes to turn purchased heart-shape boxes into tabletop accessories like those shown next to the candle holders.

Instructions for all projects in this section begin on page 72.

A quilter's choice and placement of fabrics often are compared to the artist's use of paint on canvas, but inspiration works both ways. The quilter's feel for color and pattern also can inspire the painter's brush.

An imaginative arrangement of shapes and colors transforms chunky hearts into bright, stylized blossoms on the cozy quilt pictured *opposite.*

Because the shapes are simple, with moderate curves and not-too-sharp corners, this coverlet is an ideal appliqué project for a beginning patchworker.

Hearts have always been a staple component of folk art designs, and are traditionally favored for decorating children's furniture and playthings. The purchased wooden stroller, *above right,* features a design of plump red hearts, borrowed from the quilt pattern, *opposite.* Hearts are traced onto the back, front, and wheels of the stroller, then each shape is outlined with woodburning to set the pattern.

For a soft wash of color that's reminiscent of an antique finish, stain each heart with fabric dye to allow the wood grain to show through. Finish the piece with Danish oil or a protective coat of polyurethane, if you wish.

A similar design and the same techniques work well for all sorts of children's toys and furniture, from carts to cradles.

For the cheerful floorcloth spread before the fire, *below right,* transfer the entire quilt block pattern directly onto canvas with an artist's brush and sponge-painting techniques. The cloth can be made any size, and you can enlarge or reduce the block pattern to fit the available space.

Or, instead of painting a floorcloth, stencil the block pattern directly onto the kitchen floor. To set off the floor treatment, trim your kitchen cabinet doors with the same motif.

Simple leaf and stem designs like the Ohio Blue Leaf pattern shown here are among the most versatile and easy to adapt of all appliqué motifs.

Using two pattern pieces—a stem and a leaf—vine patterns are wonderfully easy to adapt to new uses. Simply moving the pieces around or changing their size makes them suitable for borders and linear trims of all kinds.

The sprightly patterned quilt from which the Ohio Blue Leaf design is lifted, *opposite,* features sky-blue calico appliquéd on a white quilted background—one of the all-time-favorite color schemes of quiltmakers, past and present. This color combination is repeated for the painted chair and appliquéd bed linens, *above and below left,* but soft red and gray wools are combined to give the design an entirely different look on the little girl's appliquéd jumper, *below left.*

With paint and fabric appliqués, secondhand or unfinished furniture takes on a customized country look, as shown on the chair. To create this side chair, paint a single horizontal portion of the pattern across each slat of a ladder-back chair, then outfit the seat with an appliquéd cushion that repeats one entire block of the pattern.

Purchased plain white sheets benefit from a similar custom treatment. Appliquéd motifs are a handsome and inexpensive way to give bargain-basement sheets, towels, and pillowcases the look of designer linens. But always be sure that the appliqués are cut from preshrunk fabrics and that they are similar in fiber content and care requirements to the items you plan to embellish.

Notice that the central cluster of leaves is turned sideways on the chair designs, and on the appliquéd linens. This adjustment extends the length of the horizontal pattern without disturbing the proportions of the design. Similarly, the stems are curved upward on the little girl's jumper, to complement the cut of the bodice.

Appliquéd floral patterns, like the graceful daisy motifs on this quilt, are wonderful inspiration for decorating all sorts of personal accessories and home furnishings.

Blossoms that took endless hours to appliqué by hand on the quilt, *right,* seemed to bloom in next to no time on the machine-appliquéd tea cloth and matching napkins, *opposite.*

By altering the length of the stem and varying the number and position of the flowers and leaves, you can adjust the elements of this design to fit any size and shape of cloth. If you'd prefer a border rather than a center pattern, try arranging stems and flower clusters in a softly scalloped pattern around the edges of the cloth, similar to the design stitched along the quilt border.

To turn teatime into a special event, design a one-of-a-kind tea set to match your tablecloth. Even if you're only a novice ceramist, you can purchase basic greenware shapes for pot and cups, paint the designs at home, then take the set into a commercial ceramics studio to have the pieces fired.

For those whose passion is hand stitchery, here's a surprise: These sunny daisy designs—like many patchwork patterns—work equally well as cross-stitched patterns and lose nothing in the translation (see the bib of the young lady's apron, *opposite*). Or work the design in satin stitches, if that's more to your liking.

Lovely rose motifs and lyrical swag designs from an elegant nineteenth-century quilt find new life and a new look as decorative accents in a contemporary home.

The magnificent antique quilt, *above,* is one of the many patch-work masterpieces displayed in the Woodlawn Plantation collection in Mount Vernon, Virginia. (See page 10 for more information on the Woodlawn Plantation and on "Nelly's Needlers," a devoted group of needle artists who lovingly restore quilts and other textile treasures in this collection.)

The relatively simple Whig Rose and Swag designs used on this quilt are enhanced by incredibly fine workmanship and the rich texture of hand quilting. The flavor of the original is captured in charming adaptations of the motifs used to embellish the cozy window nook, *opposite.*

The rose motifs used on the pillows are two sizes. The star pattern, on a 12-inch-square pillow, is actually two of the swag crowns pieced back to back. In place of the elaborate quilting found on the coverlet, the pillows are embellished with a single row of outline quilting around each of the motifs.

A stenciled version of the swag motif frames the window seat.

HEARTS AND FLOWERS TO APPLIQUÉ

Friendship or Sampler quilts, in which every square is worked in a different pieced or appliquéd pattern, provide a wealth of design ideas for patchwork enthusiasts.

A unique and valuable piece in the Woodlawn Plantation's permanent stitchery collection is this stunning sampler coverlet, *opposite,* stitched about 1852. It consists of both pieced and appliquéd designs that are suitable for stitchers of varying skills. Some are simple patterns of pieced squares, but others are complex enough to challenge the most experienced quilter. From this quilt alone, an imaginative crafter could create patchwork-inspired decor for an entire household.

This 42-square quilt boasts 42 different patchwork designs, three of which have been adapted for other projects, *right.*

A traditional Friendship block design (one on which the quilter usually entered her signature in ink or stitchery on the center block) makes a handsome fabric mirror frame, *above left.*

Repeats of a modified Fleur-de-Lis pattern trim the curtain, *above right.* A variation of the Rose of Sharon quilt pattern graces the needlepoint footstool, *below.*

To stimulate your imagination, study other patchwork patterns—in this book and at quilt shows and shops—with an eye for the many ways they may be adapted for other crafts projects.

Miniature Heart Quilt

Pages 60-61

Finished size is 26½ x30½ inches

Materials

⅞ yard of muslin
¼ yard of gray-and-white pindot fabric
⅜ yard of burgundy print fabric
1 yard of backing fabric
Scraps (at least 4 inches square) of 30 print fabrics (hearts)
Cotton batting
3¼ yards of black double-fold bias tape

Instructions

To piece the quilt top: From muslin, cut a 20½ x24½-inch rectangle. Cut two 1¼ x20½-inch strips from pindot fabric.

Stitch the strips to the short sides of the muslin piece, using ¼-inch seams. Press seams toward the gray fabric.

Cut two 1¼-inch-wide gray strips long enough for the remaining sides. Stitch in place. Repeat this process with 2¾-inch-wide burgundy border strips.

Using a ruler and a water-erasable pen, mark 4-inch squares on the muslin (quilting lines).

Cut batting and backing fabric to size. Sandwich batting between top and backing; baste together. Machine- or hand-quilt along the marked lines. Then, stitch around the inside edge of the quilt top next to the gray border. Quilt in the ditch between gray and burgundy borders.

For heart appliqués: Using the heart pattern for the heart quilt on page 73 as a guide, trace and cut out a template measuring about 3½ inches at the widest part.

Using a water-erasable pen or a *light* pencil, trace around the template onto the wrong side of each print fabric. Lay each print fabric atop a matching scrap of muslin, right sides facing, and stitch them together around the heart shape. Cut out each heart, leaving a ¼-inch seam allowance. Make 30.

In the center back of each heart, *through the muslin only,* cut a slit large enough to turn the heart right side out. Clip curves, turn, and press; whipstitch opening closed.

Center the hearts within the quilted squares on the quilt top. Hand-appliqué by catching the outside edge of the *top* fabric only. Outline-quilt around each heart.

To finish the quilt: Using black, double-fold bias tape, bind the edges of the quilt. Attach a muslin sleeve or narrow strip of nylon fastening tape to the top of the wrong side of the quilt for hanging if desired. (To prepare quilts for hanging, see page 191.)

Heart Place Mats

Pages 60-61

Finished size is about 16x18 inches

Materials

(For two place mats)

½ yard each of four print cotton fabrics in coordinating colors
½ yard of 45-inch-wide polyester fleece

Instructions

To make a pattern for the place mat, fold a large sheet of paper in half and cut a half heart that is about 14 inches high and 8 inches wide at the widest point. Open out the pattern. On a second sheet of paper, trace around the heart shape, then draw a second outline that is 1 inch beyond the original heart shape.

For each place mat: Using the *larger* pattern, cut out one heart from fleece.

Choose the fabric you want for the center, dominant part of the place mat. From this fabric, cut one heart using the *smaller* pattern. Center the fabric heart on the fleece and sew the layers together ¼ inch from the edge of the heart.

To frame the center heart, cut a heart from a second fabric, using

the *larger* pattern. Then pin the large fabric heart, right side up, to the place mat, matching edges of the fabric heart with edges of the fleece heart. This will conceal the smaller fabric heart. Baste along the previous line of stitching.

Reverse-appliqué the large heart by cutting away *only the top layer of fabric* ½ inch inside the basting line. Turn under ¼ inch along the inside raw edge of the top heart and blindstitch it to the lower fabric layer. Remove the basting thread.

From a third fabric, cut a back for the place mat, and bind edges with 1½-inch-wide bias strips cut from the fourth print fabric.

Repeat the above steps for each place mat, varying the selection of fabrics for center, border, backing, and bias binding for each mat.

Heart Candlesticks

Page 61

Materials

1¼-inch-thick pine (hearts)
½-inch-thick pine (bases)
Jigsaw or coping saw
Drill with ¼- and ¾-inch bits
¼-inch-diameter dowel
Sandpaper, wood glue
Pastel shades of enamel paint

Instructions

To make a 4¼-inch-high candlestick, first make a template from the heart-shape pattern on page 73 (pattern piece B). Center and trace the heart onto a 4-inch square of 1¼-inch-thick pine. Do not cut out the heart shape yet.

On the edges of the block, mark the center top and bottom points of the heart. Drill a ¾-inch-diameter hole 2 inches deep into the center top for the candle.

Drill a ¼-inch-diameter hole ½ inch deep into the center bottom of the block. Use this hole to fasten candlestick to its base.

With a jigsaw or coping saw, cut out heart. Sand until smooth.

To make a base for the heart, cut a 1x2-inch piece from ½-inch-thick pine. Bevel the edges.

To attach the heart to the stand, drill a ¼-inch-diameter hole through the center of the base. Put a drop of wood glue into the hole in the bottom of the candlestick, then insert a 1-inch length of ¼-inch dowel to connect the base to the heart. Let the glue dry, then paint as desired.

To vary candlestick size, trace a larger or smaller heart onto a larger or smaller square of pine.

COVERED BOXES
Page 61

Materials
Purchased heart-shape boxes
Dollhouse wallpapers or other decorative papers
White glue
Ribbon, lace, and floral trims

Instructions
Cut papers to fit the boxes, using papers in different combinations on the same box, if desired. Glue the papers in place. Conceal seams by gluing on ribbons and lace. Glue on floral trims as desired.

HEART QUILT
PAGE 62
Finished size is 67x82½ inches

Materials
2 yards of red fabric
1½ yards of red print
9 yards of muslin
Batting
Water-erasable transfer pen
Cardboard or plastic for templates

Instructions
The quilt top is made by appliquéing 20 muslin blocks with heart motifs, setting them together on the diagonal (four appliquéd blocks wide, five appliquéd blocks long) with 12 plain squares of muslin, and adding a border.

To begin, make templates for the full-size pattern pieces, *above*. Use these templates to trace a full-

Full-Size Pattern

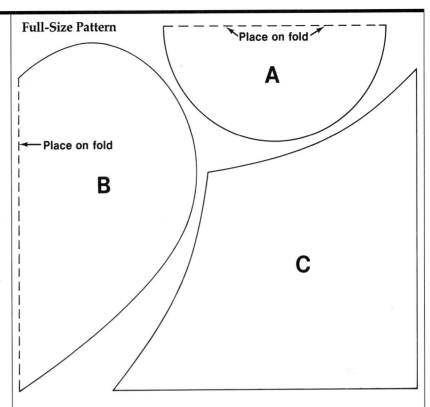

size, master pattern block onto an 11-inch square of paper (refer to photo for positioning). From cardboard, cut an 11½-inch square. This is the template for the muslin block. On tissue paper draw an 11-inch square. Draw two diagonal lines across the square, from corner to corner, to form an X. Use the larger half-square triangle for the sides; use the smaller quarter-square triangle for the corners. Add ¼-inch seam allowances and cut out templates.

Lay templates on the wrong side of the fabric and trace around them with a pencil. Cut pieces as follows: From muslin, cut four quarter-squares, 14 half-squares, and thirty-two 11½-inch squares. From solid red fabric, cut two 3x69-inch and two 3x84½-inch border strips. Set them aside.

Using a water-erasable pen, trace pattern pieces A and B onto the right side of the red fabric; trace pattern piece C onto the right side of the red print. Cut out 80 of each pattern piece, adding ¼ inch for seam allowances.

To appliqué, lay each muslin square over the master pattern. Using a water-erasable pen, trace outlines onto the muslin blocks.

Turn under seam allowances on appliqués and baste or press. Clip curves. Position appliqués on 20 muslin squares; stitch in place. (For more information on appliqué techniques, see Chapter 8.)

To assemble the quilt top, lay out the blocks and triangles on the floor, referring to the photograph to see how they are positioned.

Beginning in one corner and working diagonally across the quilt, stitch a corner triangle and two side triangles to one appliquéd block to complete Row 1. Stitch three blocks together and add a side triangle to each end to complete Row 2. Stitch Row 1 to Row 2. Continue in this manner until all blocks and triangles are joined. Press the seams to one side. Add border strips.

Piece backing fabric to size and baste backing, batting, and quilt top together. Outline-quilt close to the edges of the appliqués; quilt decorative motifs in the plain blocks. Finish edges as desired.

HEART DOLL STROLLER
PAGE 63

Materials
Purchased wooden doll stroller
Red and coral fabric dyes
Woodburning tool
Danish oil or satin-finish
    polyurethane
Graphite paper

Instructions
Adjust size of heart from pattern on page 73 to fit the stroller.

Using graphite paper, transfer hearts to the back, front, and wheels of the stroller. Draw grid lines around the hearts (see page 63). Woodburn outlines of the hearts and grid lines.

Apply red dye to the hearts and coral dye to the grid area. Let dry.

Rub the stroller with Danish oil, or finish it with polyurethane.

HEART FLOORCLOTH
PAGE 63
Finished size is 28x40 inches

Materials
28x40-inch piece of canvas
White latex paint
Red acrylic paint
Paintbrush, small sponge
Clear acrylic finish

Instructions
The floorcloth is made by coating canvas with latex paint, then painting and sponging the design on the cloth, using red paint.

Paint one side of the canvas with two coats of white latex. Let dry. Using a pencil, lightly mark off a 2-inch-wide border around the cloth, then divide the remaining area into six 12-inch squares with *light* pencil marks.

Make templates for each full-size pattern piece, using the pattern on page 73. Trace around the templates to transfer the pattern onto the floorcloth as shown in the photograph.

Paint hearts solid red. For other shapes, dip edge of sponge in red paint and sponge designs lightly. Paint the border red. Let dry. Protect the painted floorcloth with several coats of clear acrylic.

OHIO BLUE LEAF QUILT
PAGE 65
Finished size is 82x82 inches

Materials
6½ yards of white fabric
2½ yards of blue fabric
5 yards of backing fabric
Batting

Instructions
This quilt is constructed of sixteen 17-inch-square pattern blocks. Each block has a crisscross stem with 24 appliquéd leaves.

For master pattern: On brown paper draw a 17-inch square. Add ¼-inch seam allowances. Referring to the photograph, draw two ½-inch-wide stems in an X shape on the 17-inch square pattern.

Using the full-size pattern, *below*, make a leaf template. Trace leaf shapes onto the master pattern, positioning leaves as shown in the photograph.

For the leaves: Trace 384 leaves onto blue fabric, allowing at least ½ inch between leaves; cut out the leaves, adding ¼-inch seam allowances. Clip curves and baste under seam allowances.

For the stems: From blue fabric, cut out thirty-two 1x18½-inch stems. Turn under ¼-inch seam allowances along the sides of each stem; press.

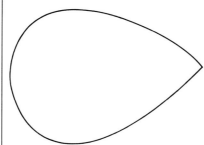

Full-Size Pattern

For the border strips: From white fabric cut four 7½x82½-inch strips (this includes ¼ inch for seam allowances).

To assemble blocks: Cut out sixteen 17½-inch blocks from white fabric. Pin stems onto white blocks and slip-stitch in place.

Pin leaves to stems. Baste, then hand-appliqué in place. Repeat until all 16 blocks are completed. Remove basting.

Arrange completed blocks in four rows of four blocks. Sew together. Sew border strips to the appliquéd blocks, mitering corners. Piece backing to size. Baste top, batting, and backing together. Quilt and finish as desired.

CHAIR CUSHION
PAGE 64

Materials
White and blue fabric to cover the
    top and bottom of the cushion
Blue fabric for appliqués
Piping
2-inch-wide foam for cushion
Batting
Water-erasable marking pen

Instructions
Trim foam slab to fit chair seat. Trace outline of cushion onto white and blue fabric, using water-erasable marking pen. Cut out shape, adding ½-inch seam allowances. Cut out backing.

From the same fabric, cut a 3-inch-wide boxing strip the length of the perimeter of the cushion.

Follow instructions, *above*, for assembling one block of the Ohio Blue Leaf Quilt to cut and appliqué the cushion top. Adjust the length of stems and placement of leaves to fit cushion size.

Note: For a padded effect, baste batting to the wrong side of cushion before appliquéing. If you prefer, cut out stems and leaves *without* seam allowances, and machine-stitch appliqués in place.

Finish cushion with piping. Assemble into a box pillow, leaving one side open. Wrap foam with a layer of batting; insert into cushion and stitch the opening closed.

APPLIQUÉD LINENS
PAGE 64

Materials
Purchased sheet and pillowcases
Blue fabric for appliqués

Instructions
Fourteen leaves and a pair of 6-inch-long stems are appliquéd by hand or machine to the hem of each pillowcase. (If the hem of the purchased pillowcase is not wide enough to accommodate the pattern, make your own cases from sheeting or yard goods.)

For the hem of the top sheet, arrange repeats of the same pattern for the pillowcases across the width of the sheet.

APPLIQUÉD JUMPER
PAGE 64

Materials
Purchased wool jumper with plain bodice (or pattern and yard goods)
Red fabric for appliqués

Instructions
Adjust length and shape of stems and size of leaves to fit attractively on the bodice. Appliqué shapes by hand or machine, as desired.

DAISY CHAIN QUILT
PAGE 67
Finished size is 76x92 inches

Materials
9½ yards of 60-inch-wide muslin (top and backing)
2¾ yards of yellow fabric
Scraps of orange and green cotton
9 yards of green bias binding
Green embroidery floss
Batting

Instructions
This quilt is made by stitching the scalloped center section to the striped border, then appliquéing daisies, leaves, stems, and buds onto the assembled quilt top.

Enlarge the diagram on page 76 onto a 40x48-inch sheet of graph paper. This is the master pattern for one quadrant of the quilt.

For border strips: Cut fifty-one 3¾x20½-inch border strips *each* from yellow fabric and muslin (102 strips total). Measurements include ¼-inch seam allowances.

For the scalloped center section: Cut out a template for the center section. Trace the outline onto muslin fabric, flopping along the dashed lines to complete. Add ¼-inch seam allowances. Cut out the piece, seaming the fabric down the center, if necessary.

For the appliqués: Make leaf and flower templates from full-size patterns on page 76. Cut out shapes as follows: 62 daisies and 12 buds from yellow fabric; 60 leaves and 12 stamens from green; and 62 daisy centers from orange.

Note: Add seam allowances to all pieces if you plan to hand-appliqué flowers; omit seam allowances for machine appliqué.

To assemble the border: Alternating muslin and yellow strips as shown on diagram, sew 28 strips together for *each* long side of the quilt and 23 strips together for *each* short side. *Note:* Each long strip begins with a muslin strip and ends with a yellow strip. One short strip begins and ends with a muslin strip; the other begins and ends with a yellow strip. Press seams toward yellow strips.

Stitch border strips together, mitering the corners; cut away excess fabric and press seams open.

To prepare quilt center: Staystitch along seam lines of center section; clip curves. Fold seam allowances under and press.

To assemble quilt top: Lay the striped border out flat; position the muslin center in place. Slipstitch the center to the striped border; trim seam allowances.

To position appliqués: *Note:* Baste under seam allowances on all pieces for hand appliqué.

Position daisies where indicated by Xs; pin in place. Cut green bias binding strips long enough to connect daisies and cover scalloped edges (add ¼ inch on both ends to tuck under the daisies). Cut extra green strips to attach buds to daisies. Pin stems in place. Position leaves at random, tucking end of leaf under daisy to dashed line (shown on diagram). Pin two buds at each corner cluster of flowers and two extending from two daisies on each side of the center motif (refer to photograph for position of appliqués). Pin green stems (to attach buds to daisies) in place.

To appliqué motifs: Machine-zigzag or hand-buttonhole stitch the stems and leaves. Stitch daisies and buds in place. Stitch centers atop daisies and stamens atop buds. With two strands of green floss, embroider leaf veins.

Piece backing to size. Baste the top, batting, and backing together. Quilt and finish coverlet.

TABLECLOTH AND NAPKINS
PAGE 64

Materials
Purchased 70-inch-diameter white linen tablecloth
Purchased white linen napkins
½ yard of dark yellow print fabric
⅛ yard of light yellow print fabric
½ yard of green fabric
Yellow and green thread
Fusible webbing

Instructions
The tablecloth is made using the full-size patterns for the Daisy Chain Quilt on page 76.

(Continued)

Full-Size Pattern

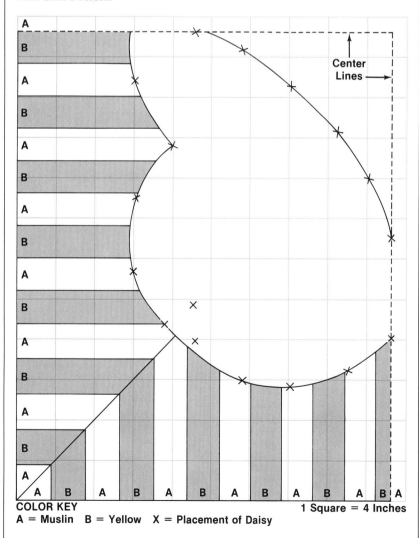

Center Lines →

COLOR KEY
A = Muslin B = Yellow X = Placement of Daisy

1 Square = 4 Inches

(Continued)

All appliqué work is done by machine.

From dark yellow fabric, cut 24 daisies, eight buds, and enough 1-inch-wide bias binding to go around tablecloth and napkins. From light yellow fabric, cut 24 flower centers. From green, cut 22 leaves and 3½ yards of ⅜-inch-wide bias strips. Do *not* add seam allowances to appliqué pieces.

For the tablecloth: With the water-erasable pen, mark the position of daisies, buds, leaves, and green strips. Corner buds are about 13 inches from cloth edge, and daisies lie along a gentle curve of green strips patterned after the center of the quilt.

Using fusible webbing, position the daisies, daisy centers, buds, leaves, and strips on the tablecloth, tucking ends of the green stem strips under the daisies; machine-satin-stitch in place, using matching thread. Stitch leaf veins with green thread. Bind edge with pieced yellow binding.

For napkins: In one corner of each napkin, position a daisy and two leaves as desired. Anchor in place with fusible webbing; machine-satin-stitch around the edges. Add leaf veins and a center in each flower. Bind edges with yellow bias binding.

❖

BIB APRON INSET
PAGE 66
Finished size of inset is 6½ x 6½ inches

Materials
10-inch square *each* of white broadcloth and 14-count waste canvas
Purchased bib apron (or pattern and yardage as required)
Embroidery floss (see color key)

Instructions
Baste the waste canvas atop the broadcloth. Using two floss strands and following the chart, *opposite*, cross-stitch the design.

Outline petals with gold back-stitches; outline leaves with dark green. Remove canvas; press inset.

Turn under raw edges and slip-stitch inset to apron bib. Frame with strips of fabric if desired.

◆

DAISY CERAMICS
PAGE 66

Materials
Purchased bisque teapot and cups
Gold, green, and orange under-
glazes
Clear glaze, brushes

Instructions
Remove any dust from each piece, using a clean brush.

Referring to the pattern, *opposite above,* draw daisies onto the teapot (refer to photograph). Draw stripes around each cup.

Apply three coats of an under-glaze for each area of color. Allow to dry thoroughly.

In a paper cup, mix clear glaze with water to the consistency of milk. Pour the thinned glaze *inside* the lid, teapot, and spout, rolling it around until the insides are completely coated. Return excess glaze to the paper cup.

With a clean brush, apply two coats of clear glaze, undiluted, to the outside of the lid and teapot, and completely over each cup.

Glaze-fire all pieces to cone 06 at a local hobby ceramics studio.

◆

WHIG ROSE QUILT
PAGE 69
Finished size is 97x97 inches

Materials
Cotton fabrics in the following amounts and colors: 8 yards of white, 4 yards of red, 2 yards of green, ⅔ yard of pink
5½ yards of 54- or 60-inch-wide fabric for the backing
Quilt batting
11 yards of green bias binding

1 Square = 1 Stitch

COLOR KEY
⊠ Yellow
⊡ Gold
◪ Medium Green
◕ Dark Green

Instructions
The quilt is made by appliquéing a rose onto twenty-five 10½-inch white blocks, setting squares together on the diagonal with 16 plain white blocks, and adding a border appliquéd with swags.

Cutting the blocks and borders: To avoid piecing the border strips, cut them out first. From white fabric, cut two 12x74¼-inch strips and two 12x97¼-inch strips. These measurements *include* ¼-inch seam allowances.

To make the patterns for half-squares and corners for the quilt, on graph paper draw a 10½-inch square. Then, draw two diagonal lines across the square to form an X. Use the large half-square triangle for sides; use the smaller quarter-square triangle for corners. Add ¼-inch seam allowances to the triangles; cut out the templates. Cut out a template for the square (11 inches—includes ¼-inch seam allowances).

From white fabric, cut 41 squares, 16 large triangles (for

quilt sides), and four small triangles (for corners).

Cutting the appliqués: Enlarge the patterns shown on the grid on page 78, and cut templates for each pattern piece. These patterns do not include seam allowances.

Trace pattern pieces onto the right side of the fabrics. Adding ¼-inch seam allowances, cut the appliqués as follows: *From red,* 25 small roses, 25 large roses, 200 rosebuds, 20 swags, four corner shapes, and 20 diamonds; *from green,* 400 rosebud coverings, 40 diamonds, and four 3¼-inch squares for the corners of the quilt; and *from pink,* 25 medium-size roses.

Appliquéing the blocks: Appliqué 25 blocks with roses and rosebuds, referring to photograph and quilt block diagram on page 78.

(Continued)

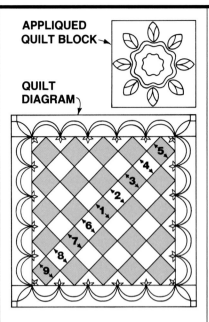

APPLIQUED QUILT BLOCK

QUILT DIAGRAM

(Continued)

Assembling quilt top: First lay out the blocks and triangles on the floor and refer to the photograph to see how pieces are positioned.

Beginning in one corner, stitch a corner triangle and two side triangles to an appliquéd square to complete the first strip. For the second strip, stitch three squares together, beginning and ending with an appliquéd square; add a side triangle to each end.

Continue stitching squares and triangles together following the diagram, *right.* Make nine strips. Each strip should begin and end with a triangle sewn to an appliquéd square; alternate white squares with appliquéd ones.

Beginning with the longest (center) strip, join strips lengthwise in the order indicated by the numbers on the quilt diagram.

When the quilt center is assembled, add borders using ¼-inch seam allowances. Appliqué the swags, corners, and diamonds in place (see photograph). In each corner, appliqué a green square, using ⅛-inch seam allowances.

Piece backing to size. Baste appliquéd top, batting, and backing together. Quilt and finish edges.

❖

QUILT PATTERN PILLOWS
PAGE 68

Materials

⅓ yard of fabric for each pillow front and back
Assorted red and green fabric scraps for appliqués
Polyester fiberfill
Piping or ruffling

Instructions

Enlarge the rose, bud, and diamond pattern pieces for the Whig Rose Quilt, *right.*

For rose pillow: Trace and cut out rose and rosebud appliqués, adding seam allowances. Position pieces on pillow front and appliqué as directed for Whig Rose

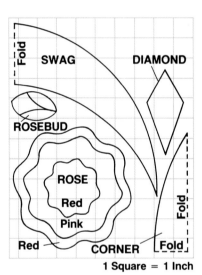

Fold
SWAG
DIAMOND
ROSEBUD
ROSE
Red
Pink
Red
CORNER
Fold
Fold
1 Square = 1 Inch

Quilt, page 77. Add piping or a ruffle. Sew pillow front to back. Turn, stuff, and stitch closed.

For star pillow: Cut six diamonds with seam allowances. Piece diamonds together into a star, then appliqué to pillow front. Sew into a pillow.

❖

STENCILED WINDOW SEAT TRIM
PAGE 68

Materials

Clear plastic for templates
Red and green paint
Paintbrush

Instructions

Enlarge swag, diamond, and corner pieces from Whig Rose Quilt pattern, *left,* to the size needed for the area you plan to trim.

Cut a template for each piece from plastic, and trace around the pieces onto the surface. Paint, referring to the photograph for colors. Let dry thoroughly.

❖

FRIENDSHIP SAMPLER QUILT
PAGE 70
Finished size is 82x94 inches

Materials

5½ yards of background fabric plus scraps for appliqués, *or* forty-two 13x13-inch appliquéd quilt blocks (this includes ½ inch for seam allowances)
Four 2½x88-inch and four 2½x95-inch red fabric strips
Four 3x92-inch white fabric strips
Quilt batting
5½ yards of fabric for backing

Instructions

This coverlet consists of 42 different quilt block patterns. Four patterns from the quilt are given in quadrants in the diagram, *opposite.* Refer to patterns throughout this book for other suitable designs.

Piece or appliqué a total of 42 different 13-inch-square quilt blocks, or have each block worked by a different individual.

To piece the quilt top: Join the quilt blocks in six vertical rows of seven blocks each; then sew the six rows together along the long edges. Use ½-inch seam allowances throughout.

For the border, join four short red strips to the raw edges of the quilt center. Miter the corners and cut away excess fabric. Repeat the procedure to add the white border and outer red border strips.

To finish the quilt: Piece backing to size. Baste the top, batting, and backing together. Quilt and finish as desired.

MIRROR FRAME
PAGE 71
Finished size is 13½x13½ inches

Materials
½ yard *each* of beige fabric and muslin
⅜ yard of red print fabric
16-inch square of quilt batting
13½-inch square of foam-core board
2½ yards of red piping
Masking tape
Plastic lids or cardboard for templates
13-inch-square mirror

Instructions
Enlarge the pattern (upper left-hand corner of the diagram, *above*) onto tissue paper. This is one quarter of the block design. Flop the design along the dashed lines to complete the pattern.

From beige fabric, cut a 16-inch square. Make a 13½-inch square in the center of the fabric and transfer the pattern, centered, onto the right side of the fabric.

Cut the leaf-shape template from a plastic lid or cardboard. On the right side of the red print fabric, draw around the template 12 times, leaving at least ½ inch between shapes. Cut out the leaves, adding ¼-inch seam allowances.

Baste under seam allowances and hand-appliqué leaves to the fabric square, following traced outlines. Sandwich batting between the appliquéd block and the muslin. Quilt around all the appliquéd shapes with red thread ¼ inch from the appliquéd seams.

Next, machine-baste along the curved inside edge of the pattern, and stitch the piping to the mirror center. Cut out the center shape, leaving ¼-inch seams. Clip into corners. Turn the raw edges to the back; press. Stitch piping around the edges of the 13½-inch square.

Cut a 13½-inch square from foam-core. Trace the opening for the mirror onto foam-core, following the pattern shape; cut out.

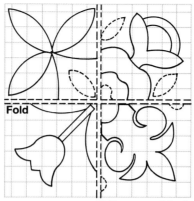

Fold

1 Square = 1 Inch

Position the quilted mirror front on the foam-core and tape the edges of the fabric to the back of the foam-core. Then tape the mirror to the back of the frame.

Cut a 14-inch square of red or beige fabric for backing; press under ¼-inch seam allowances.

Layer the backing (wrong side up) and the mirror and mirror frame (right sides up) atop one another; stitch the backing to the mirror frame. Attach loops for hanging.

FLEUR-DE-LIS CURTAINS
PAGE 71

Materials
Purchased curtains or pattern and yardage for curtains
Red cotton fabric for appliqués
Fusible webbing
Embroidery floss and ⅜-inch-wide red satin ribbon

Instructions
Enlarge the fleur-de-lis pattern (lower right-hand corner of the diagram, *above*) onto brown paper; cut out a template.

Calculate the number of repeats you will need for curtain borders, then cut fleur-de-lis motifs from the red fabric together with matching shapes of fusible webbing. Space the motifs evenly across the width of the curtain and fuse the motifs in place. Machine-appliqué around all raw edges of each motif.

Topstitch rows of ribbon along the top and bottom edge of the motifs. Couch a 6-ply strand of red embroidery floss ¼ inch above the top ribbon, if desired.

FLORAL NEEDLEPOINT FOOTSTOOL
PAGE 71

Materials
10½x10½-inch footstool with a removable cushion (available at needlecraft stores)
15x15-inch piece of 10-count needlepoint canvas
3-ply wool yarn in green, red, pink, and white
Tapestry needle, masking tape
Stretcher strips or needlepoint frame

Instructions
The diagram, *below*, represents one quarter of the design. Transfer the pattern onto graph paper, using felt-tip marking pens. Flop the diagram to complete the pattern.

Cover the canvas edges with masking tape. Mount canvas on stretcher strips or on a needlepoint frame. Using all three plies of yarn, work the design in basket-weave or continental stitches. Stitch the color areas of the design first, then fill in the background with white, stitching a 2½-inch border around the entire design.

Block the needlepoint. Stretch the blocked canvas over the footstool cushion and use a staple gun to secure it, or have the footstool professionally finished.

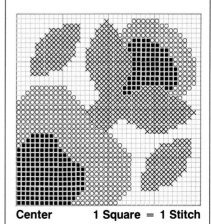

Center　　**1 Square = 1 Stitch**

COLOR KEY
⊠ **Green**　　⧄ **Pink**　　■ **Red**

79

WORKING WITH LOG CABIN BLOCKS

Among the most popular of traditional patchwork motifs, the Log Cabin block also is one of the easiest to construct. And yet the range of visually sophisticated patterns possible with this single, simple-to-piece block intrigues beginners and expert stitchers alike.

PIECING COURTHOUSE STEPS

There are two different ways to piece the basic Log Cabin block. The simpler of these is the Courthouse Steps variation illustrated on these two pages.

Log Cabin patterns are ideal for novice patchworkers because they are easy to piece by hand or machine, and they require only a single template, for the center square around which each block is constructed. The narrow logs of fabric used for the remainder of the block are cut or torn in long strips and then snipped to size as the block is built.

This simple arrangement of squares and rectangles can be manipulated into an astonishing variety of designs simply by altering the way individual blocks are pieced and arranged into an overall pattern.

Unlike most pieced patchwork patterns, the Log Cabin block is always stitched to a foundation—usually a square of muslin or lightweight cotton. Because of the stability created by this backing, the narrow pattern pieces, and the number of seams on each pattern block, Log Cabin designs are often left unquilted. Instead, they are simply backed and tied, or tacked, like the Courthouse Steps table mat, *right.*

Step-by-step instructions for piecing the Courthouse Steps design are on the opposite page.

1

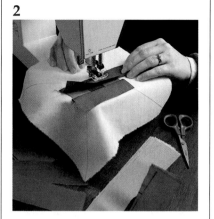

2

3

4

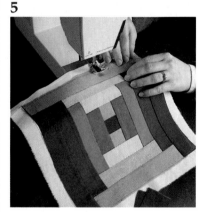

5

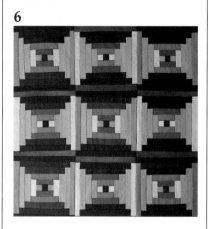

6

❖

1 To piece the Courthouse Steps version of the Log Cabin pattern, first cut a muslin backing square the size of the finished block, adding ¼-inch seam allowances.

Find the center of the square by drawing a diagonal line from the lower right to the upper left corner, using a pencil or washable marker. Draw a second line from the lower left to the upper right corner. Where these two lines intersect is the center of the square.

Next, cut a small square of fabric for the center of the block, adding ¼-inch seam allowances. To mark the center of the square, fold it in half diagonally, then into fourths, and press.

Match the centers of the small square and the muslin square. Pin and baste the center square to the muslin, or tack it in place with a spot of fabric glue, as pictured.

2 Cut or tear a substantial supply of light and dark fabric strips to the width you wish the logs of the block to be, again adding ¼-inch seam allowances. The strips may be any length, because they will be trimmed to the correct size as the block is constructed.

Pin strips of similar value (light or dark) to the top and bottom of the center square. Trim the ends even with the edges of the square and sew the strips in place. Press seams away from the center.

3 Alternate between adding pairs of logs to the top and bottom and then to the sides of the square until the block is the desired size.

4 As shown in this set of pot holders, the colors selected for each set of strips and the order in which they are pieced determine the design of the finished block.

5 The Courthouse Steps pattern is traditionally pieced with all dark fabrics on the top and bottom and all light fabrics on the sides, or vice versa, creating the illusion of steps surrounding the center square.

6 For this traditional version of the overall Courthouse Steps pattern, multiple blocks like those constructed in Step 5 are assembled from 1-inch-wide logs (finished size), with all of the dark strips running from top to bottom and all of the light strips running from side to side.

The appealing table mat pictured opposite is pieced according to the same principles, using ½-inch-wide strips of assorted light and dark print fabrics.

Directions for the Courthouse Steps table mat are included in the instructions that begin on page 92.

PIECING LIGHT-AND-DARK BLOCKS

By far the most common and versatile version of the Log Cabin block is the Light-and-Dark, or spiral, construction illustrated here.

Like the Courthouse Steps design explained on the preceding pages, the Light-and-Dark set of the Log Cabin block consists of a center square surrounded by logs of plain or patterned fabric. But instead of building the block by adding strips to the top and the bottom of the square, and then to the sides, begin constructing the Light-and-Dark block with a single strip sewn to one edge of the center square.

Piece each succeeding strip so it is perpendicular to the preceding strip, working around the center square in a circular fashion until the block reaches the desired size.

For most Log Cabin designs using this method of block construction, the block is divided into two triangular sections; one half is executed in dark fabrics and the other in light fabrics. By manipulating the final placement of the individual blocks, it is possible to create dramatic and startlingly different visual effects.

The wall hanging, *opposite,* is one example of an unusual arrangement of Light-and-Dark blocks. Other, more traditional block arrangements are illustrated on the following pages.

❖

1 To piece a Light-and-Dark block, first baste or tack a small square of fabric to the center of a muslin backing square, as described for the Courthouse Steps block on page 83. Then, with right sides together, pin and machine- or hand-stitch a *dark* strip to one side of the center square, using ¼-inch-wide seams. Trim the strip so that it is exactly as long as the square is wide.

Select a second *dark* fabric strip; pin it to an adjacent edge of the square, perpendicular to the first.

Note: In the example, *right,* the block is rotated in a counterclockwise direction as each strip is added. It does not matter whether you work in a clockwise or a counterclockwise direction, but you should be consistent, and construct each subsequent block in the project in the same fashion.

For the third log of the block, select a *light* fabric strip, position it perpendicular to the preceding strip, trim, and sew in place as before. Repeat for the fourth log.

2 Continue adding logs to the square in the same manner until the block reaches the desired size.

3 Note the arrangement of light and dark fabrics in the completed block. Because the spiral assembly process began with a short, dark strip and finished with a longer, light strip, the dark triangular half of the block is somewhat smaller than the light half.

Pattern designs can be varied in interesting ways by beginning with light strips rather than dark. Or, piece a dark strip first, followed by two light strips and then a second dark strip. Repeat this sequence until the block is completed, and the proportions of the dark and light halves of the block are changed again.

To explore the effects of different piecing arrangements on the overall patterns of Log Cabin quilts, study photographs and samples of antique designs.

1

2

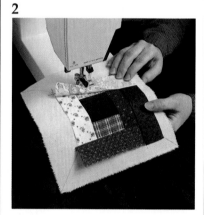

3

Careful attention to the piecing and positioning of each block is crucial to the success of these exciting Log Cabin variations.

Traditionally, the center of each Log Cabin block is a red or warm-colored square, representing the cabin hearth, and the light and dark strips represent the firelight and shadows surrounding the hearth. Both the Barn Raising design used on the Mennonite quilt, *above*, and the block arrangement called Light-and-Dark used on the boxes, *opposite*, make effective use of this traditional color scheme.

In the Barn Raising pattern, solid diamonds of dark and light fabric seem to radiate from a central diamond shape. (The absence of floral fabrics and the sophisticated, though subtle, color progres-sion in this quilt are typical of Amish and Mennonite quilts of the late nineteenth and early twentieth centuries.)

Print fabrics spark the Light-and-Dark pattern boxes, *opposite*. As in the center diamond of the Barn Raising Quilt, matching corners of each of four squares meet at the center point of the design on the large square box and on the rectangular glove box.

The arrangement of lights and darks on the smaller square box creates the illusion of a Straight Furrow design. For more on this pattern, please turn the page.

Strong primary shades and luminous pastels lend new vitality to the familiar Log Cabin variations used for the folding screen and tea cloth pictured here.

The individual blocks in these handsome projects are pieced in the traditional Light-and-Dark arrangement described on page 83, but outsize pattern pieces and innovative color schemes make them decidedly contemporary.

Instead of using a single color in all the center squares of the Straight Furrow design, *left*, the designer of this patchwork screen varied the color of each square, blending it with the color range of the rest of the block—greens, blues, reds, and oranges.

The dark half of the block is flopped from the upper right to the lower left corner on every other block across the top row of four green squares. The order of the Light-and-Dark arrangement is reversed for the next horizontal row of blue squares. The position of the blocks continues to switch back and forth across the third and fourth rows, creating a strong diagonal pattern of light and dark shadings across the width of the screen.

For the tea cloth, *opposite*, hand-dyed strips of lavender, blue, gray, and pink are arranged around a large blue center square on each block. All of the blocks are identically positioned and pieced in this simplest of all variations of the Log Cabin pattern.

STITCHING THE PINEAPPLE VARIATION

Piecing logs of fabric on the diagonal, rather than perpendicular to the center square, creates a challenging Log Cabin variation known as the Pineapple pattern.

A widely recognized symbol of hospitality in colonial times, the pineapple is a recurrent motif in the decorative and textile arts of the period. Among the most imaginative interpretations of this popular fruit is the Log Cabin pattern named in its honor and illustrated by the table runner, *above.* The angularity of the design echoes the spiky leaves and chunky shape of the pineapple itself.

The piecing for the Pineapple pattern is more complex than for other Log Cabin designs, and the finished block is exceptionally dynamic. Other regional names for this design are Maltese Cross and Windmill Blades.

As with other Log Cabin designs, the size and impact of the Pineapple block depend on the width, colors, and number of fabric logs used to construct it.

Instead of using two dark and two light strips for each round of logs (as in the Courthouse Steps and the Light-and-Dark squares pictured on the preceding pages), four strips *each* of light and dark fabrics are used for one complete round of the Pineapple block.

Instructions for completing one block of the Pineapple design used for the table runner, *above,* follow. Use ¼ inch for seam allowances throughout.

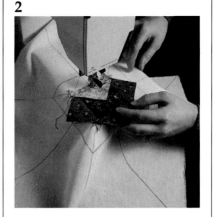

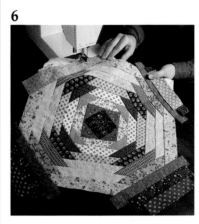

1

❖

1 First, cut a 15½-inch square muslin base for each block. To locate the exact center of the square, draw diagonal lines from corner to corner on the square, using a water-erasable pen. Draw a second pair of lines through the center of the square from top to bottom and from side to side. These two pairs of perpendicular lines will help you to orient each succeeding log of the square accurately.

To further assist in positioning the first pieces of the Pineapple design, use your erasable pen to mark off a 4-inch square in the center of the muslin piece, with edges parallel to the outer edges of the muslin square. Then measure and mark a second square, 5½ inches on a side. Draw this second square on the diagonal.

To begin piecing, baste a 3-inch square of dark printed cotton in the center of the muslin, on the diagonal, as shown.

2 Cut four right-angle triangles (2¾ x 2¾ x 3⅞ inches) from the medium-blue print fabric (measurements include seam allowances). With right sides facing, pin the triangles to the edges of the square; stitch them in place. Press triangles away from the center. (Edges of triangles should fall approximately along the marked edges of the 4-inch square drawn on the muslin in Step 1.)

3 Cut a selection of 1½-inch-wide strips of light and dark print fabrics. Starting with a light-colored strip, cut four 4-inch-long logs. Match the raw edges of the logs to the raw edges of the triangles (and marked square); pin and stitch all four logs in place.

4 Using the previously marked 5½-inch square as a guide, align raw edges of four 3¼-inch-long, dark logs with markings. Pin and stitch the logs in place. Trim away excess fabric beneath the strips, if necessary, and press the strips away from the center.

5 Mark next two sets of guidelines for the strip placement, measuring and marking each square exactly 1¼ inches beyond seam lines of preceding strips.

6 Continue to add rounds of dark and light strips until the block reaches the desired size. Complete the corners by adding dark strips until the corner of the muslin is completely covered. Trim edges of the logs to match the edges of the muslin lining square.

For instructions on how to assemble the Pineapple design table runner pictured *opposite,* turn to page 93.

COURTHOUSE STEPS

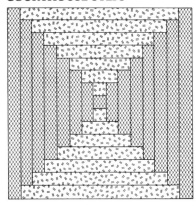

LIGHT-AND-DARK SQUARE

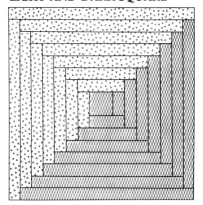

PINEAPPLE

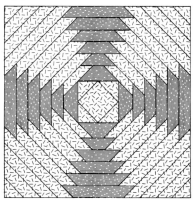

❖

COURTHOUSE STEPS TABLE MAT
PAGE 82
Finished size is 24x24 inches

Materials
23-inch square *each* of polyester
fleece and backing fabric
½ yard of lightweight muslin
Scraps of light and dark fabrics
2⅔ yards of 1-inch-wide lace

Instructions
The mat consists of 16 blocks,
each 5½ inches square and pieced
from ½-inch-wide logs. To begin,
cut sixteen 6-inch muslin squares
and sixteen 1-inch squares (centers). Cut 1-inch-wide strips of
light and dark print fabrics.

To make one block: Following directions on page 83, piece five
rounds of light and dark strips.
Make 16 blocks.

To assemble mat: Join completed
blocks into four rows of four
blocks each; stitch rows together.
   Back mat with fleece; stitch lace
⅛ inch from edges of mat. With
right sides facing, sew backing
fabric to mat on three sides. Turn,
press, and slip-stitch fourth side.

❖

LIGHT-AND-DARK SQUARES WALL HANGING
PAGE 84
Finished size is 22x30 inches

Materials
Scraps of assorted print fabrics in
light and dark colors
⅛ yard of black cotton for centers
½ yard of print border fabric
1 yard *each* of lightweight batting
and backing fabric
Gold metallic thread (hearts)
3¼ yards of bias binding

Instructions
Piece and quilt each 4-inch-
square block in one operation by
stitching through batting and
backing fabric at the same time.
   To begin, cut twenty-four 1½-
inch squares of black fabric (centers), 5-inch squares of backing
fabric, and 4½-inch squares of
batting. Cut 1-inch-wide light
and dark fabric strips for logs.

For each block: Baste batting,
centered, to wrong side of backing
fabric. Following directions on
page 85, piece block with three
rounds of logs, beginning with
two light, followed by two dark
strips, for each round. Make 24.

To join blocks: Follow arrangement shown in photograph. Fold
under raw edges and slip-stitch
blocks (front and back) into rows.
Join rows in same fashion.

For borders: Cut two 3½x16½-
inch pieces *each* from border fabric, fleece, and backing. Matching

raw edges, pin pieces to top and
bottom of quilt, layering backing
fabric (right side up), quilt top
(right side up), batting, and border
fabric (wrong side up). Stitch. Repeat for sides of quilt, using
3½x24½-inch strips.

To finish: Trim borders to size
and quilt. Bind edges with bias
binding. Embroider gold hearts in
black center squares.

❖

BARN RAISING QUILT
PAGE 86
Finished size is 75x90 inches

Materials
3 yards of light fabrics, 5 yards of
dark fabrics
½ yard of red for centers
5 yards of lightweight muslin
5 yards of fabric for backing
6½ yards of bias binding

Instructions
The quilt consists of 120 blocks,
each 7½ inches square, arranged
in 12 rows of 10 blocks each. Each
block consists of a 1½-inch center
square surrounded by three
rounds of 1-inch-wide logs.
   Using the photograph as a
guide, plan the position and color
of each block on graph paper.
   Cut 120 two-inch red squares
and 120 eight-inch muslin
squares. Cut light and dark fabrics
into 1½-inch-wide strips. Referring to your graph paper pattern
and the assembly diagram for the
Light-and-Dark square, *above center,* construct blocks in appropriate
color combinations.

Join blocks into rows; stitch rows together to complete the top.

Piece backing fabric to size; baste to top. Quilt along seams or tie, as desired. Bind edges.

LOG CABIN BOXES
PAGE 87

Materials
Scraps of light and dark prints
Scraps of red fabric for centers
Muslin, lining fabrics
Lightweight foam-core board
Batting or polyester fleece

Instructions
For the large, square Barn Raising box: Piece 20 Light-and-Dark Log Cabin squares onto batting-covered muslin squares.

For the sides and top of the box, sew four squares together so the light halves of the squares meet in the center (see photograph). Line assembled blocks with contrasting fabric, leaving one side open. Create a sixth lined square from plain muslin for the box bottom.

Cut squares of foam-core board to size, pad with batting, and slide into the Log Cabin pockets. Slip-stitch the fourth side closed.

To assemble box: Slip-stitch sides to bottom. Fold up sides to form corners; slip-stitch. Slip-stitch top to one side of the box.

Piece and assemble other boxes in a similar manner.

STRAIGHT FURROW FOLDING SCREEN
PAGE 88

Materials
Purchased folding screen
Solid-color fabrics in various shades, lightweight muslin
Graph paper, colored pencils

Instructions
Each of the 15-inch-square pattern blocks consists of a 3-inch-square center and four sets of 1½-inch-wide logs. The screen has four panels, each four blocks high. Adjust number and size of blocks to suit size of screen.

Referring to the photograph for inspiration, use colored pencils and graph paper to map out colors for each block. For each block, cut and sew a 3½-inch-square center and 2-inch-wide logs onto a 15½-inch square of muslin backing. (Use ¼-inch seams.)

Regardless of color combinations used, arrange Light-and-Dark blocks for a Straight-Furrow pattern as follows: position dark half of squares alternately between lower left and upper right, creating diagonal rows (furrows) across the surface.

Attach the rows of pieced blocks to the panels of the screen and frame with strips of molding.

LIGHT-AND-DARK CLOTH
PAGE 89
Finished size is 44x44 inches

Materials
½ yard *each* of 6 light and 6 dark pastel fabrics
¼ yard of blue fabric (centers)
½ yard of blue-gray fabric for inner border
1¼ yards *each* of muslin and backing fabric

Instructions
For each block: Cut and sew a 3½-inch square of blue fabric to the center of a 9½-inch muslin square. Surround with three rows of 1½-inch-wide dark and light fabric strips, using colors suggested by the photograph. Make nine.

To assemble: Join blocks into three rows of three squares each; orient all nine blocks in the same direction, as shown. Border the cloth with 3-inch-wide strips of medium-blue fabric. Then piece 2x6½-inch strips of fabric in random colors for the edge of the cloth. Sew in place, mitering corners. Line completed cloth.

PINEAPPLE TABLE RUNNER
PAGE 90

Materials
1 yard of muslin
1 yard of print fabric for backing
Scraps of light and dark fabrics
Lightweight fleece

Instructions
Each block is 15½ inches square. Piece three, using instructions on page 91. Join blocks, pad with fleece, and line with backing fabric. Bind edges with bias strips.

STRAIGHT FURROW QUILT
PAGES 80-81

Materials
Scraps of light and dark fabrics
Lightweight muslin and backing fabric
Bias binding, batting

Instructions
Cut and piece Log Cabin square pattern blocks to the desired size, using how-to instructions for the folding screen, above.

Assemble the quilt top in a pattern of diagonal rows. Sandwich batting between top and backing; baste, and quilt as desired. Finish edges with bias binding.

FRAMED LOG CABIN BLOCKS
PAGE 81

Materials
Scraps of light and dark fabrics
Lightweight muslin, batting
Purchased frames, cardboard

Instructions
Piece Log Cabin pattern blocks to the size of your choice, following assembly diagrams, *opposite,* and how-to instructions on pages 82-91. For each block, cut cardboard to size, pad cardboard with batting, and stretch pattern blocks in place. Frame as desired.

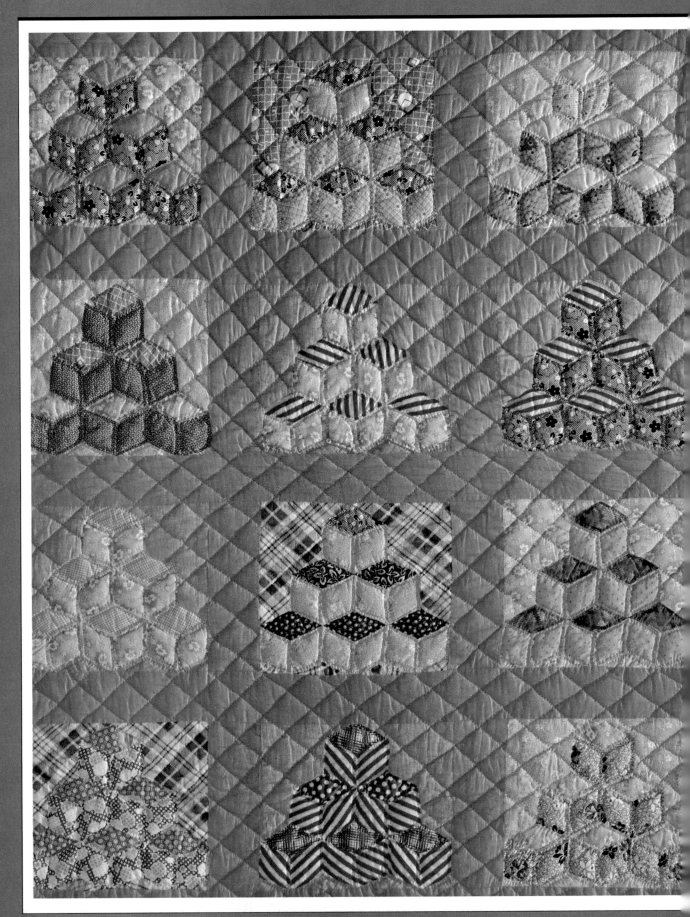

GROWING UP
WITH PATCHWORK

Patchwork
brings to life a special warmth and
color that children thrive on.
Here's an inspired collection of
quilts and coverlets, plump stuffed
animals, and a painted patchwork
picture to make, plus an appliquéd
alphabet to enliven everything
from building blocks to book bags
for your favorite youngsters.

PATCHWORK GIFTS
TO MAKE FOR BABIES

**Welcome a newborn
with a lovingly pieced and stitched
present designed especially with
him or her in mind. Here and on the
following pages, you'll find a
selection of crib quilts and other
patchwork accessories sure
to delight both mother and child.**

A baby shower offers the perfect occasion for friends and family members to collaborate on a one-of-a-kind crib quilt like the one shown here. Each of the nine blocks on this quilt was machine-appliquéd ahead of time, then personalized with hand embroidery after baby's arrival.

When planning a similar quilt, decide on a common color scheme so that all contributed blocks will be compatible, then let your collective imaginations go to work. You can adapt the block patterns used here or let every participant design his or her own. To make this a true friendship quilt, each block should be signed by the person who stitched it.

Nine 12-inch blocks, 3-inch-wide sashings, and 5-inch-wide borders were used in this 52-inch-square quilt. You can adjust the size and number of blocks and the width of sashings on your quilt to accommodate the number of stitchers who plan to participate.

Extra blocks, or a duplicate block, can be used to personalize a purchased baby book or photograph album, like the one on the table at far left. The book cover can be appliquéd ahead of time, with space left for the child's name and birth date to be embroidered at the last minute.

Instructions begin on page 102.

Little ones love color and pattern the way flowers love sunshine. This patchwork teddy and pinwheel crib quilt are ways to introduce a touch of both to the nursery.

The stout little patchwork bear, *opposite,* is the ideal companion for a child's first excursions into the land of make-believe. The bear's body is machine-pieced from sturdy cotton prints and plumped with washable stuffing, and his ever-cheerful features are appliquéd and embroidered to last, at least through several seasons of childhood, if not forever.

Unexpected colors and oversize prints are combined to lively effect on the pinwheel-pattern crib quilt, *above.* The sharp pastel shades in the quilt fabrics are repeated on the painted pastel pillow nestled below it in the rocker.

Either of these projects would bring a welcome splash of color to baby's room, yet neither is restricted to nursery duty. Both quilt and pillow can remain part of the decor of a child's room long after other reminders of "baby days" have been tucked away.

(For general instructions on painted patchwork, turn to pages 266-267.)

Here are more
showstoppers for baby
showers—adorable
appliquéd gift bags,
a clown crib toy,
and a spectacular
Mother Goose quilt to
paint and stitch.

Artful presentation enhances any gift, and sweet appliquéd bags, *above left,* make the tokens inside seem extra special. What's more, these colorful catchalls come in handy after baby's arrival, storing odds and ends within easy reach of the crib or changing table.

The calico cat, gingham dog, and fluffy lamb are classic kid-pleasing motifs that you'll want to repeat on other items as well. Bibs, rompers, and T-shirts are all good candidates for these easy-to-stitch appliqués.

Suspended from a sturdy elastic cord, the chunky alphabet block character, *above right,* will dance all day, delighting a child with every movement. When you make this cheerful clown, personalize the block with baby's initials.

Finally, what more appropriate gift for a nursery than a winsome Mother Goose coverlet, *opposite.* The Mistress of Rhyme and six of her favorite subjects are painted on muslin squares, embroidered and embellished, then joined with pieced and appliquéd blocks to create this delightful crib quilt or wall hanging.

As with the designs on the gift bags, *above,* the patterns used on the painted blocks adapt easily to other uses. You might try wood-burning the central square onto baby's toy box, then accenting portions of the design with transparent stain or paint. Or enlarge any of the smaller figures and stitch them into soft, huggable pillow dolls.

1 Square = 1 Inch

BABY BOOK
PAGE 96

Materials

Purchased album
Plaid fabric for cover and lining
Muslin for backing
Fabric scraps for appliqués
⅓ yard narrow cording
Purchased floral appliqués
Embroidery floss in various colors
Dressmaker's carbon paper
Batting, water-erasable pen

Instructions

To make a paper pattern for the album cover, draw a rectangle equal to the height of the album (top to bottom) and the circumference (from the front edge of the front cover around to the front edge of the back cover).

Draw a second, smaller rectangle with the exact dimensions of the album cover; this will be the pattern for front and back linings. Add ½-inch seam allowances to both patterns. Cut one large rectangle *each* from plaid fabric, batting, and muslin; cut two smaller rectangles from plaid fabric.

Hem one vertical edge of each of the smaller lining pieces. With right sides facing, place one small hemmed rectangle atop each end of the larger rectangle, matching raw edges. Baste the linings to the cover along the top, sides, and bottom.

Stack the pieces as follows: batting rectangle, large plaid rectangle with lining pockets facing up, and large muslin rectangle. Sew the layers together using ¼-inch seams. (The extra ¼ inch in the seam allowance will permit the cover to slip onto the album easily.) Leave an opening for turning.

Clip the corners, trim batting close to the seam, turn, and press. Slip-stitch the opening closed.

For appliquéd design: Enlarge pattern for baby rattle block, *opposite center.* Center and transfer design to front of album cover using dressmaker's carbon. With erasable pen, write baby's name and birth date in the center of the design. Using two strands of floss, outline-stitch the name and date.

Trace and cut out appliqué shapes, adding ¼-inch seam allowances to each piece. Cut matching shapes from batting without adding seam allowances. Baste batting piece to wrong side of each appliqué shape. Set aside.

Cover narrow cording with bias fabric and slip-stitch lengths of fabric-covered cord between bead positions on the album cover, as indicated on the pattern.

Now baste under seam allowances and appliqué beads in place, carefully concealing edges of cord. Outline-stitch around edges of each appliquéd bead, and embellish beads with rows of satin or running stitches, as desired.

Complete the design by adding floral appliqués atop selected beads and sewing a double row of running stitches ½ and ¾ inch inside the outer edges of the front cover. Slip cover onto the book.

FRIENDSHIP QUILT
PAGES 96-97
Finished size is 51½ inches square

Materials
3 yards of blue fabric for backing, sashes, and borders
1 yard of white cotton for blocks
Scraps of assorted prints, plaids, and solids for appliqués
1 yard of contrasting plaid for binding and trim
12 yards of narrow cording
Embroidery floss
Scraps of ribbon and lace, plus small buttons and assorted appliqués for accents
Water-erasable pen
Batting, fusible webbing

Instructions
This quilt consists of nine 11½-inch appliquéd squares. As pictured, some blocks are appliquéd by hand and others by machine; designs can be executed in whichever method you prefer. For hand appliqué, add ¼-inch seam margins to all pieces; for machine appliqué, omit seam allowances.

Use scraps of fusible webbing to anchor shapes as you stitch.

Arrange blocks in three rows of three squares each; assemble with 3-inch-wide sashing strips and 5½-inch-wide borders.

To begin: Enlarge patterns, *opposite,* and use erasable pen to trace each design in the center of a 12-inch square of white fabric. Also use pen to outline appropriate messages or signatures on each square (see notes on individual blocks, below).

Next, trace and cut appliqués from appropriate fabrics. Appliqué shapes to each block, following suggestions below. (See page 248 for embroidery stitches.)

◆ BUNNY RABBIT: Embroider dashed lines on body in brown stem stitches. Work mouth in red stem stitches and eye in brown satin stitches with a white highlight. Couch strands of green yarn for flower stems and embroider stamens with red French knots. Use a purchased white pom-pom for bunny's tail, if desired.

◆ BEAR AND WAGON: Embroider eye, eyebrow, nose, and seams on bear's head and paws with floss. Sew bows of satin ribbon atop packages; add buttons to centers of wheels on wagon. Embroider baby's name on the side of the wagon, if desired.

◆ SHEEP: Use French knots for the eyes; work tails and flowers in satin stitches. Sew green rickrack along edges of fabric hills. On one sheep, stitch "I love Ewe," and on the other, satin-stitch a heart and the quilter's name.

◆ LITTLE BOY: Work boy's and bear's eyes in black French knots; use stem stitches for mouth. Satin-stitch the bear's nose, inside of ears, and paws, and the swirl on the lollipop in the little boy's hand. Add decorative buttons at the top of the overalls, if desired.

◆ BABY RATTLE: Couch decorative cord between beads on the rattle. Appliqué and lightly stuff each bead. Outline-quilt around beads with contrasting floss and embroider baby's name inside the circle of the rattle. Frame the design with 1-inch-wide strip of contrasting fabric, if desired.

◆ LITTLE GIRL: Appliqué all shapes in place. Add lengths of lace and ribbon trim to hem of skirt and decorate collar and front of dress with small purchased appliqué flowers. Add a satin bow to hair and smaller bows to shoes and basket.

◆ HOUSE: Sew shapes in place. Embroider "Sweet Dreams" on cloud to the left of the house and add the child's name above the house. Add other embroidered details to roof, windowpanes, flowers on lawn, rays of sun, and so forth, as desired.

◆ DUCKLING: Work raindrops and eye in satin stitches. The swirl on the snail and details on the duck's feet are stem stitches; running stitches embellish the hat. Add a tiny ribbon bow to top of hat.

◆ CLOWN (in lower right corner of quilt; not visible in photograph): Embroider clown's features in running stitches. Add tufts of yarn for hair. Stitch one letter of baby's name in each of the balls the clown is juggling, adding or subtracting balls to accommodate name.

(Continued)

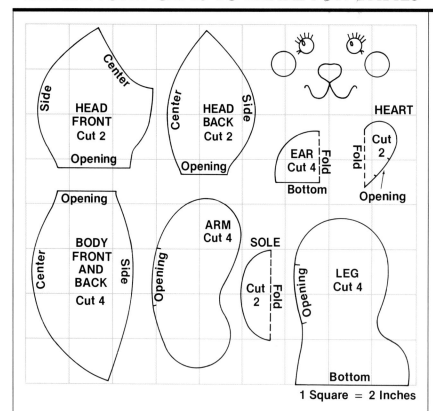

1 Square = 2 Inches

(Continued)

To assemble quilt: Cut and piece 12 yards of ½-inch-wide bias binding from plaid fabric. Stitch bias strips together into one long strip, then use the strip to cover narrow cording.

Tack covered cord along seam lines of each of the nine completed quilt blocks.

Arrange blocks in three rows of three squares each. Use 3½-inch-wide strips of blue fabric to join square into rows and rows into quilt top (use ¼-inch seams).

Cut 6-inch-wide strips of blue fabric for the borders and stitch them to the sides, top, and bottom of the quilt; miter the corners.

Cut and piece blue fabric to size for backing.

Layer backing, batting, and appliquéd top together; pin. Baste layers securely together from top to bottom, side to side, and on the diagonal between opposite corners. Quilt or tack layers together as desired.

Cut and piece 5⅔ yards of 1½-inch-wide bias binding from plaid fabric and bind edges of quilt.

❖

PATCHWORK TEDDY BEAR
PAGE 98
Finished size is 12 inches high (seated)

Materials
⅔ yard muslin for backing
Assorted pastel fabric scraps
Black and yellow scraps of washable felt
White and black embroidery floss
Dental floss, fiberfill
Scraps of ribbon

Instructions
To make yardage for the bear, piece fabric squares into rectangles large enough to accommodate patterns. Follow directions below.

First cut out a 2½-inch-square cardboard or plastic template. (This measurement includes ¼-inch seam allowances.) Trace and cut out a total of 276 squares of pastel fabrics. Using ¼-inch seams, piece squares together in 12 rows of 23 squares each to form a 24x46-inch patchwork rectangle. Press seams open.

Enlarge patterns, *above,* and make paper patterns. All patterns include ¼-inch seam allowances.

From muslin, trace and cut out two body shapes, one head back,

one head front, two legs, two arms, two ears, and one sole. Flop patterns and cut out a *second* set of muslin lining pieces.

Cut the same pieces from patchwork fabric, carefully positioning patterns so that seams between squares will match up along center and side seams of completed bear. (Study the photograph to see how fabric patches are aligned.) Baste a matching muslin backing piece to the wrong side of each patchwork shape.

Body, head, and face: Stitch center seams of two body pieces together for front of bear; repeat for back. (*Note:* Sew all seams twice with small machine stitches for durability.) Stitch front to back along sides and bottom. Clip seams, turn body right side out, and stuff firmly with fiberfill through neck opening.

Next, stitch center seams of head backs and head fronts. Sew together curved edges of each pair of ear pieces. Clip, turn, and lightly stuff ears. Gather bottom edge of each ear and machine-baste to head front along seam line, positioning each ear about 2 inches from center seam line.

Stitch head front to back along seam lines, leaving neck open. Clip seams, turn, and stuff head.

Stitch head to body, using dental floss and tiny whipstitches for added strength.

Cut two eyes and one nose from black felt. Cut two yellow cheek circles from yellow felt. Slip-stitch nose, eyes, and cheeks to head, using matching threads. Use two strands of white embroidery floss and satin stitches to embroider eye accent. Work mouth in stem stitches, using three strands of black floss, and use a single strand of floss and straight stitches for eyelashes.

Arms and legs: Stitch legs together in pairs, leaving bottoms open for sole pieces and tops open for turning. Stitch soles to bottoms of legs. Clip seams, turn, and stuff; slip-stitch opening closed. Stitch legs to body with dental floss, po-

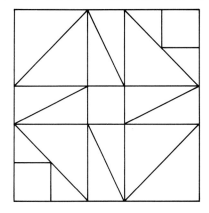

sitioning legs so that bear appears to be sitting.

Stitch arms, leaving openings at shoulders for turning. Clip, turn, stuff, and stitch openings closed. Sew arms to body with dental floss.

To finish: Embroider paw markings with three strands of black embroidery floss. Cut two hearts from calico fabric. Stitch hearts together, turn, and stuff. Add a loop of narrow ribbon and a small bow to heart and tack the heart to the bear's paw. Tie a pretty ribbon around the bear's neck to complete the design.

PINWHEEL PATTERN CRIB QUILT
PAGE 99
Finished size is 56x36 inches

Materials
2½ yards total of pink, blue, yellow, and green prints, checks, and solids for pieced blocks
1¾ yards of print fabric (backing)
1 yard of contrasting fabric for borders
White crochet cotton
Quilt batting
Cardboard or plastic lids for templates

Instructions
The quilt shown consists of fifteen 10-inch squares. Blocks are arranged in five rows of three squares each and finished with a 3-inch-wide border of contrasting fabric.

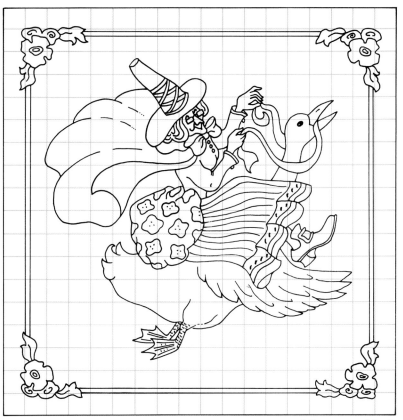

1 Square = 1 Inch

For a similar quilt, enlarge the quilt block pattern, *above*, to size on graph paper and make cardboard or plastic templates for each shape.

Trace and cut the pattern shapes from desired fabrics (study color photograph for inspiration); add ¼-inch seam allowances to all pieces.

Piece a total of 15 blocks and assemble them into five rows of three blocks each. Stitch rows together to form quilt top.

Cut 4-inch-wide strips of contrasting fabric for borders.

Note: The extra width of the borders will be folded to the back of the quilt as a self-binding for the edges.

Stitch border strips to top, bottom, and sides of quilt top (¼-inch seams).

Press the quilt top. Cut batting and backing to size. Layer top, batting, and backing together and baste. Using white crochet cotton, quilt or tack the design as desired.

To finish, trim batting and backing to 56x36 inches. Turn under raw edges of border fabric and slip-stitch to back of quilt.

MOTHER GOOSE QUILT
PAGE 100
Finished size is 46x46 inches

Materials
¾ yard of muslin
1 yard of purple-pink calico
1 yard of pink pindot cotton
¼ yard of purple pindot cotton
2¾ yards of pink plaid (for backing and nine-patch squares)
Fabric paints in assorted colors
Permanent fine-tip brown marking pen
Graph paper, water-erasable pen
Embroidery floss, ribbons, purchased floral appliqués, pom-pom, and lace
Purple pearl cotton
Embroidery hoop
Batting

Instructions
All measurements include ¼-inch seam allowances.

(Continued)

1 Square = 1 Inch

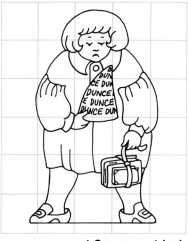

1 Square = 1 Inch

1 Square = 1 Inch

1 Square = 1 Inch

1 Square = 1 Inch

1 Square = 1 Inch

(Continued)

For nursery rhyme blocks: With erasable pen, draw six 6½-inch squares and one 18½-inch square on muslin. Do *not* cut out. (Complete all painting and decorative stitching before cutting blocks.)

Enlarge the Mother Goose design on page 105 and the six nursery rhyme figures, *left,* to size and trace them onto muslin squares. Trace over the outlines of each design with fine brown permanent marker.

Paint designs with textile paints (refer to the photograph for color suggestions). When the paint is completely dry, press squares on wrong side to set colors.

Use simple embroidery to highlight the designs. For best results, limit embellishments to details, such as flowers and facial features. Trim designs with pompoms, ribbons, and purchased appliqués, if desired. Cut blocks from fabric and set aside.

For appliquéd heart blocks: Cut four 6½-inch squares of purple/pink calico. Cut out a 3-inch heart-shape template. Trace and cut four hearts from pink pindot fabric, adding ¼-inch seam allowances. Baste under raw edges and appliqué a heart to the center of each purple square.

For nine-patch blocks: Make a 2½-inch-square cardboard template. Cut 40 squares each from purple pindot and plaid fabrics. Cut 10 squares from the pink pindot fabric for the centers of the blocks. Referring to the photograph for placement, piece the nine-patch blocks; set aside.

For border triangles: First draw a 6-inch square on graph paper. Divide the square in half diagonally, then divide one of the resulting triangles in half again.

Cut out the large triangle (half of the square) to use as a pattern for border triangles, and use the smaller triangle (one-quarter of the square) as a pattern for the corner triangles.

Cut templates for the large and small triangles from cardboard or plastic, if desired.

Cut 12 large triangles and four small triangles from purple and pink calico, adding ¼-inch seam allowances; set aside.

For sashing strips: From pink pindot fabric cut four 6½x34½-inch strips. With erasable pen, write across the strips as follows: "Old Mother Goose when" (first strip), "She wanted to wander" (second strip), "Would ride through the air" (third strip), "On a very fine gander" (fourth strip).

Using purple pearl cotton and outline stitches, embroider each border strip.

Assembly of quilt top: Refer to the photograph for placement of squares around central block.

To begin, piece together two short strips, each consisting of one heart block stitched between two nine-patch blocks. Stitch one of these strips to top and one to bottom of the Mother Goose block.

Next, assemble two strips consisting of a single heart block stitched between two nursery rhyme blocks (strips to the left and right of Mother Goose block in the photograph).

Sew one large triangle to both ends of each strip (refer to photo for positioning), then stitch these strips to each side of the Mother Goose block.

Assemble the remaining triangles and pieced and painted blocks to complete the corners of the top.

For borders, first stitch the "Old Mother Goose . . ." strip to the left side of the pieced top. Sew the "Would ride . . ." strip to the right side of the top. Next, stitch a nine-patch square to both ends of each of the two remaining border strips, then sew these strips to the top and bottom of the quilt.

To finish: From the pink plaid, cut and piece a 47-inch square of backing fabric. Layer backing,

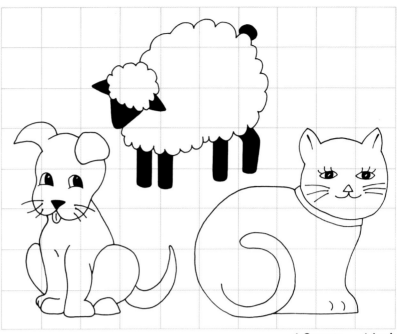

1 Square = 1 Inch

batting, and quilt top together and baste. Machine-quilt around border design of Mother Goose block, in the seam lines between Mother Goose block and the six-inch blocks, in seam lines around sashing strips, and around each appliquéd heart.

Use pearl cotton to tie the quilt on the plaid (reverse) side at all points where blocks and triangles meet. Trim backing to size.

For the binding, piece four calico strips to measure 1½x47 inches. With right sides facing, sew strips to quilt top. Press under raw edges and slip-stitch binding to back of quilt, mitering corners.

GIFT BAGS
PAGE 101
Finished size is 6½x13 inches

Materials
⅜ yard each of two cotton prints and of fusible webbing
Pinking shears
Embroidery floss
Scraps of print fabrics and ribbons for appliqués

Instructions

To make bag: Use a paper lunch bag as a pattern. Cut the bag apart to make two separate pattern

pieces: Cut down the center back of the bag and then cut out the bottom. Add 1-inch seam allowances to the center back edges of the top pattern and add ¼-inch seam allowances to all other edges.

Cut top and bottom bag patterns from each of the two coordinating print fabrics and from the fusible webbing. With wrong sides facing, fuse fabrics together. Overlap the 1-inch-wide back seam allowances on the bag top and fuse together.

With the lining side out, fold bag in half and press to make sharp creases on the two sides. Stitch along both sides ⅛ inch in from fold to within 2 inches of the bottom edge. Then, with right sides facing, pin and sew bottom piece to bag top. Turn.

Again using a lunch bag as a model, fold in sides of the fabric bag; press firmly to establish its shape. Trim top of bag with pinking shears; cut out the half-circle at center top with plain scissors.

To appliqué bag: Make your own appliqué designs or select one of the animal patterns, *above*. Enlarge pattern to fit the size of the bag.

(Continued)

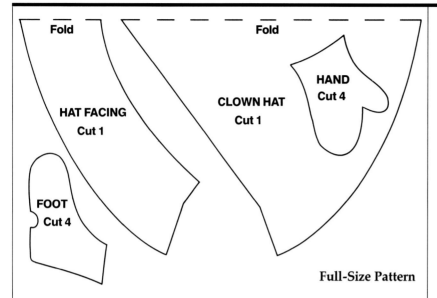

Full-Size Pattern

(Continued)

Cut designs from fabric, adding ¼-inch seam allowances to all pieces. Center and position appliqué approximately 1¼ inches above the bottom seam line of the bag. Turn under raw edges and stitch shape in place. Embellish with embroidery, ribbon, bows, and other trims as desired.

❖

CLOWN BLOCK CRIB TOY
PAGE 101
Finished size is 5x8 inches

Materials
3x36-inch strip of fabric for body
Scraps of contrasting fabric for hat and strips outlining block
6x36-inch strip of organdy
Narrow rickrack
Scraps of white and purple felt for hands, head, and shoes
1 yard each of four 1-inch-wide pastel satin ribbons
Scraps of grosgrain ribbon
1-inch-diameter foam ball
Scraps of yarn for hair and tassel
Red and black embroidery floss
Polyester fiberfill

Instructions
Patterns, except hands and feet, include ¼-inch seam allowance.

For body: Trace full-size patterns, *above.* From body fabric, cut five 3x3-inch squares, and two 3x1¾-inch rectangles.

With right sides facing, sew four squares into a strip. From contrasting fabric, cut 1-inch-wide bias strips as follows: four 2½-inch-long strips and two 10½-inch-long strips. Press under raw edges, lengthwise. On right side of body seams, sew bias strips over each seam and edge these strips with rickrack.

Using grosgrain ribbon, form a letter in the center of one square; hand-sew in place (clown front).

Complete fourth seam on cube and add rickrack and bias tape to this seam.

With right sides together, stitch fifth square to make top of cube, leaving one side open for turning.

Whipstitch around shoes and hands, leaving an opening for stuffing; stuff. Place the two shoes along seam line of the two rectangular body pieces and sew seam. Sew this square to body to complete the cube.

Turn cube right side out, stuff firmly and hand-sew the opening closed. Stitch hands to sides. Add rickrack and bias strips to the top and bottom edges of body, pleating strips at corners to fit.

For head: Wet a 4-inch square of white felt and pull over the foam ball to shape. Let dry; remove ball. With three strands of embroidery floss, make French knots for eyes and nose; work outline stitches for mouth. Fill felt shape with fiberfill. Wrap a ½-inch-wide strip

of felt around the bottom of head to form neck. Clip excess material below neck. Tack the head to the top of the cube.

For hat: Stitch hat facing to hat, right sides together. Sew the hat seam, leaving a ⅜-inch-wide opening at top. Turn and trim edge of brim with rickrack.

Make a pom-pom from yarn; leave tying ends uncut. Slip the ends of the pom-pom through the top of the hat. Sew the ends to the opening to secure. Tack the hat in place atop the head.

For hair: With yarn, make loop stitches around the face and neckline and tack in place.

For collar: From the organdy, cut one strip 3¼ inches wide. Fold under ¼ inch on one length of organdy. Fold under ¼ inch in the opposite direction on the other side of the length. Trim to within ⅛ inch and stitch ⅛-inch ribbons atop the trimmed edges. Fold the strip almost in half (do not overlap the ribbon edges). Repeat for the remaining 2¾-inch-wide strip. Lay the folded edges atop each other and hand-gather. Tack in place around clown's neck.

Add a length of narrow ribbon for hanging, if desired.

❖

BABY BLOCKS QUILT
PAGES 94-95
Finished size is 72x73½ inches

Materials
Scraps of assorted cotton prints for blocks
36 pieces of fabric for backgrounds of blocks, each 10x10¼ inches
2⅛ yards of pink cotton for sashing strips
8½ yards yellow bias binding
4¼ yards muslin for backing
Batting

Instructions
Quilt consists of 36 blocks arranged in six rows of six blocks each. Blocks are assembled with

3-inch-wide pink sashing strips; edges of quilt are bound with yellow bias strips.

Each square of the quilt is composed of six pieced baby blocks arranged in a pyramid and appliquéd to a 9½x9¾-inch background block.

To make one pattern block: Using full-size diamond pattern on page 161, trace and cut out six diamond shapes from one fabric (A) and 12 diamonds from a second fabric (B) for each set of blocks. Add ¼-inch seam allowances to all pieces.

Following instructions on page 133 for assembling diamonds into hexagonal blocks, piece together one A diamond and two B diamonds to form one block. Make a total of six baby blocks.

Stitch these six blocks together into a pyramid shape, as shown in the photograph, and appliqué the pyramid to the center of a 10x10¼-inch background piece. (The base of the pyramid should parallel the longer edge of the background piece.)

Stitch 36 pattern blocks, referring to the photograph for color suggestions.

To assemble quilt: Arrange the pieced and appliquéd blocks in six rows of six squares each and join with 3½-inch-wide pink sashing strips (measurements include ¼-inch seams).

Piece backing fabric to size. Layer and baste backing, batting, and pieced top together; quilt as desired. Finish the edges of the quilt with yellow bias binding.

❖

PAINTED PATCHWORK FARMYARD WALL HANGING
PAGE 95

Materials
1 yard muslin
Textile paints and brushes
Scraps of fiberfill
Three Velcro fasteners
Batting

1 Square = 1 Inch

Instructions
Enlarge patterns, *above,* to size and trace onto muslin with water-erasable pen or light pencil.

Paint farmyard background (field, fence, and sky) with textile paints, following painting tips on pages 20-21 and 267.

On separate scraps of muslin, paint cow, sheep, and pig. When all painted pieces are thoroughly dry, set designs by pressing gently on the wrong side.

To construct wall hanging, cut out painted background animals, leaving ½-inch seam allowances around all pieces. Lay painted background on table, painted side up. Place a matching piece of plain muslin on top of the scene, followed by a layer of batting. Pin, baste, and stitch all three layers together around the perimeter of the design, leaving an opening at the bottom for turning. Trim seams, turn, press gently, and slip-stitch opening closed.

Hand- or machine-quilt along cloud line and edge of grass, and then tack at various other points across design.

Next, back each of the three farm animals with muslin. Stitch, trim seams, turn, and stuff with scraps of fiberfill. Slip-stitch the openings closed.

Arrange animals as desired on background panel and mark positions. Stitch one-half of a Velcro fastener to the back of each animal and a matching half of the fastener to the spot on the background panel where the animal is to be attached.

Attach rings or loops of muslin to the back of the painted scene for hanging. The child can then play with the animals and snap them on and off the background scene or reposition them at will.

PICTURE-BOOK PATCHWORK FOR CHILDREN

Youngsters of all ages will adore this collection of quilts and patchwork playthings featuring familiar motifs from a child's own world. Each of the pieced and appliquéd designs on these pages will inspire dozens of other patchwork projects as well.

What child could resist the merry assortment of lions and tigers and bears romping across this delightful quilt. The fierce wild animals that Dorothy and her companions feared to meet on their way to the Emerald City turn out to be an unexpectedly friendly bunch in this fanciful interpretation of that well-loved episode in "The Wizard of Oz."

Each of the nine cuddly animals is captured on a muslin block in a combination of machine appliqué and hand embroidery. The tigers' stripes are painted on to complete the picture.

Embroidered muslin borders frame the animals and repeat the line that is the source of inspiration for this appliquéd menagerie.

And the appliquéd animals, in turn, inspired the trio of plump stuffed creatures keeping guard over the quilt. Each three-dimensional creature is almost two feet long, stitched from cotton prints and firmly stuffed with fiberfill. The animals' features are appliquéd and embroidered, and the tiger's stripes, as on the quilt, are painted on with textile paints.

Any of these animal designs also would make a charming appliqué for a child's jacket, jumper, shirt, or book bag. Instructions begin on page 116.

Stitch these whimsical alphabet blocks into a host of imaginative projects to brighten a child's room and help him learn his ABCs at the same time!

Each letter of this appliquéd alphabet is accompanied by a kid-pleasing design, often with a humorous twist: B's baby bear carries balloons, K's kangaroo flies a pair of kites, and H's grinning hippo wears her heart on her chest.

Letters and accompanying motifs are cut from sturdy fabrics in bright primary colors and machine stitched to 12-inch squares of background fabric. The squares then can be mixed, matched, and sewn together to make any or all of the projects pictured on these two pages.

In the youngster's bedroom, *opposite,* eleven alphabet blocks are pieced together with green sashing strips and borders to form a tailored dust ruffle along one side and across the foot of the bed. Four more squares are backed and stuffed to make toss pillows for the bed. (What a great way to make a name for your child!)

Three squares have been sewn into storage pockets on the wall

hanging above the bed, and another is pieced into the front of a patchwork toy tote hanging on the wall at far left.

For the storage box on the rug, five alphabet blocks and one plain square are backed with contrasting fabric, lined with stiff cardboard, and assembled into a cube.

The foam-stuffed hassock, *above left,* is constructed the same way.

Use a child's initial block to make a personalized cover for his scrapbook, photograph album, or school notebook, as pictured *above.*

Any and all of the alphabet blocks can be stitched in colors and combinations of your choice, to spell out a child's name, his school, hometown, and so forth. Picture motifs also can be appliquéd without accompanying letters to embellish clothing and other items for your favorite youngster.

Countrified patchwork
pillows, a sampler quilt,
and an amusing pair
of school portraits that are
easy to personalize
make appealing accents
for a child's room.

The spectacular red, beige, and blue quilt, *left,* is truly a patchwork tour de force. An imaginative mingling of appliqué and piece-work techniques, it achieves the effect of a sampler quilt within a more formal framework of a repeated geometric pattern and minimal color scheme.

Each 15-inch block is based on a blue and beige nine-patch Ohio Star design. The pieced stars are combined with appliquéd corner squares, featuring a series of traditional and not-so-traditional motifs (hearts, apples, tulips, whales, and birds). The center of each star is an entirely separate, carefully pieced, 5-inch-square pattern block—and each of these center pattern blocks is different from all the others.

The eight completed star blocks—each different in the details of composition but identical in basic piecing—are sashed with strips of blue pindot fabric and framed in a lively sawtooth border of red and beige triangles.

Each square of the star blocks is simply outline quilted, and the blue sashing strips are quilted in a pattern of interlocking hearts. The

sawtooth border is quilted "in the ditch" (along the seams), and the wide blue border features a woven braid design.

This twin-size quilt manages to interpret traditional patterns in a delightfully contemporary way, making it a standout in almost any setting.

In a strictly traditional vein, Sunbonnet Sue and Overall Sam make picturesque appliqués for a pair of muslin pillows, *opposite.*

For more contemporary portraits, turn to the boy and girl at the blackboards in the appliquéd pictures, *above.* While she practices her numbers, he sketches the alphabet. To lend these pictures a pleasingly personal air, select fabrics for the hair and clothing that match your own youngsters' coloring and favorite outfits.

1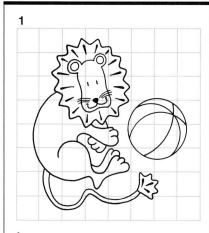

2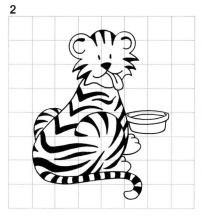

3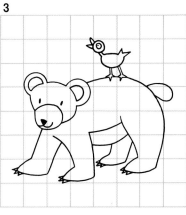

4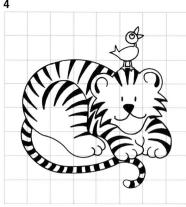

5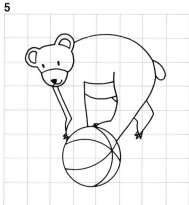

6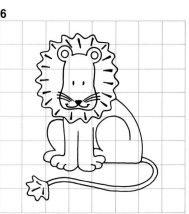

7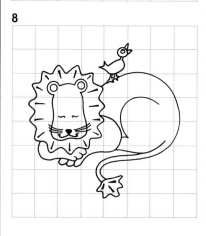

8

9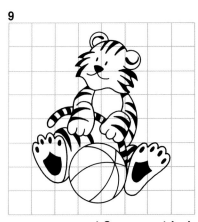

1 Square = 1 Inch

❖

LIONS, TIGERS, AND BEARS QUILT
PAGES 110-111
Finished size is 54 inches square

Materials
4½ yards of muslin
⅔ yard of green floral print
½ yard of brown floral print
¾ yard of plaid fabric
¼ yard *each* of fabric for bears, lions, and tigers

2 skeins green No. 5 pearl cotton
Fabric scraps for noses, feet, balls, dish, and birds
Embroidery floss
Fusible webbing, typing paper
Black laundry marker, batting

Instructions
Cut and piece a 55-inch square of muslin for backing; cut four 37x8½-inch strips of muslin for borders. Set aside. Cut nine 8½-inch squares of muslin for blocks.

To make blocks: Enlarge patterns, *above;* trace onto appropriate fabrics. Pin fusible webbing to backs of fabrics; cut shapes from fabric and webbing at the same time.

For bears, cut separate muzzles, ear centers, tummies, and bodies.

For lions, cut separate heads, bodies, manes, ear centers, tails, and tail ends.

For tigers, trace patterns onto fabric; transfer stripes with pencil or erasable pen. Before cutting shapes, either embroider stripes with black floss or color them using a laundry pen. Make separate tiger heads, tails, bodies, and foot pads (for design No. 9).

Cut out all appliqués and fuse shapes to muslin squares. With pencil or dressmaker's carbon, draw the inside detail lines for each animal. (Facial features and birds' legs and beaks will be hand embroidered. Other details are machine satin-stitched.)

To machine-appliqué, set machine for narrow satin stitches. Use threads that match fabrics, except stitch lines on balls in contrasting thread. Slip typing paper beneath each square as you stitch, to avoid puckering. Embroider inside detail lines with narrow rows of satin stitches first, then cover outlines of each appliqué shape.

Tear away paper; press block.

For hand-embroidered details, use stem and straight stitches for facial features and small accents; fill larger areas with satin stitches. Use black floss for facial features. For bee, use a double strand of black and orange floss to make a bullion knot for the body. Wings are loops of black floss. Trace bee's flight using black running stitches. Cut a tiny circle of white felt for bird's eye and attach with a French knot.

To assemble quilt: Cut the following border strips from plaid fabric: four strips 3½x11½ inches and four strips 3½x19½ inches. Cut identical strips from green floral print fabric.

Arrange blocks in three rows of three squares each; assemble with green and plaid sashing strips arranged in a lattice pattern. (See photograph.) Pin, baste, and sew blocks and sashing strips together, using ¼-inch seams. Set aside.

For embroidered borders: Center and trace the phrase "Lions and Tigers and Bears! Oh My" onto the four 8½x37-inch border strips; embroider with pearl cotton, using stem stitches.

Cut four 1½x55-inch pieces of brown print fabric and four 8½-inch squares of green floral print. Assemble narrow brown strips, green squares, and embroidered muslin panels to form quilt borders; attach to quilt top. Use ¼-inch seams throughout.

Cut batting to size. Layer muslin backing, batting, and quilt top; baste. Quilt as desired.

Trim backing and batting; fold raw edges of quilt top to back and slip-stitch in place.

LION AND TIGER STUFFED ANIMALS
PAGE 111
Finished size is approximately 20 inches long, 13 inches high, and 16 inches wide

Materials
1¾ yards of peach print (lion)
1¼ yards of yellow print (tiger)
Black fabric paint, brush (tiger)
¼ yard of fleece (each animal)
Black felt scraps, dental floss
Black and white embroidery floss
2½ pounds fiberfill (each animal)

Instructions
Patterns include ¼-inch seam margins. Enlarge patterns on pages 118–119; cut out. *Flop patterns for right and left side* as necessary (body, legs, and head backs). Trace seam markings onto wrong side of fabric; trace facial features and outlines for tiger stripes onto right side of fabric. Sew all seams and darts twice for extra strength.

Cutting and marking: For each animal, cut patterns from print fabric as indicated. Also cut one tail strip measuring 5½x27 inches. Also cut four ears and one face shape from fleece. Baste fleece shapes to wrong side of fabric shapes; handle each as one piece.

Also cut black felt eyes and nose for each animal.

For lion, cut a mane 10x44½ inches and tail 9x17 inches.

For the tiger, mark areas to be painted with light pencil lines, using photograph as a guide for placement of stripes. (Paint stripes

on tail and whiskers before assembly; paint stripes on body, legs, and head *after* animal is assembled and stuffed.)

To assemble body and back legs: Stitch toe darts; clip centers and press open. Sew gathering stitches along curved edge of foot dart (at base of each leg). Pin dart edges together; adjust gathers, and stitch. Press seam toward foot.

Sew curved edge of back legs and back inner foot together along Xs; press seam toward leg.

Pin leg to body, matching dotted lines and dot at point C. Sew with body on top, beginning at wide end of small seam; clip seam, then pin leg to body, matching dashed lines. Beginning at wide end of small seam, sew around foot; end at A. Clip seam.

Underbodies: Sew toe darts for inner front feet. Clip centers, trim, and press open. Sew underbody darts; clip and press. Sew straight edge of inner front feet to front openings, easing to fit; clip and press seams toward feet.

Gather along back leg openings. Pin and sew underbody to body from neck front to back leg openings, matching foot darts.

Restitch inner corner of front feet; clip. Pin back inner feet to underbody; adjust gathers and sew. Stitch from A to C on both sides of center back seam, joining back edge of underbody to bottom back edge of upper body.

Sew body backs together from B to C; clip, turn, and stuff. Stuff body and legs firmly, beginning with toes and working toward neck. Using dental floss, gather neck opening and tie off.

Tails and toes: For tiger's tail, sew long sides and one end of tail strip together, rounding end. Trim, turn, and stuff.

For lion's tail, use pointed pattern to trace six points the length of the tail (align bottom of point pattern with long raw edge of tail strip).

(Continued)

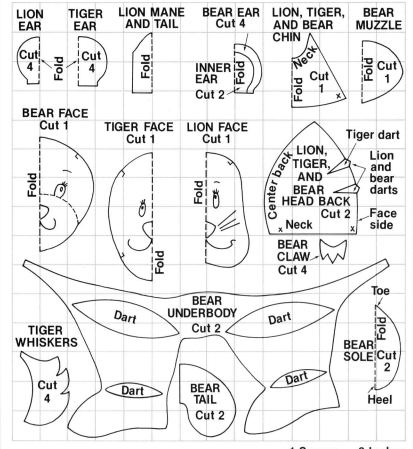

LION EAR — Cut 4 / Fold

TIGER EAR — Cut 4 / Fold

LION MANE AND TAIL — Fold

BEAR EAR — Cut 4 / Fold / INNER EAR — Cut 2 / Fold

LION, TIGER, AND BEAR CHIN — Neck / Fold / Cut 1 / x

BEAR MUZZLE — Cut 1 / Fold

BEAR FACE — Cut 1 / Fold

TIGER FACE — Cut 1 / Fold

LION FACE — Cut 1 / Fold

LION, TIGER, AND BEAR HEAD BACK — Cut 2 / Center back / Tiger dart / Lion and bear darts / Face side / x Neck x

BEAR CLAW — Cut 4

TIGER WHISKERS — Cut 4 / Dart / Dart

BEAR UNDERBODY — Cut 2 / Dart / Dart

BEAR TAIL — Cut 2 / Dart

BEAR SOLE — Cut 2 / Fold / Toe / Heel

1 Square = 2 Inches

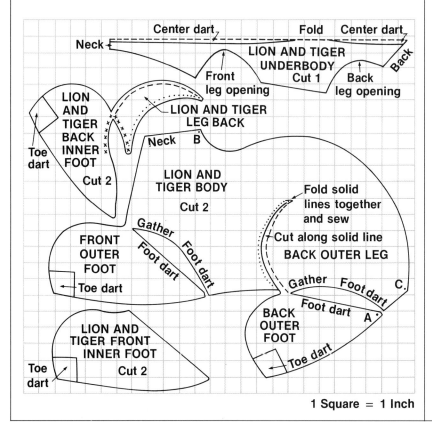

Center dart / Fold / Center dart

Neck

LION AND TIGER UNDERBODY — Cut 1 / Front leg opening / Back leg opening / Back

LION AND TIGER BACK INNER FOOT — Cut 2 / Toe dart

LION AND TIGER LEG BACK / Neck / B

LION AND TIGER BODY — Cut 2

FRONT OUTER FOOT — Toe dart / Gather / Foot dart / Foot dart

Fold solid lines together and sew / Cut along solid line — BACK OUTER LEG / Gather / Foot dart / C. / Foot dart / A.

BACK OUTER FOOT — Gather / Foot dart / Toe dart

LION AND TIGER FRONT INNER FOOT — Cut 2 / Toe dart

1 Square = 1 Inch

(Continued)

With right sides facing, join short ends of strip. Fold strip in half lengthwise (right sides facing); machine-sew along jagged tops of points (do not stitch sides of points). Trim, clip, turn ruffle right side out, and press.

Gather raw bottom edge of ruffle; draw up. Join long sides of tail strip. Insert gathered ruffle into end of tail strip and stitch. Turn and stuff tail. Sew lion and tiger tails to bodies, using dental floss.

Using a long needle and black floss, sculpture toes on each foot, sewing from toe dart on bottom of foot up to top of toes (see photograph for placement of stitches).

Heads and faces: Whipstitch eyes and nose to face. Stitch features with floss. Use black stem stitches for mouths, white satin stitches for eye highlights, and black straight stitches for eyelashes.

For tiger, paint ear fronts; for lion, embroider inner ear circles (refer to photograph).

Stitch ears together in pairs; clip, turn, and press. Pleat bottom center of each ear. Baste ears to face pieces, matching raw edges.

For tiger, join whiskers in pairs; clip and turn. Baste whiskers to face pieces, slightly overlapping ears and matching raw edges.

For lion's mane, trace 15 points onto wrong side of mane ruffle strip. Stitch and assemble mane as described for tail ruffle, above. Sew points, trim, clip, and turn. Gather, pin, and baste mane to face piece, matching raw edges.

Sew head back darts. Stay-stitch neck edge. Sew center back seam. Stitch chin piece to head back, matching Xs. Sew face piece to head back, matching center points of face at top and chin.

Turn head right side out; stuff firmly. Use dental floss to gather neck opening; tie off. Use dental floss to sew head to body, positioning head so it faces to one side (see photograph).

To finish tiger, adjust pencil marks for stripes on tiger's head, body, and legs. Paint stripes with black fabric paints or acrylics. To avoid bleeding, do not dilute paint or saturate brush. Allow paint to dry thoroughly in one area before moving on to the next.

Trim animals with colorful satin ribbon bows, if desired.

❖

STUFFED BEAR
PAGE 110
Finished size is 21 inches long, 20 inches high, and 11½ inches wide

Materials
⅞ yard of rust print fabric
⅛ yard contrasting print for muzzle, ear centers, soles, and tail
¼ yard polyester fleece
Black felt scraps, dental floss
Black and white embroidery floss
2½ pounds polyester fiberfill

Instructions
Note: Read general directions for Lion and Tiger stuffed animals before proceeding.

Cutting and marking: Enlarge patterns, *opposite* and *above right;* cut out bodies, head backs, face, chin, and ears. From contrasting print, cut out muzzle, inner ears, soles, and tails. Also cut out face piece, muzzle, and ears from the fleece. Baste fleece to backs of matching shapes; handle as one piece.

From felt, cut out eyes, nose, and claws. Transfer markings for features to face piece and muzzle.

Body, underbody, feet, and tail: Stitch underbody darts; clip. Join underbodies along center seam. Sew one side of pieced underbody to each body piece, from toe of back foot to heel of front foot. Clip seams. Sew from heel of back foot to end of underbody; clip seam. Sew remaining top seam of body pieces together; clip seam. Stitch soles to feet; clip seams and turn body right side out. Stuff body firmly with fiberfill, working from toes up to neck.

Use dental floss to gather neck opening; tie off.

Stitch felt claws to toes. Sew tail pieces together; leave straight

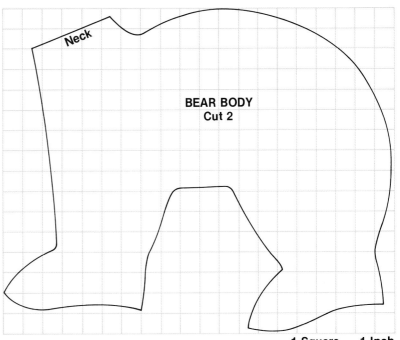

Neck

BEAR BODY
Cut 2

1 Square = 1 Inch

edge open. Clip, turn, and stuff; use dental floss to stitch the tail to the body.

Head and face: Press under seam margin on muzzle; appliqué muzzle to face, matching chin line. Whipstitch eyes and nose to face. Embroider features, add ears, and attach head to body, as described for lion and tiger, above.

❖

ALPHABET DESIGNS
PAGES 112-113

Materials
Yardage for each project
Assorted rickrack, ribbons, piping, and embroidery floss for accents and trim
Fusible webbing

Instructions
Designs are approximately 6 to 7 inches wide and 10 inches long (see patterns, pages 120-121). Cut motifs from fabrics; machine-appliqué atop background blocks. Embellish blocks with trim, ribbons, and hand embroidery, if desired. Stitch appliqués and details before sewing individual projects.

◆ BED SKIRT: Complete a sufficient number of 8½x14¼-inch appliquéd blocks to go around bed. Join blocks with narrow sashing strips; add a border, adjusting width of sashings and border to suit bed. Line skirt strips; stitch strips to fabric equal to the length and width of the mattress. Add kick pleats of plain fabric at corners of skirt, if desired.

◆ PILLOWS: Appliqué designs to fabric; border with piping and sew into pillows.

◆ TOY BOX: Stitch five 13-inch appliquéd squares and one plain square. Assemble into a box (see box instructions, pages 92-93).

◆ POCKET WALL HANGING: Stitch three appliquéd blocks to a fleece-backed, rickrack-trimmed 13x31-inch rectangle of fabric; leave tops of blocks open to make pockets. Add a casing at the top for a dowel for hanging.

◆ TOY BAG: Piece an appliquéd block in the center of a patchwork design of desired size. Line bag and add grosgrain drawstrings.

◆ SOFT CUBE: Construct as for Toy Box, except trim edges with rickrack rather than piping; omit cardboard. Stuff cube with shredded foam; slip-stitch sides closed.

(Continued)

119

1 Square = 1 Inch

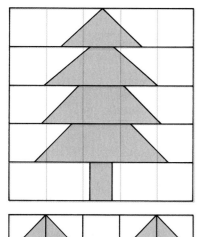
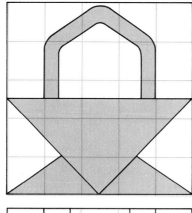
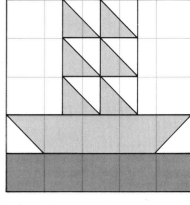

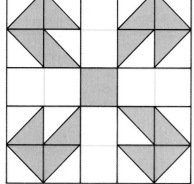
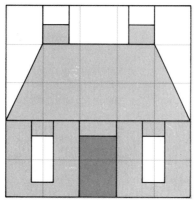
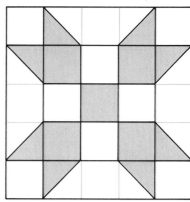

1 Square = 1 Inch

(Continued)

◆ BOOK COVER: Construct cover following instructions for cover on page 102. Appliquéd letter of your choice to front of book.

SAMPLER QUILT
PAGES 114-115
Finished size is 59x97 inches

Materials
5 yards beige pindot fabric
3½ yards navy blue pindot
1½ yards burgundy print
¼ yard solid burgundy
⅓ yard beige, blue, and burgundy print; quilt batting

Instructions
Quilt consists of eight pieced and appliquéd 15-inch-square Ohio Star blocks. Blocks are arranged in four rows of two blocks each and set with 4-inch-wide sashing strips, 3-inch-wide sawtooth inner border, and 5½-inch-wide outer border. Use ¼-inch seams.

1 Square = 1 Inch

To begin: Piece beige pindot backing to 60x98 inches; set aside. Cut blue pindot sashes and borders as follows: four 4½x15½-inch strips, five 4½x34½-inch strips, two 4½x80-inch strips, two 6x60-inch strips, and two 6x87-inch strips. Set sashes and borders aside.

Enlarge the Ohio Star pattern on page 154 to 15 inches square.

Each of the nine patches that make up the block will be 5 inches square (finished size).

To complete one block: Trace and cut out eight beige and eight blue pindot triangles, adding seam allowances. Assemble triangles into four squares (star points) composed of two beige and two blue triangles each. Set aside.

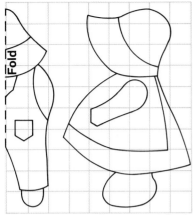

1 Square = 1 Inch

For center square of each block, enlarge patterns, *opposite;* piece into 5-inch squares. For the two remaining centers, piece a 5-inch-square Ohio Star and a 5-inch-square 25-patch block composed of small burgundy and navy blue squares. See photograph for colors on other center squares.

Next, cut four 5½-inch squares of beige pindot fabric for corners of each star block. Enlarge one of the appliqué patterns *(opposite);* cut four identical motifs from burgundy print (add seam margins). Appliqué one design to each corner block. (Embroider apple stems, legs and beak on bird, and blow spout on whale.)

Stitch hearts in corners of three blocks. For star block with pine tree pattern in center, appliqué small clusters of hearts on two corner squares and birds on remaining corners. See photograph for placement of corner squares and arrangement of completed blocks. Assemble blocks with 4-inch-wide sashes and inner borders of navy blue pindot fabric.

For sawtooth border: Divide a 2x3-inch rectangle diagonally to make a template for sawtooth triangle. Trace, cut, and piece burgundy print and beige pindot triangles to form border strips. For corners, piece 3-inch squares from beige and burgundy triangles.

To complete quilt: Add 5½-inch-wide borders of navy pindot fabric. Baste backing, batting, and top together; quilt as desired. Bind edges of quilt with 1½-inch-wide bias strips of navy pindot fabric.

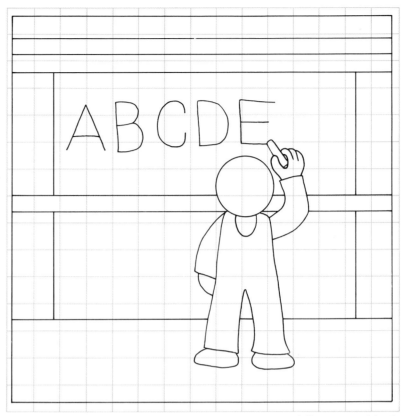

1 Square = 1 Inch

SUNBONNET SUE AND OVERALL SAM PILLOWS
PAGE 114
Finished size is 15 inches square

Materials
⅓ yard white fabric
⅓ yard polyester fleece
1 yard red print fabric
¼ yard *each* solid blue and blue gingham
Fiberfill, scraps of lace and embroidery floss

Instructions
Enlarge patterns, *above;* transfer to the centers of 11½-inch white squares. Cut appliqués from appropriate fabrics, adding ¼-inch seam allowances to pieces. Stitch appliqués in place. Trim Sue's hat with lace and Sam's hat with an embroidered hatband.

Back appliquéd squares with fleece; quilt designs as desired.

Cut and piece a 5x80-inch red strip for each ruffle. Fold strip in half lengthwise, gather raw edges, and baste to top. Using red print for backing, sew designs into pillows. Stuff with fiberfill.

SCHOOL DAYS WALL HANGINGS
PAGE 115
Finished size is 15 inches square

Materials
½ yard of white canvas
Black fabric for blackboard
Assorted fabric scraps and trims
Fusible webbing, frame

Instructions
Enlarge pattern, *above;* transfer to a 15-inch square of canvas. (To transform boy figure into girl figure, shape hair into a bob, cut overalls off at skirt length, and add legs between shoes and skirt.)

Cut out appliqués; zigzag-stitch in place. Sketch letters or numbers on blackboard; machine-zigzag over lines. Frame as desired.

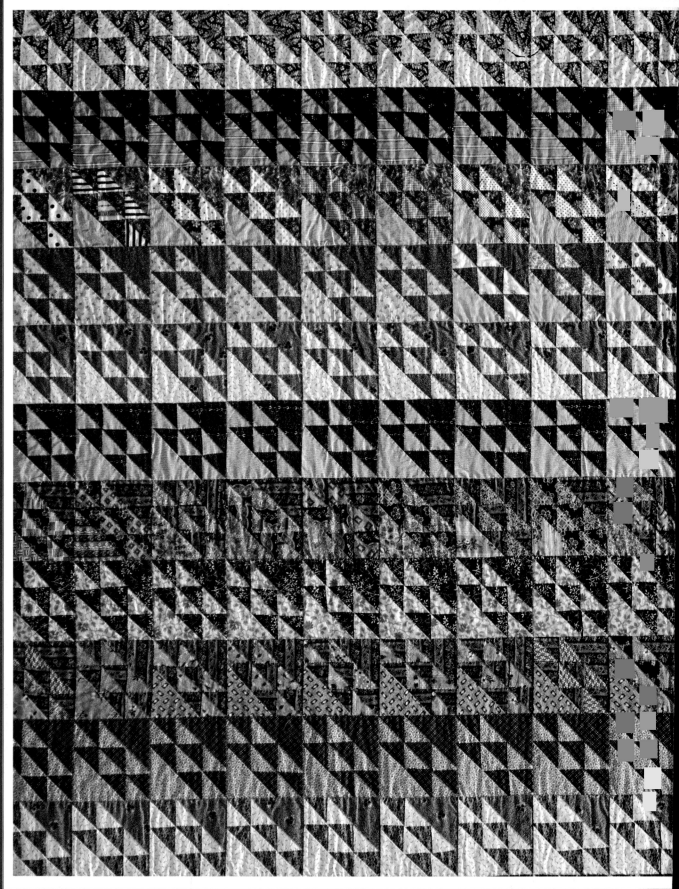

PIECING ON THE BIAS—
TRIANGLES, DIAMONDS,
AND HEXAGONS

Learning to
control fabric pieces that are cut
on the bias—and thus more apt to
stretch out of shape—is an
essential step toward perfecting
your patchwork skills. Used alone
or in combination with simple
squares and rectangles, this trio of
geometric shapes can more than
triple the possibilities in your
pattern repertoire.

CREATING PATTERNS WITH TRIANGLES

The bench pad and tote bag pictured here are used to illustrate two different ways of piecing right-angle triangles as part of a patchwork design.

One of the more versatile shapes in the patchwork repertoire, the right-angle triangle is used alone or in combination with squares and rectangles to create hundreds of different patterns.

Piece two right-angle triangles together along the diagonal to form a square—the basis for the random-patch pattern used on the settle bench pad, *above*.

Stitched back to back, the same two triangles form a larger triangle—or one half of a large square, as in the Yankee Puzzle pattern on the tote bag pocket, *left*.

1

2

3

4

5

6

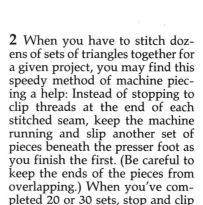

◆

1 The most important point to remember when working with right-angle triangles, or any shapes that have one or more bias edges, is that, whenever possible, the bias edge(s) should face toward the inside of the pieced block. And wherever possible, the edge(s) of pieces cut on the grain of the fabric should fall toward the *outside* of the block, to ensure stability and minimize stretching.

Keep this principle in mind as you position templates on fabric and stitch triangles together for all your patchwork projects.

For most patterns, it is best to trace and cut triangular pieces so that the short legs of each triangle fall on the horizontal and vertical grain lines of the fabric.

2 When you have to stitch dozens of sets of triangles together for a given project, you may find this speedy method of machine piecing a help: Instead of stopping to clip threads at the end of each stitched seam, keep the machine running and slip another set of pieces beneath the presser foot as you finish the first. (Be careful to keep the ends of the pieces from overlapping.) When you've completed 20 or 30 sets, stop and clip the sets apart.

3 Press all squares open (press seams toward the darker triangle). Stitch squares into rows, then stitch rows together to make sufficient pieced fabric to cover the cushion.

4 Cutting and piecing right-angle triangles for the Yankee Puzzle pattern on the tote bag pocket, *opposite,* requires a slightly different procedure. Because the triangles are to be pieced in such a way that

the diagonal of each triangle ends up on the *outside* edge of each pattern block, this edge should be cut on the straight grain of the fabric.

When planning any patchwork pattern involving triangles, always study the way the pattern block is pieced, then decide how to lay out and cut pattern pieces.

5 To piece the four-patch Yankee Puzzle pattern, stitch eight sets of dark and light triangles together along one short leg. Press seams toward the dark side of each pair.

Next, piece two sets of triangles together along the new diagonal, matching seams carefully, to form a square. Make four squares.

6 Stitch the squares together to form the completed Yankee Puzzle block.

For complete how-to on the bench pad and tote bag, turn to page 136. For how-to on the star-pattern crib quilt (on the back of the bench), see pages 154-161.

Using only three colors and three graduated sizes of triangles, you can create dozens of different pattern blocks to make your own version of the patchwork sampler wall pictured here.

All of the pattern blocks on the wall, *right,* are simple to piece, but perhaps the simplest is the Windmill block, used for the two smallest pictures, upper left and lower right. For this pattern, a small light blue and a small white triangle are pieced back to back to form a larger triangle. This pieced triangle is then stitched to a large dark blue triangle to form one square of the four-patch block.

Just below the Windmill block, on the left in the photograph, is a pattern called the Colorado block. Based on a 16-patch design, the Colorado block is pieced entirely from one size of triangle in two colors.

In the lower left corner of the photograph, resting on the shelf, stands a Flock of Geese block. Another four-patch design, this pattern uses two sizes of triangles in two colors to evoke the grace and symmetry of flocks of geese in flight.

Similarly, the long, horizontal pattern at the bottom of the photograph, called Flying Geese, uses the strong contrast of light and dark triangles to depict the outspread wings and a follow-the-leader formation of migrating birds. Frequently used in combination with solid blocks for an entire quilt top, this design also makes an attractive border or sashing design.

Finally, there is the over-scaled pattern called Marion's block, pieced from triangles in three colors and three sizes.

Any one of these patterns can be stitched large or small, with or without sashing strips between the blocks, and pieced alone or along with other blocks for a sampler quilt.

To experiment with patterns while planning your own sampler wall, work with graph paper and colored pencils to test the effects of different arrangements of triangles in assorted colors and sizes.

TURNING TRIANGLES INTO DIAMONDS

Piecing equilateral triangles is the first step in learning to work with finished pattern blocks that are other than square in shape.

Equilateral triangles are the basis for a number of more advanced patchwork shapes, including diamonds, hexagons, and many star designs. Learning to accurately cut and piece this shape will vastly increase your pattern repertoire.

As with all patchwork, precision cutting and piecing is crucial to the success of patterns involving equilateral triangles and other geometric shapes derived from them. These shapes are especially "unforgiving" in the sense that inaccuracies of even ⅛ inch may be magnified and multiplied in the course of piecing an entire quilt top. This inevitably results in mismatched seams, pattern blocks that will not lie flat, and a generally unsatisfying patchwork experience.

To avoid disappointment, mark and cut pattern pieces carefully, replace worn templates often, press fabric after each piecing step, and always match points and seams with special care.

1 At first glance, the Birds-in-Air Quilt, *opposite,* appears to be composed of random rows of dark and light triangles. However, the overall pattern is actually carefully constructed from diamond-shape blocks.

First, dark and light triangles are stitched together to form diamonds. These small diamonds are then assembled to form larger diamond-shape blocks. Finally, these blocks are stitched together to complete the quilt top.

To keep the patchwork shapes as stable as possible, make sure that one edge of each basic triangle shape is traced and cut parallel to the grain of the fabric. Cut nine dark and nine light triangles for each large diamond block in the pattern. *Note:* Clear plastic graph paper—available in quilt shops— is especially useful for drafting reusable geometric templates.

Carefully pin one light and one dark triangle together along the grain edge. Stitch triangles together, matching seam lines. (Do *not* run stitching into the seam allowance; this will enable you to press seams in any direction required as the pieces are assembled into more complex blocks.)

2 Piece a total of nine diamonds from the light and dark triangles. Press all seams toward the dark triangles. Next, lay out these nine diamonds in a large diamond shape, with all dark points facing in one direction and light points facing in the opposite direction.

To assemble diamond block, first stitch nine small diamonds into three diagonal rows of three diamonds each (press seams in one direction). Next, piece these three strips into the larger diamond shape; again, press seams in one direction.

3 Finally, join the large diamond blocks into diagonal rows and assemble the rows to form quilt top. (Instructions begin on page 136.)

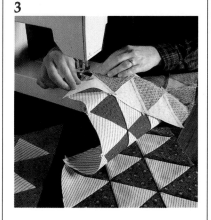

PIECING TUMBLING BLOCKS

A trio of diamonds in light, medium, and dark tones are pieced together to form each hexagonal shape, the basic building block of this popular traditional pattern.

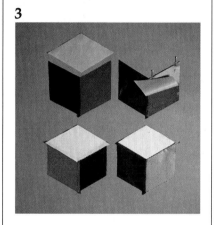

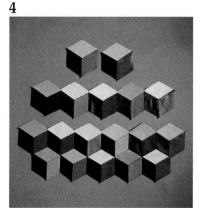

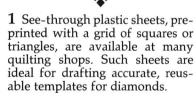

The dramatic and strikingly three-dimensional quality of the Tumbling Blocks pattern is most apparent when smooth, light-reflecting fabrics are pieced into the design, as in the stunning jewel-tone silks and satins used for the Victorian era, crib-size quilt top, *opposite.*

Consistent use of a black diamond as the darkest third of the hexagon, plus careful attention to placement so the dark, medium, and light faces of each block are oriented always in the same directions, makes this a particularly effective example of the Tumbling Blocks design. A similar play of light and pattern can be achieved with less expensive polished cotton fabrics, used to piece the how-to steps, *above right.*

It is important to note here that there are two diamond shapes most commonly used in patchwork. A relatively wide diamond (with 60-degree and 120-degree angles) is used for Tumbling Blocks, other hexagonal designs, and six-point star patterns. A longer and narrower diamond (with 45-degree and 135-degree angles) is used primarily for eight-point stars.

❖

1 See-through plastic sheets, pre-printed with a grid of squares or triangles, are available at many quilting shops. Such sheets are ideal for drafting accurate, reusable templates for diamonds.

Trace and cut an equal number of light, medium, and dark fabric diamonds for this pattern.

2 Since accurate matching of points and angles is essential, Tumbling Blocks is most successfully pieced by hand. Pin and stitch along seam lines, from point to point. To facilitate turning and pressing, do *not* extend stitching into seam allowances.

The hexagonal blocks should be pieced in the same sequence, to ensure that light, medium, and dark facets will fall on the same side of each block.

3 Sew together medium and dark diamonds; press the seams toward the dark diamond. Next, set lightest diamond in place, matching points and angles. Pin and sew along one side, from inner corner to outer point. Repeat along second side, again sewing from center point to outer edge of hexagon (this eliminates bunching at point where seams meet). Press seams toward darker diamonds.

4 Assemble completed hexagons into rows, always keeping light, medium, and dark diamonds in the same relative positions. Stitch blocks into rows, then join rows together, always pressing seams toward darker fabric pieces.

To make a Tumbling Blocks coverlet, see page 137.

STITCHING HEXAGON FLOWERS

A recurrent shape in traditional English patchwork, the hexagon probably originated in mosaic patterns of the Middle East.

Grandmother's Flower Garden pattern, also called Mosaic, enjoyed widespread popularity during the late nineteenth and early twentieth centuries. It was especially common during the depression era, when quiltmaking again became a necessity in many American homes. Pieced from tiny hexagonal patches, this pattern can make thrifty use of even the smallest scraps of fabric.

In earliest examples of the design—and indeed, in most quilts dating from the depression years—each flower block was pieced from a different set of three print fabrics, with the only unifying factor being the color of the hexagonal patches that made up a "path" among the "flowers."

Whether each block is pieced from different scraps of calico, or all flowers repeat a single color scheme (as in the contemporary quilt pictured *opposite*), the Flower Garden pattern remains a perennial favorite among American quilters.

❖

1 Grandmother's Flower Garden is essentially a one-patch design—a single pattern piece is used throughout. To ensure accurate piecing, replace cutting- and seam-line templates as soon as they become worn.

Note: If you've had practice tracing and cutting pattern pieces, you may prefer to use a single stitching-line template, trusting your now-experienced eye to judge ¼-inch seam allowances. But if you feel less than confident about your ability to "guesstimate" seam allowances, use the two-template method described on page 25.

Whichever template method you use, orient the templates so that the two parallel sides of the hexagon are always aligned along the horizontal or vertical grain line of the fabric.

Cut and thread together the hexagons required for each flower block: one center patch, six patches for the first row, twelve patches for the second row, and eight muslin hexagons for a part of the path around each flower.

2 To assemble a block, stitch one of the first circle of hexagons to the center hexagon. Stitch *only* from seam line to seam line, leaving seam allowances free so that fabric may be pressed in whichever direction creates the least bulk on the design. *Note:* Although it is possible to piece large hexagons by machine, hand-piecing assures greater accuracy and is recommended to all but the most experienced machine stitchers.

Continue to add hexagons until the first round of petals is completed. Press seam allowances to one side and in toward the center of the flower (see photograph). Repeat for second row of petals.

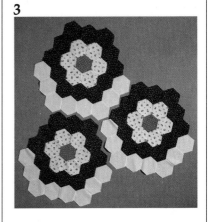

3 To assemble flowers into quilt top, add eight muslin hexagons to outer edge of each flower. For quilt instructions, see page 138.

SETTLE BENCH CUSHION
PAGE 126

Materials

Assorted scraps of light and dark print, plaid, and striped fabrics
2-inch foam slab, cut to size and shape of bench seat
Fabric for backing
Print piping
Flat buttons (optional)

Instructions

Make templates for right-angle triangles of the desired size (finished size of triangles on cushion shown is 4 inches on each right-angle leg). Cut and piece triangles to make sufficient yardage to cover seat cushion, following basic piecing instructions on page 127.

Carefully trim pieced yardage to size and shape of cushion, adding ½-inch seam allowances on all sides. Cut a matching piece of backing fabric.

Next, pin and stitch pieced or purchased print piping on right side of fabric around seam lines on pieced top and bottom panel.

To make boxing strip, cut 1x3-inch strips of light and dark fabrics and stitch together along long edges to make a pieced strip 3 inches wide and long enough to encircle cushion. Sew boxing strip between top and bottom pieces of the cushion cover (use ½-inch seams). Leave one edge open. Insert foam pad and slip-stitch the opening closed.

If desired, use a long upholsterer's needle, buttonhole thread, and flat, decorative buttons to tuft bench cushion at evenly spaced intervals across the surface of the cushion. Draw thread through the button, all the way through the cushion, out the back, and then back up to the top several times. Pull thread tight enough to make slight indentations in the cushion. Tie off tightly.

YANKEE PUZZLE PATTERN TOTE POCKET
PAGE 126

Materials

Scraps of two contrasting fabrics
Muslin for backing
Lightweight batting
Purchased tote bag or yardage and commercial pattern for tote

Instructions

Enlarge pattern on page 139 to desired size and make template for right-angle triangle.

Cut and piece Yankee Puzzle pattern block of the desired size, following basic piecing instructions on page 127. Add a contrasting fabric border of the desired dimensions.

Back the pieced block with batting and muslin backing fabric and quilt as desired. Trim batting, turn under raw edges, and slip-stitch front and backing of block together.

Hand- or machine-stitch completed Yankee Puzzle pocket to front of tote bag.

QUILT BLOCK PICTURES
PAGES 128-129

Materials

Scraps of white and two shades of blue fabric
Muslin for backing
Batting
Cardboard or foam-core board for backing each picture
Purchased frames

Instructions

Enlarge quilt block patterns of your choice (see page 139) to desired size and cut out triangular templates as required.

Cut and piece pattern blocks, following general instructions on page 127. Back each completed block with batting and muslin and quilt as desired (optional).

Back pictures with a matching square of cardboard or foam-core board; frame as desired.

BIRDS-IN-THE-AIR QUILT
PAGE 130
Finished size is 90x90 inches

Materials

5 yards of assorted dark print fabrics (blues, reds, browns)
5 yards of assorted light prints
5½ yards of fabric for backing
½ yard of blue or other dark fabric for side and corner triangles
10 yards of bias binding
Batting
Yarn or pearl cotton for tufting

Instructions

The quilt pictured consists of 104 large diamond shapes, each pieced from nine light and nine dark equilateral triangles, plus 18 half-diamonds along top and bottom edges. Sides of quilt top are pieced with dark blue triangles.

To begin: Enlarge patterns for basic triangle (A) and for side piece (B), *opposite right,* to size and cut templates for both shapes (patterns include ¼-inch seam allowances). For pattern piece B, flop the pattern along dashed line to complete side triangle pattern.

For corner pieces of quilt top, cut a right-angle template from pattern piece B, including ¼-inch seam allowance along right-angle edge.

Trace pattern piece A onto fabric; cut a total of 114 sets of nine triangles each from light and dark fabrics.

Using ¼-inch seam allowances, stitch nine light and nine dark triangles together to make each of 105 large diamonds, following basic piecing instructions on page 131. Take care to see that all dark triangles point in one direction and all light triangles point in the opposite direction.

Next, piece and stitch 18 half-diamond shapes (to fill out top and bottom rows of quilt). Nine of these will consist of six light and three dark triangles, and the other nine will have six dark and three light triangles.

Finally, cut 10 large blue triangles (pattern piece B) for sides of quilt, and cut four blue corner pieces (right-angle triangles cut with template B).

To assemble quilt top: Lay out blue corners and side triangles, pieced diamonds and half-diamonds into diagonal strips, as shown in assembly diagram, *above right.* Work from upper left corner down toward lower right corner of quilt top. Note that Rows A (a blue corner piece) through G appear twice in the piecing, and Row H is repeated three times.

Pin and stitch each strip in the sequence, pressing all seams in one direction. Then pin and stitch strips together to complete quilt top.

To finish quilt: Piece backing to size. Baste backing, batting, and pieced top together and quilt or tuft, as desired. Trim the raw edges and bind with pieced or purchased bias binding.

TUMBLING BLOCKS QUILT
PAGES 132-133
Finished size is 49x54 inches

Materials
3½ yards of black satiny fabrics (such as taffeta, silk, and moiré)
2½ yards of medium-color fabrics (brown, purple, blue, green, gray)
2½ yards of light-color fabrics (light or bright green, yellow, blue, tan, red, ecru, pink, rose)
Lightweight batting

Instructions
Quilt pictured is composed of 19 rows of hexagonal blocks—nine rows of 13 complete blocks each, and nine rows of 12 complete blocks with a half-block at each end. The top (nineteenth) row is pieced with a horizontal half-diamond along top edge, and bottom edge of quilt is pieced with horizontal half-diamonds as well.

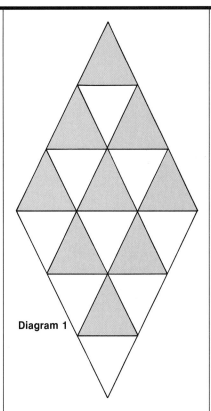

Diagram 1

To begin: Make templates from the full-size diamond pattern on page 138. Also use the diamond shape to make three additional templates: a horizontal half-diamond, a vertical half-diamond, and a quarter-diamond.

Cut and piece a 50x55-inch rectangular piece of black fabric for backing. Set aside.

To piece quilt top: Trace and cut the following diamond shapes, adding ¼-inch seams to all pieces: 247 black diamonds, 247 medium-color diamonds, and 225 light diamonds. Also cut 26 horizontal half-diamonds and 20 vertical half-diamonds from light fabric.

Piece a total of 225 complete hexagonal blocks, following general instructions on page 133.

Piece the blocks into nine rows of 13 blocks each and nine rows of 12 blocks each, keeping all light diamonds on top, black diamonds to the left, and medium diamonds to the right in each row. Piece together half-blocks consisting of a dark- or medium-color full diamond and a light-color vertical half-diamond for the ends of each of the nine 12-block rows. Stitch these end blocks in place. Stitch rows together, alternating rows

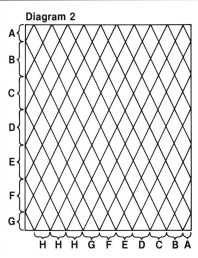

Diagram 2

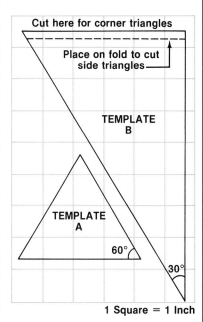

Cut here for corner triangles

Place on fold to cut side triangles

TEMPLATE B

TEMPLATE A

60°

30°

1 Square = 1 Inch

with 13 full blocks and rows with half-blocks at each end. Next, cut and piece a top row of 12 blocks, with a black diamond, a medium-color diamond, and a light-color, horizontal half-diamond at the top of each block, creating an even edge for the quilt top.

Piece ends of this row with a single black or medium-color diamond and a light-color quarter-diamond. Add the top row to the pieced top. Piece horizontal half-diamonds along bottom edge.

To assemble quilt: Layer backing, lightweight batting, and pieced

(Continued)

137

Full-Size Patterns

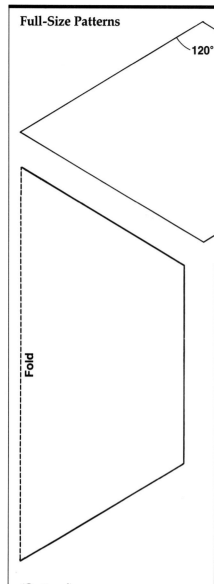

Fold

(Continued)

top together and baste. Quilt as desired (outline quilting, ¼ inch in from seam lines, is suggested). Trim backing and batting to size. Turn under raw edges and slip-stitch backing and top together.

◆

GRANDMOTHER'S FLOWER GARDEN QUILT
PAGE 134
Finished size is 89x109 inches

Materials
5¾ yards of brown print
3 yards of white print
¾ yard of pink print
3 yards of muslin
6½ yards of backing fabric
Batting

Instructions
As pictured, the Grandmother's Flower Garden Quilt consists of 32 separate flower blocks or rosettes joined by a path of muslin hexagons. Each block is made by joining 19 individual hexagons as follows: one pink for center, six white print for first row of petals, and 12 brown for second row.

To begin: Use the full-size, half-hexagon pattern, *left,* to make the templates. Trace and cut the following pieces, adding ¼-inch seam allowances to each piece: 32 hexagons for center, 204 hexagons for first round of petals, 414 hexagons for second round, and 372 muslin hexagons for joining paths and borders.

To assemble quilt: Assemble 19 complete rosettes, following general piecing instructions on page 135. Also piece six half-blocks, consisting of two pink hexagons and five brown hexagons each.

Arrange completed rosettes and muslin paths in seven rows of blocks—rows of five blocks alternate with four-block rows. Use half-blocks and plain muslin hexagons to complete borders, as pictured on page 134.

Piece backing to size. Baste the backing, batting, and pieced top together and quilt as desired (outline quilting, ¼ inch inside seam lines of each hexagonal shape, is suggested). Trim the batting and backing. Turn under raw edges of backing; topstitch and slip-stitch edges together.

NORTH WINDS QUILT
PAGES 124-125
Finished size is 81x81 inches

Materials
4½ yards of assorted dark print fabrics
4½ yards of assorted light fabrics
4 yards of backing fabric
Batting
9 yards of bias binding

Instructions
The quilt pictured on pages 124-125 consists of 324 pieced blocks, each 4½ inches square. Blocks are arranged in 18 rows of 18 blocks each. All 18 blocks in each row are pieced from the same (or similar) two fabrics—one light and one dark. Fabrics change from row to row. To make a similar quilt, follow instructions below.

To begin: To make templates for the two right-angle triangles required to piece the North Winds block, trace and cut out a 1½-inch square and a 3-inch square. Cut each of these squares in half diagonally and use resulting triangles as pattern templates.

For each row of 18 blocks, cut 18 large dark and 18 large light triangles, adding ¼-inch seam allowances to each piece. Next, cut 90 small dark and 90 small light triangles from the same two fabrics used for the larger triangles.

To piece quilt top: Piece together one large light and one large dark triangle, plus five each of the small light and dark triangles, following piecing diagram, *opposite.*

Piece 18 blocks from each combination of two fabrics. Stitch blocks together end to end to complete one row of the quilt top.

Make 18 rows in the same manner. Stitch the rows together to complete the quilt top.

To assemble quilt: Piece backing to size. Baste backing, batting, and pieced top together and quilt as desired. Bind the raw edges.

MOSAIC PATTERN SWEATER FRONT
PAGE 125

Materials
Scraps of light and dark print
  fabrics
Purchased cardigan sweater

Instructions
Light and dark right-angle triangles are pieced together along the
diagonal to form 1-inch squares.
Squares are pieced together into
fabric, and fabric is appliquéd to
the front panels of a purchased
cardigan sweater.

Note: Any pieced patchwork
composed of random fabric scraps
would be equally appropriate for
similar projects. You might also
consider using yardage from old
or damaged quilts or from pieced,
unquilted tops.

To piece fabric: Trace and cut out
a 1-inch square of cardboard. Cut
the square in half diagonally to
make triangular templates. Trace
and cut out approximately 200
light and 200 dark triangles, adding ¼-inch seam allowances to
each piece.

Stitch one light and one dark
triangle together to form each
block; assemble completed blocks
to make sufficient yardage to cover the front panels of purchased
sweater (see pattern, *right*).

Use tracing paper to make a
pattern for the right and left
fronts of sweater. Cut pattern
shapes from pieced mosaic fabric,
adding ½-inch seam allowances
all around. Baste under raw edges
on fabric pieces.

Remove buttons from one side
of sweater, pin and slip-stitch
fabric shape in place. Replace buttons. Repeat for opposite side of
sweater. Use scraps of fabric or
contrasting bias binding to bind
buttonholes.

Quilt or tack pieced fabric to
sweater front, as desired.

YANKEE PUZZLE

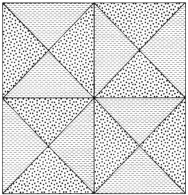

1 FLOCK OF GEESE

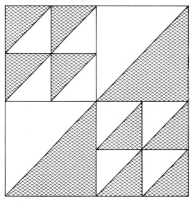

2 COLORADO BLOCK

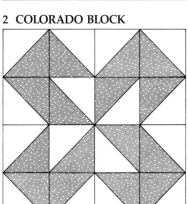

3 WINDMILL

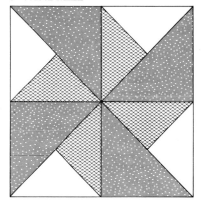

4 MARION'S CHOICE

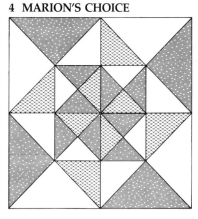

5 FLYING GEESE

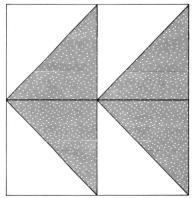

NORTH WIND

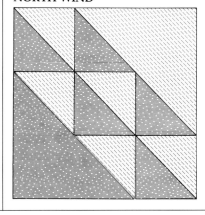

MOSAIC

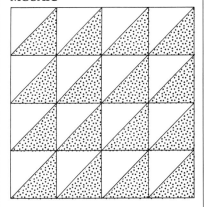

PATCHWORK STARS—
A GALAXY OF
FAVORITE DESIGNS

Based upon
artful arrangements of the simplest
geometric shapes, the sampling
of star patterns in this chapter
represents a test of, and tribute to,
the skill and patience of any stitcher.

PATCHWORK STARS— A GALAXY OF FAVORITE DESIGNS

Diamonds or triangles and squares are the building blocks for patchwork stars. Perhaps the earliest star motif to appear in patchwork was the aptly named Variable Star. A classic 16-patch arrangement of squares and triangles, this simple, eight-point design is the basis for dozens of patchwork patterns.

The earliest American quilts featuring the Variable Star date from the mid-seventeenth century, and most were made in New England. Originally, the star appeared almost exclusively as a border motif, but by the mid-eighteenth century, this versatile block had been developed by creative patchworkers into an astonishing variety of patterns, both one-of-a-kind designs and perennial favorites.

Among the simplest of these variations is the center medallion design used for the handsome Amish Star Quilt, *left.* Pieced from an imaginative mix of deep red and subtly shaded cotton fabrics, this particular pattern makes an ideal scrap-craft project. An assembly diagram for the quilt appears in the instructions (which begin on page 154), but the number, width, and color of strips used to piece the borders around the central motif can be adjusted easily to suit available materials.

(Also pictured in the photograph, *left,* is a striking double Nine-Patch quilt in blue, black, and soft green fabrics. For instructions for piecing Nine-Patch designs, see Chapter 2: "Learning to Piece with Squares and Rectangles," pages 22-39.)

Depending on the
size and set of the blocks,
and the colors used to
piece the pattern,
the effect of the Variable
Star design can be
radically altered.

Each small star block on the crib quilt, *opposite*, is pieced in exactly the same way as the large, center medallion star on the Amish Quilt, page 142. Here, however, the dark calico stars are set off against a lighter ground, and the multiple star blocks are set on the diagonal, alternating with solid muslin blocks, so the stars appear almost like crosses against the light background.

Called variously Evening Star, Texas Star, and Lone Star, this pattern also is known as Tippecanoe and Tyler Too—named for the campaign slogan used by William Henry "Tippecanoe" Harrison and his running mate, John Tyler, in the Presidential race of 1840.

From the mid-nineteenth century on, the names Variable Star and Ohio Star have been used almost interchangeably to identify star patterns pieced from squares and triangles. However, the true Ohio Star pattern—used for the blue-and-white coverlet, *left*—is based on a nine-patch, rather than a 16-patch, block.

The central patch on each side of the block is pieced from four triangles, creating both the star points and the corners of the central square-within-a-square design of the block.

Among the most complex and intriguing elaborations of the basic Variable Star block is the design pictured here, known interchangeably as the Feathered Star or Sawtooth Star pattern.

This magnificent, intricately pieced blue-and-white quilt is a comparatively recent (1924) rendition of the Feathered Star pattern—so named because each point of the basic Variable Star block is embellished with an airy feathering of smaller triangles. This picotlike edging is enlarged and repeated in the bold, sawtooth arrangement of pieced triangles around the center border strip.

Sawtooth and Feathered Star quilts appeared with increasing frequency during the late nineteenth and early twentieth centuries. Many accomplished quilters apparently welcomed the challenges posed by the precision cutting and piecing that this pattern demands. Some of the finest patchwork examples of the design date from this period.

Most early examples of the pattern appear as an overall arrangement of repeated blocks. Often the star blocks were less than 12 inches across and the feathered edges were pieced from minute triangles, measuring no more than 1/2 inch on a side.

The bold, medallion-style version of the design shown here is an enlargement of this traditionally small-pieced pattern, foreshadowing the contemporary impulse to make big images, to draw large.

When planning a Feathered Star design of your own—whether the medallion quilt pictured here or a more traditional assemblage of smaller blocks—it is a good idea to trace at least one quarter of the pattern block full size before you begin.

Trace, cut, and stitch all pattern pieces for the block, with extra-special attention to accuracy. And even though all the seams and pieces in the pattern are straight-edged, it is advisable to piece the blocks by hand, particularly the smaller triangles, to ensure that all points and angles are absolutely precise.

A second basic star form from which a whole constellation of other star patterns derive is the eight-point Lemoyne Star. The design is based on a single diamond pattern, repeated in matching or contrasting colors.

The Star of Lemoyne pattern, shown in its simplest version on the quilt, *left,* was named for Pierre and Jean-Baptiste Lemoyne. Reputedly a dashing pair of French Canadian explorers, soldiers, and statesmen, the Lemoyne brothers are credited, among other things, with founding the city of New Orleans in 1718.

In the English-speaking territories, the same pattern became known by the anglicized name of Lemon Star. By either name, it has remained one of the most enduringly popular star patterns in every part of the country for well over two centuries.

And because the piecing of the diamond shapes allows for expansion of the basic star in a variety of ways, the Lemoyne Star is also the foundation of some of the most breathtaking of all pieced patchwork patterns, including the much-loved Star of Bethlehem design pictured on pages 152-153.

The multihued stars set into nine-inch blocks on the pastel coverlet, *left,* are not difficult to piece. But, as with all star patterns, precision cutting and stitching are crucial to the success of the pattern. For variations of this simple block, you might experiment with using only two colors for the alternating spokes on each star. Or, for a totally different effect, try piecing light-colored stars against a dark background and omit the sashing.

The quilt pictured here is trimmed with an edging of Prairie Points, alternating squares of peach and white fabric folded into triangles and stitched along the outer edge, between the border and backing. A charming finish for any quilt, they are especially effective on star-pattern designs.

Two quite different designs—an enormous single star and a vibrant field of small, exquisitely pieced stars—illustrate the wonderful versatility of the Lemoyne Star block.

This economy-size Lemoyne Star, cut and pieced from pre-quilted fabric and appliquéd to a pieced and prequilted background, *above,* is one quick and easy way to achieve big-image impact with this appealing star design. In contrast, the elegant constellation of stars on the stunning blue-and-white quilt, *opposite,* takes many hours and much patient stitching to complete—it is a real labor of love.

Each block of this handsome variation of the Blazing Star pattern begins with a center Lemoyne Star composed of eight blue diamonds. Four additional rows of diamonds radiate from the center motif to construct the larger star pattern.

Though a wider range of colors is more common in the Blazing Star patchwork pattern, the restrained use of blue and white here underlines the sophistication of this particular design. The same pattern is called Harvest Sun in parts of the Middle West, and Ship's Wheel in Massachusetts.

Perhaps the most popular star design is the challenging Star of Bethlehem pattern, in which hundreds—sometimes thousands—of tiny diamonds are pieced together to form a single, magnificent central motif.

Many antique, and stunningly handsome, examples of the Star of Bethlehem pattern exist today because of its popularity with serious quilters since the first quarter of the nineteenth century. And no wonder. Planning, piecing, and quilting this pattern is an exciting creative challenge that accomplished stitchers find hard to resist.

A finely honed sense of color is essential to the success of this pattern. For example, in the Amish quilt pictured here, radiant shades of blue, pink, and yellow—eight fabrics in all—have been arranged so that the colors seem to pulse from the center of the design.

Although all Star of Bethlehem quilts combine fabrics of different colors in the center star motif, not all succeed in achieving the vibrancy of this unusual quilt.

Cutting and stitching the Bethlehem Star is every bit as challenging as choosing the fabrics, for a *single* mistake can destroy the balance of the design. If the angles of the diamonds are off by even a few degrees or the pieces are not assembled accurately, the quilt top will curl or buckle as it is stitched, and no amount of pulling or pressing will make it lie flat.

Yet with careful cutting and piecing, and judicious pressing between each step, even a novice can successfully complete a magnificent Star of Bethlehem quilt.

Traditionally, the Bethlehem Star is outline quilted, with rows of fine stitching parallel to the seams of the diamonds in the design. Yet in the large, plain blocks in the corners, in the triangles between the star points, and (in the example shown here) along the borders, there is ample space for the elegant quilting motifs beloved by master stitchers. And Amish quilts such as this one are frequently characterized by elaborately quilted backgrounds.

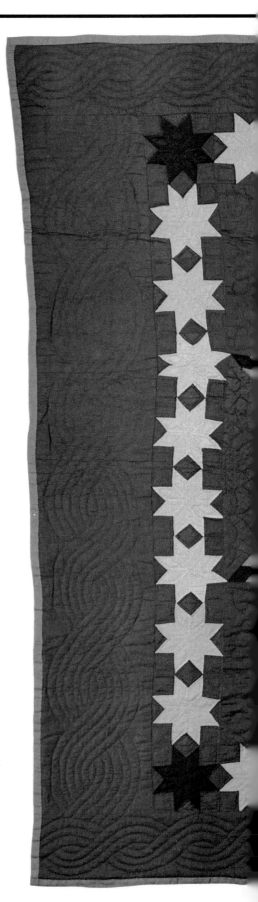

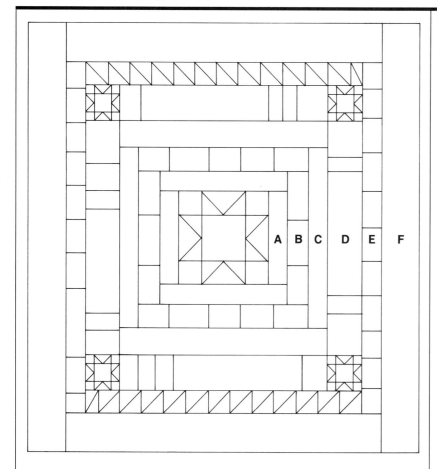

VARIABLE STAR AMISH QUILT

PAGE 142

Finished size is 74x79 inches

Materials

Cotton fabrics in the following amounts and colors: ¼ yard *each* of pink, gray, off-white, and beige; ⅓ yard of sky blue; ⅔ yard *each* of red and gold; 1 yard of brown; 2¼ yards of navy blue; 4½ yards of backing fabric

Batting

9 yards of bias seam binding

Instructions

The quilt consists of a center star block and six concentric borders (A–F) pieced from random-size squares, rectangles, and triangles. (Note that four of the squares consist of small star blocks.) The diagram, *above*, shows the layout for a similar quilt, but you can adjust the sizes and shapes of border pieces to suit your fabrics and preferences.

To begin: Transfer pattern, *above*, to graph paper, to make a master pattern.

Referring to the master pattern, trace and cut out templates for each pattern piece.

Note: When cutting and piecing the center Variable Star medallion and the triangle border strips, make sure that all right angles measure exactly 90 degrees, to ensure accurate piecing.

Trace templates onto fabrics, using fabrics of your choice. Cut out all pattern pieces, adding ¼ inch for seam allowances.

To piece the Variable Star medallion: When piecing this or any other star pattern, stitch *only* along seam lines. Do *not* stitch beyond the corners or points (and into seam allowances) of squares, triangles, or diamonds. This will facilitate piecing and pressing.

Visually divide the star into three horizontal segments, or strips. Piece each strip as a unit, then stitch the strips together to form the star.

For the top segment, begin with the center unit (star points). Stitch two right-angle triangles to each side of a large right-angle triangle, making a rectangle. Then, stitch one small square on each end of the pieced rectangle to complete the top strip of the Variable Star. Repeat for the bottom strip of the star.

To form the center strip, begin with the end units (star points). Piece two small and one large triangle together to make rectangles for each side of the strip. Then, stitch these two rectangles to each side of the large center square.

To assemble the star, stitch the three strips together, matching all seams carefully to ensure that corners are square. Press seams to one side.

To complete quilt: Cut and piece successive borders (A–F) around center star medallion, following the diagram. Attach shorter side bands first, then add strips to top and bottom. Continue until the pieced top is completed. (Assemble the small corner star blocks as described for the center Variable Star medallion block above.)

Piece backing to size. Baste the backing, batting, and pieced top together and quilt as desired. Finish raw edges with strips of pieced or purchased bias binding.

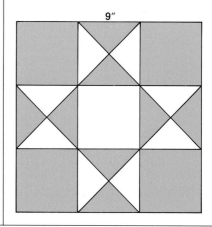

9"

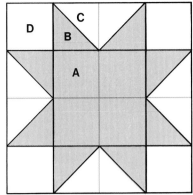

1 Square = 1 Inch

OHIO STAR QUILT

PAGE 144
Finished size is 65x81 inches

Materials
3¾ yards of assorted white fabrics for borders, sashing, and blocks
3 yards of assorted blue fabrics
5 yards of backing fabric, batting

Instructions
This quilt consists of thirty-five 9-inch squares (15 plain squares and 20 pieced star blocks) assembled with sashing and borders. To alter the size of the quilt, adjust the number of squares or rows and/or the size of the borders.

To begin: From white fabrics, cut four 3½x66-inch sashing strips, two 9½x60-inch borders, and two 4½x84-inch borders.

To make templates for pieced star blocks, trace and cut out two 3-inch cardboard squares. Set one aside and divide the other diagonally into fourths, to make triangular templates for the star points.

To piece star blocks: Trace and cut 80 blue squares, 20 white squares, 160 blue triangles, and 160 white triangles. Add ¼-inch seam allowances to all pieces.

Visualize each star block as a Nine-Patch design. Referring to the diagram, *opposite below,* piece two white and two blue triangles together to form each of the four center side squares of the Nine-Patch pattern. Stitch one pieced square between two blue squares for the top row of the block. Repeat for bottom row of block.

Next, piece one white square between two pieced squares for the middle row of the block. Piece all three rows together to form one complete block. Make a total of 20 star blocks.

To assemble quilt: Cut out fifteen 9½-inch white squares for plain blocks. Stitch three plain blocks between four star blocks to make each of five rows.

Sew four 3½-inch-wide sashing strips between the five rows of blocks. Use ¼-inch seams; trim sashing strips as required.

Add 9½-inch-wide panels to top and bottom of quilt, and stitch 4½-inch-wide border on each side. Piece backing to size, and baste backing, batting, and pieced top together. Quilt as desired. Finish edges with strips of pieced or purchased bias binding.

VARIABLE STAR CRIB QUILT
PAGE 145
Finished size is 41½x53 inches

Materials
2½ yards of muslin for piecing and backing
Scraps of assorted calico prints for stars and border squares
Batting

Instructions
The rectangular center panel of the crib quilt is composed of 35 star blocks and 24 muslin squares set into diagonal rows. Each row is finished with muslin triangles. The center panel is circled with a 4-inch-wide muslin border, followed by a narrow border of pieced squares and triangles, and a final border of muslin strips.

To begin: Enlarge Variable Star pattern, *above,* and cut templates for each of the four pattern pieces (corner square, small triangle, large triangle, and center square).

(Continued)

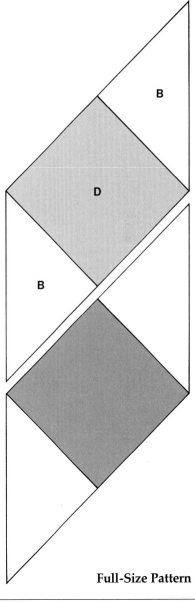

Full-Size Pattern

155

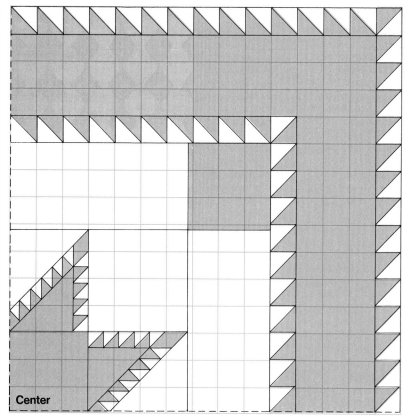

Center

1 Square = 2 Inches

(Continued)

Trace and cut two 4-inch cardboard squares. Use one as a template for the plain muslin squares. Cut the other in half diagonally and cut one of the resulting triangles in half again to make templates for large border and small corner triangles for center panel.

Cut two 4½x50-inch muslin strips and two 4½x40-inch muslin strips for inner borders. Cut two 2x44-inch and two 2x56-inch muslin strips for outer borders.

To piece star blocks: Trace and cut pieces for 35 stars. (Cut pieces A and B from calico; cut pieces C and D from muslin.) Add ¼-inch seam allowances to all pieces.

Hand-piece star blocks, following instructions for piecing the Variable Star medallion on the Amish Quilt on page 154.

To assemble quilt top: Trace and cut twenty-four 4½-inch muslin squares, 20 large muslin triangles for borders, and four small corner triangles (add ¼-inch seam allowances to all pieces). Lay the

triangles, muslin squares, and pieced squares out on the floor or a table and then stitch them together, following the piecing diagram, *top right,* on page 155. Press seams carefully.

Next, join 4½-inch-wide muslin border strips to the top, bottom, and sides of the pieced top; miter corners.

To make pieced border insert: Using full-size patterns on page 155, cut 116 calico squares (D) and 232 muslin triangles (B). Piece one triangle on both sides of each square, as shown.

Next, piece together 33 of these square-and-triangle strips for each side border, and stitch 25 strips together for each top and bottom border. Press carefully. Pin and baste pieced border strips to outer edges of muslin borders, easing to fit. Cut and stitch small triangles at corners to piece borders, if necessary.

Sew 2-inch-wide muslin border strips to sides and to top and bottom of quilt top; miter corners.

To assemble quilt: Cut muslin backing and batting ½ inch smaller all around than pieced top. Center and baste backing, batting, and top together. Quilt as desired. Fold raw edges of muslin border to back; slip-stitch.

❖ ❖ ❖

Feathered Star Quilt
PAGES 146-147
Finished size is 90x90 inches

Materials
9 yards of white fabric for pieced quilt top and backing
3 yards of blue fabric for star and borders
Batting

Instructions
The feathered star at the center of this design is an elaboration of the Variable Star block. Small blue and white triangles, and one diamond, are pieced in strips and joined to each star point. The star is then assembled as for the Variable Star block (see page 154).

Assemble the center star block first, then piece the remainder of the quilt from the center outward.

To piece the top: Transfer the pattern, *left,* to graph paper for reference. Enlarge each pattern shape to desired size and make templates as required.

For each star point, cut and piece blue and white triangles and one blue diamond for the feathered edging. Stitch to blue triangle for star point. Make eight feathered points.

Cut four white corner squares, four white triangles, and one large blue center square and piece together with feathered triangles to form star block. Following diagram, add white borders and blue corner squares, followed by blue and white sawtooth-edged border. Finish with 15½-inch-wide white border strips.

Piece backing to size. Baste the backing, batting, and pieced top together and quilt as desired. Finish raw edges with pieced or purchased blue bias binding.

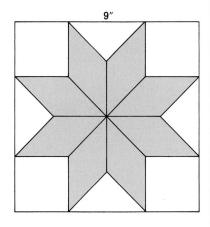

9"

LEMOYNE STAR QUILT
PAGE 148
Finished size is 72x83 inches

Materials
¼ yard *each* of 24 to 30 different
cotton print fabrics
3⅛ yards of peach fabric
4⅛ yards of white fabric
5 yards of backing fabric
Batting

Instructions
Quilt is composed of forty-two 9-inch-square pieced star blocks, framed with peach sashing strips, and finished with peach borders and an edging of white and peach prairie points.

To begin: Cut the following sashing strips and borders from peach fabric: 30 strips 2½x10 inches, five strips 2½x78 inches, two borders 4½x67 inches, and two borders 4½x86 inches. Set aside.

Cut two 2⅝-inch cardboard squares. Use one as template for corner square; cut the other in half diagonally to make templates for triangles on each block. Trace and cut templates for full-size diamond pattern A, *above right*.

For each block, cut eight diamonds from different prints, four white squares, and four white triangles. Be sure to add ¼-inch seam allowances around all pieces. *Note:* For entire quilt, cut 336 diamonds, 168 squares, and 168 triangles.

To piece star blocks: For each block, piece eight different diamonds together to form a star. *Note:* Stitch only along seam lines;

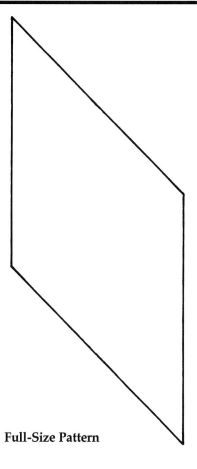

Full-Size Pattern

do *not* stitch into seam allowances. Press all seams in one direction. Add squares and triangles between star points (refer to illustration, *above left*).

Piece a total of 42 squares.

To assemble quilt top: Stitch six 2½-inch-wide peach sashing strips between seven blocks to make first row of quilt top. Make six rows of seven blocks each. Then join the rows together with longer peach sashing strips between them. (Trim sashing strips to fit, if necessary.)

For borders: Stitch shorter strips to top and bottom edges of quilt top; add longer borders to sides. Trim if necessary.

For prairie-point edging: Cut 2¾-inch squares from white and peach fabrics. Fold each square in half diagonally and then fold in half again so that all raw edges align. Press. Make approximately 84 *each* of white and peach points.

Position prairie points around outside edges of quilt top so that points of triangles face in toward center of quilt and raw edges are aligned with edges of quilt top. Baste and stitch points in place. Press seam allowance toward quilt.

To finish: Piece backing to size. Layer the backing, batting, and pieced top and baste together. Quilt as desired. Trim batting, if necessary. Turn under raw edges of backing and slip-stitch to top, covering raw edges of prairie-point border.

BLUE-AND-WHITE BLAZING STAR QUILT
PAGE 150
Finished size is 94x94 inches

Materials
5 yards of white fabric
4 yards of blue print fabric
Batting
10½ yards of blue print bias
binding

Instructions
This variation of the Blazing Star design consists of 16 blue-and-white star blocks arranged point to point in four rows of four blocks each.

A small eight-point star is appliquéd to the center of each large white square between the star blocks, and a smaller, five-point star is appliquéd to the smaller squares between the star points. Border motifs also are appliquéd.

To begin: First, cut four 6½x96-inch strips of white fabric for borders. Set aside. Next, trace and cut templates for each pattern piece. Use basic Lemoyne Star diamond pattern, *above left*, to make templates for Blazing Star and smaller Lemoyne Star appliqués.

Enlarge patterns for the small five-point star and border appliqués, page 158, and cut out templates for all pieces.

(Continued)

157

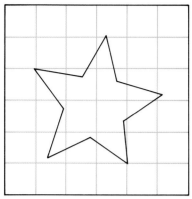

1 Square = 1 Inch

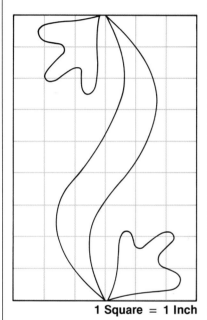

1 Square = 1 Inch

(Continued)

From white fabric, cut twenty-eight 6½-inch squares, nine 12½-inch squares, and twelve 6½x12½-inch rectangles.

To piece the pattern: Trace and cut 40 blue and 32 white diamonds for each Blazing Star motif. Add ¼-inch seam allowances all around to each shape.

For each point of the Blazing Star, join five blue and four white diamonds into three rows of three diamonds each, stitching as follows: Piece a white diamond between two blue ones to make Row 1; repeat for Row 3. Press seams toward dark pieces. Stitch a blue diamond between two white ones to make Row 2. Then stitch Row 2 between Rows 1 and 3.

Piece eight large diamonds, following the same procedure. Sew large (pieced) diamonds together to form a single star. Make a total of 16 stars.

Next, cut 120 more blue diamonds and piece nine full Lemoyne stars (eight diamonds each) and 12 half-stars (four diamonds each).

Turn under raw edges on star points and appliqué one eight-point star to the center of each 12½-inch white square. Center and appliqué a half-star to one long edge of each 6½x12½-inch white rectangle, matching the raw edges of bottom of star to raw edge of rectangle.

Finally, clip angles, turn under raw edges, and appliqué one five-point star to the center of each 6½-inch white square.

To assemble quilt top: Sew three 6½-inch appliquéd squares between points of four pieced blazing stars to form first horizontal row of the quilt top. Make three more rows in the same manner.

Next, join the four horizontal rows together by piecing 6½-inch and 12½-inch appliquéd white squares between rows (refer to photograph, page 150). Piece the appliquéd rectangles and the plain white triangles along outer edges of pieced top. Finish corners with appliquéd squares.

Cut white border strips to exact size for top, bottom, and sides of quilt top. Cut and appliqué blue border designs to each strip. Stitch borders to quilt top.

Piece backing to size. Baste the backing, batting, and top together and quilt as desired. Finish edges with blue print bias binding.

❖

"ECONOMY SIZE" LEMOYNE STAR QUILT
PAGE 151
Finished size is 79x91 inches

Materials
Prequilted navy blue mover's blanket or equivalent prequilted fabric for quilt
2 yards of deep red prequilted fabric
1½ yards of light red prequilted fabric
½ yard of prequilted purple fabric
Bias binding

Instructions
The quilt features a large Lemoyne Star made from eight large diamonds pieced from prequilted fabric. The star is appliquéd to a backing of prequilted fabric or to the center of a furniture mover's blanket (available in art supply stores in a variety of colors and sizes). Frame the star with an appliquéd border of 5-inch-wide strips of prequilted fabric in reds and purple.

To piece the star: Cut a diamond shape 30 inches long from point to point and 14 inches across at widest point. (Refer to Lemoyne Star diagram on page 157.) Using the pattern you have drawn, cut four diamonds each from the light red and the dark red prequilted fabric. Piece the diamond shapes together to form a Lemoyne Star. Alternate colors and use ½-inch seams. Press seams open and press remaining edges under ½ inch. Appliqué the star to the center of the blanket or quilt.

Cut remaining red fabrics and purple fabric into 5½-inch-wide strips. Patch strips together end to end in random lengths to make four borders (refer to the photograph). Press edges of the border strips under ½ inch on each long side. Pin and stitch borders touching points of star on all four sides. Trim borders to the desired size and finish raw edges with purchased bias binding.

STAR OF BETHLEHEM QUILT

PAGES 152-153
Finished size is 84x90 inches

Materials
6 yards of medium-blue fabric
2¾ yards of yellow fabric
¾ yard *each* of light blue, medium-pink, and maroon
½ yard *each* of lavender and light pink
6 yards of backing fabric
10 yards of medium-pink bias binding
Batting

Instructions
Each of the eight points of the Bethlehem Star is composed of 64 diamonds arranged in eight rows of eight diamonds each (see the illustration, *right*). The 32 yellow and four maroon border stars are simple Lemoyne stars, composed of eight of the same diamond pattern pieces used to piece the larger star. Following are instructions for a similar quilt.

To begin: First, cut two 11x74-inch and two 8x94-inch border strips from blue fabric. Set aside.

Next, cut two 10-inch squares of cardboard. Use one as a template for the four corner squares on the Star block. Cut the second square in half diagonally to make templates for the triangles pieced between the star points.

Trace and cut out four blue squares and four blue triangles (add ¼-inch seam allowances to all pieces). Set aside.

To piece Bethlehem Star: Make several templates from the full-size diamond pattern on page 157.

Trace and cut diamonds in the following amounts and colors, adding ¼-inch seam allowances to all of the pieces: 128 yellow (A), 80 medium-blue (B), 88 light blue (C), 72 medium-pink (D), 48 light pink (E), 64 maroon (F), and 32 lavender (G).

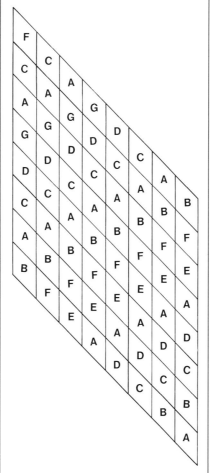

To make first point of star, arrange 64 diamonds according to the diagram, *above*. Stitch eight diamonds together for each of the eight horizontal rows, then stitch rows together to complete point. Make eight points.

To complete the star, sew the eight points together, yellow diamonds in the center. To finish the block, piece blue squares and triangles between star points.

To piece Lemoyne Star border: Cut 256 yellow and 32 maroon diamonds. Piece eight diamonds together to form each of 32 yellow stars and four maroon stars.

To piece stars into blocks, cut two 2-inch squares of cardboard and use one for the corner block template. Cut the other in half, diagonally, for triangular templates. Trace and cut 144 medium-blue squares and 144 triangles (add ¼-inch seams to all pieces). Add four squares and four triangles to each border star to complete blocks.

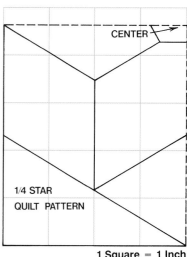

CENTER

1/4 STAR QUILT PATTERN

1 Square = 1 Inch

Sew eight yellow star blocks end to end to form top border. Sew to one edge of Bethlehem Star block. Repeat to make border for opposite edge. To make the side borders, assemble eight yellow star blocks between two maroon star blocks. Sew borders to both sides of quilt top.

To complete quilt: Stitch wider blue border strips to top and bottom of pieced quilt, and stitch narrow borders to sides. Trim the length of borders as necessary.

Piece backing to size. Baste the backing, batting, and top together and quilt as desired. Finish edges with pink bias binding.

SIX-POINT TEXAS STAR QUILT

PAGES 140-141
Finished size is 79x91 inches

Materials
6 yards (total) of assorted print fabrics for stars
Scraps of solid-color fabrics for centers
8 yards of ecru polished cotton for diamonds and backing
1½ yards of blue cotton fabric for bias binding
Batting

(Continued)

(Continued)

Instructions

This quilt consists of 13 rows of 13 stars each. To change the size of the quilt, alter the number of rows or stars in each row.

To piece star blocks: Enlarge the pattern on page 159, flopping to complete. Cut out templates.

Cut the following, adding ¼-inch seam allowances: six points for each of 169 stars (cut points for each star from the same fabric); 169 small center hexagons (assorted solid colors); and 469 ecru diamonds for joining stars.

Join six matching points together to form each star. Baste under raw edges on hexagon; pin and stitch hexagon to center of pieced star. Make 169 stars.

To assemble and finish: Lay stars out in 13 rows of 13 stars each. Using ecru diamonds, piece stars into rows and rows into quilt top.

Piece backing to size. Layer backing, batting, and top; baste and quilt. Bind raw edges.

CRYSTAL STAR HEADBOARD
PAGE 141
Finished size is 14x38 inches

Materials

2½ yards of navy pindot fabric
½ yard *each* of yellow fabric and muslin
¼ yard of light blue fabric
Artist's stretcher strips, staple gun

Instructions

Each star block is based on a 16-patch design. For twin-size headboard set three 12-inch star blocks into a border of navy pindot fabric; mount on stretcher strips.

To piece stars: Cut two 3-inch cardboard squares. Use one as template for corner squares of star block. Cut the other in half diagonally to make templates for triangular pieces of star block.

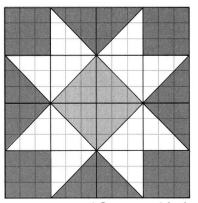

1 Square = 1 Inch

For each star block, cut 4 blue pindot squares, 12 yellow triangles, 8 blue pindot triangles, and 4 light blue triangles. Add ¼-inch seam allowances to all pattern pieces.

Join triangles into squares, then sew pieced and solid squares into star blocks, following diagram, *above.* Make three blocks.

Sew star blocks together; border with 6-inch-wide strips of blue pindot fabric. Press seams.

Layer muslin backing, batting, and pieced top; quilt as desired.

To assemble headboard: Assemble stretcher strips. Center and stretch the quilted piece over the strips; staple raw edges to back.

Cover raw edges on back of frame with blue pindot fabric. Add hanging wire.

OLD MAID'S PATIENCE QUILT
PAGES 10-11
Finished size is 112x112 inches

Materials

4½ yards of green cotton fabric (plain blocks)
2⅔ yards *each* of muslin and dark and light print fabrics (stars)
9½ yards of backing fabric
Batting

Instructions

The quilt contains 32 pieced and 32 plain green 14-inch blocks arranged in a checkerboard pattern of eight rows of eight squares each. The edges are bound with bias strips of fabric.

To begin: Cut templates for diamond, *opposite,* square (2x2 inches), and triangle (2-inch square cut in half diagonally). From green fabric, cut thirty-two 14½-inch-square plain blocks.

For pieced blocks, trace templates onto fabric (add ¼-inch seam margins). For each block, cut 16 light and 16 dark calico diamonds. Also cut 16 squares and 16 triangles of muslin.

To piece one block: Alternating colors, stitch four light and four dark diamonds into a star. Make four stars for each block. Assemble the remainder of the block following the piecing diagram, *opposite.* Make 32 blocks.

To assemble quilt: Join pieced star blocks and plain green blocks into checkerboard pattern of eight rows of eight squares each. Stitch the rows together.

Piece backing to size. Baste the backing, batting, and pieced top together and quilt as desired. Finish edges with bias binding.

LOG CABIN STAR QUILT
PAGES 6-7
Finished size is 80x98 inches

Materials

1½ yards of fabric A
1¼ yards of fabric B
2 yards of fabric C
2¼ yards of fabric D
½ yard of fabric E
1⅝ yards of fabric F
1¼ yards of fabric G
3 yards of border fabric
6 yards of backing fabric
Polyester quilt batting

Instructions

The star portion of this quilt is made using a machine-pieced strip-quilting method in place of traditional piecing. Throughout the instructions, fabrics will be referred to by letters as shown on diagrams 1–5, *opposite.*

Cut 2¼x42-inch strips as follows: two from fabric A, four *each* from fabrics B and D, and six

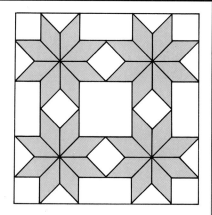

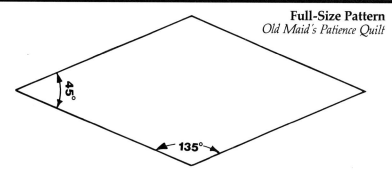

from fabric C. Measurements include ¼-inch seam allowances.

Referring to Diagram 1, sew strips A, B, C, and D together; repeat for strips B, C, D, and C. To make maximum use of the fabric, stagger strips 1¾ inches when sewing them together. Carefully press all seams to one side.

Cut a 2¼x12-inch cardboard strip to use as a template. Cut a 45-degree angle from one end of the template strip. Use this to mark and cut 16 strips from each fabric combination as shown in Diagram 2.

Each of the eight large diamonds that form the star requires four strips, two from each fabric combination. Referring to Diagram 3, sew strips together to form the eight large diamonds. Then stitch the large diamonds into pairs, join into groups of four, and finally piece the two halves of the star.

Cut four 10½-inch squares and two 11-inch squares from fabric F. Cut the two 11-inch squares in half diagonally to make four triangles. Sew triangles into top, bottom and sides of star; sew squares into corners. Set aside.

To piece Log Cabin blocks: Refer to instructions on page 85.

Piece a total of 56 Log Cabin blocks (see Diagram 4 for fabric placement and the photograph on pages 6–7 for color arrangement). *Note:* The center square is 1½x1½ inches and the logs are 1¼ inches wide. Add ¼ inch for seams.

Piece 12 Log Cabin half-blocks cut from dark fabrics. Refer to Diagram 5. (These blocks are sewn next to the inner star border.) Mark seam line and seam allow-

ance on the wrong side of the blocks. Trim off extra triangles.

To assemble quilt top: Measure the diagonal of three Log Cabin blocks (these fit along one side of the center star block).

From border fabric, cut four 2½-inch-wide strips the length of the sides of the quilt center. *Note:* Adjust width of this inner border, if necessary, so that the Log Cabin blocks will fit the border.

Stitch borders to star block, mitering corners. Sew Log Cabin half-blocks to inner border strip.

DIAGRAM 1

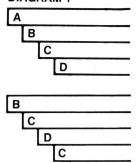

DIAGRAM 2

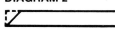

Cut along dotted lines

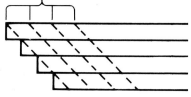

DIAGRAM 3

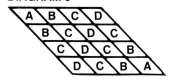

Set full Log Cabin blocks together in a Barn Raising arrangement (see pages 6–7 for placement of blocks). The quilt is eight blocks wide and 10 blocks long.

From border fabric, cut four 4½-inch-wide strips as long as sides of quilt, plus extra length for mitering corners. Join strips to quilt top, mitering corners.

To assemble quilt: Piece backing fabric to size. Layer the backing, batting, and top; baste and quilt as desired. Finish edges with bias binding.

DIAGRAM 4

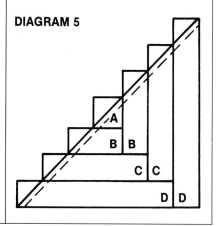

DIAGRAM 5

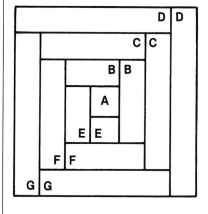

161

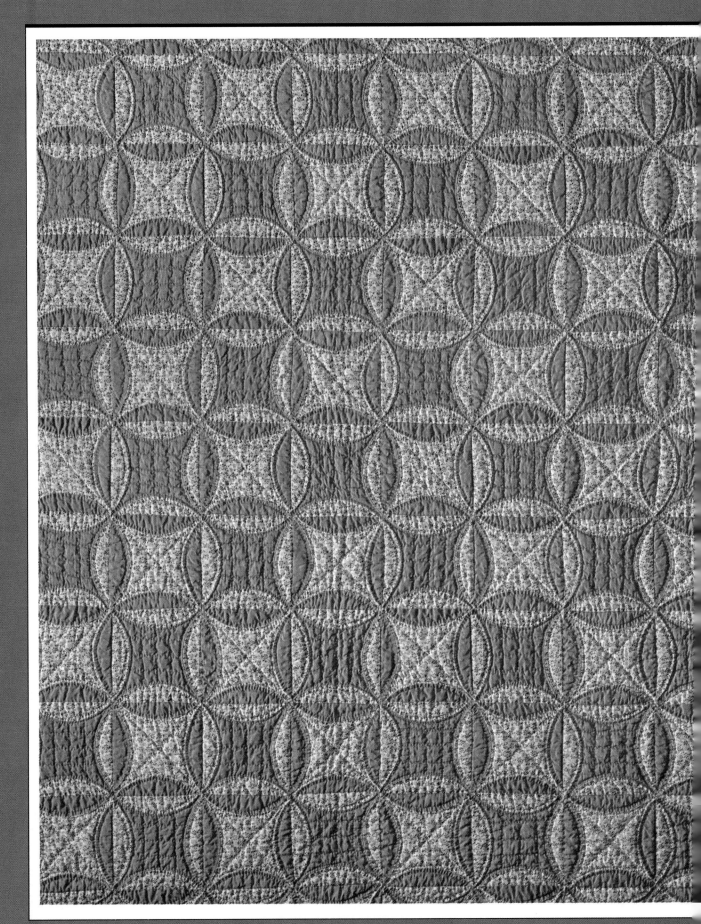

MASTERING CURVES AND APPLIQUÉD PIECES

Working with curved shapes is often considered the most difficult part of piece-work. But with practice, even a novice can learn to piece perfectly rounded arcs every time. Learning to fashion a graceful curve also is an important step in mastering the special techniques of fabric appliqué.

PIECING CONCAVE AND CONVEX CURVES

Learning to piece simple concave and convex curves adds a whole new dimension to your patchwork repertoire.

Although curves are often considered to be the most difficult form of patchwork, patience and practice assure success.

The Drunkard's Path design used for the wall hanging, *right,* is an excellent practice background for learning to piece curves. Using just two contrasting fabrics and two simple pattern pieces—a quarter-circle and a matching square from which a concave curve has been cut—it is possible to create more than a dozen different designs.

All designs derived from an arrangement of these two pattern pieces are called Drunkard's Path blocks—it's almost a generic pattern name for designs composed of squares and quarter-circles. But many of these designs have other names as well. The block *at right,* for example, is often known as the Love Ring or Nonesuch pattern. Other possible block arrangements are pictured *opposite.*

1

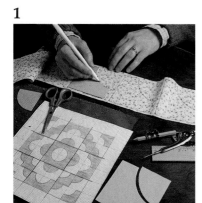

2

3

4

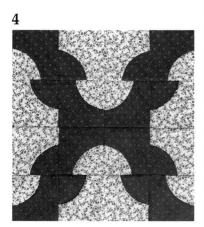

5

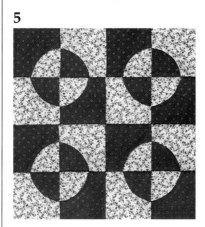

6

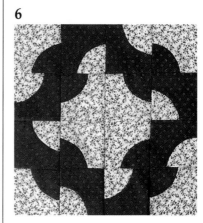

❖

1 In assembling this or any other complex patchwork pattern, you will find it helpful to sketch a master pattern on graph paper before cutting any pattern pieces. Use a contrasting marker to divide the design into manageable four-patch block arrangements to facilitate piecing. Keep this scaled drawing handy as you work.

To prepare the templates, cut a square of cardboard the size of the finished patch (3½ inches for the wall hanging, *opposite*). Next, use a compass to mark off a quarter-circle with the desired radius (2¼ inches). Carefully cut pieces apart.

Using the templates, trace eight quarter-circles on red fabric and eight on white fabric. Trace eight squares on each fabric, leaving ½ inch between shapes for ¼-inch seam allowances.

2 Although this is a pieced design, beginners will find it easiest to appliqué one curved shape to another with tiny slip stitches (stitch darker shapes over lighter ones wherever possible).

To prepare the shapes for piecing, turn under and baste ¼-inch seams on all of the *dark* quarter-circles. Also clip and baste under seam allowances on the concave curves of each *dark* square.

3 Next, lap a dark quarter-circle over the seam allowance on a light square. Pin and stitch the two parts of the patch together.

For reverse patches, lap a dark square over a light quarter-circle. Pin, stitch, and press. Complete eight patches in each color combination. (Experienced stitchers may prefer to pin the pieces of each patch together, with right sides facing. Clip and ease curves. Pin and stitch seam by hand or machine. This is the more traditional piecing method, but it is

more difficult to get a smooth, evenly curved seam this way.)

To complete the pattern block, join pieced patches following the master pattern. Using the same 16 patches, it is possible to piece a number of other designs, including the three blocks *above*.

4 Falling Timbers.

5 Mill Wheel (also known as Indiana Puzzle).

6 Solomon's Puzzle.

After you've mastered the piecing procedures outlined above, experiment with a compass, colored pencils, and graph paper to devise block arrangements of your own. Also keep in mind that curved piecing is essential for appliqué patchwork, which is explored later in this chapter.

PIECING A FAN QUILT

The ever-popular Grandmother's Fan design takes the simple square-and-quarter-circle patch one colorful step further, making wonderful use of odd-shaped fabric scraps.

Pieced from bright, bold decorator fabrics in an unexpected mix of prints and colors, the Grandmother's Fan Quilt pictured here is anything but old-fashioned. Yet the pattern dates from well before Grandmother's day. The graceful shape and romantic overtones of the Fan pattern made it a particular favorite during the Victorian era, when it was frequently pieced from elegant silks, satins, velvets, ribbons, and lace and lavishly embellished with beading and embroidery.

Also popular with quilters during the depression years, the Fan block is another design that makes especially economical use of small and mismatched fabric scraps. And the pattern looked particularly pretty pieced from the pastel floral prints so popular in the first half of the twentieth century.

As pictured here, the complete Fan block measures 12 inches square, and there are six spokes to each fan. But the size of the block and the number, color, and style of fabrics used to piece the fan shape are a matter of choice.

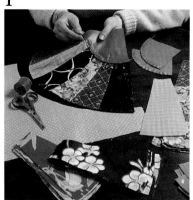

1

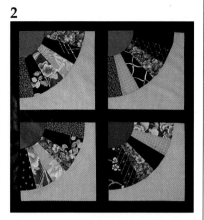

2

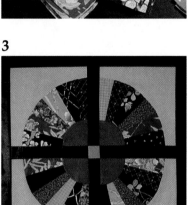

3

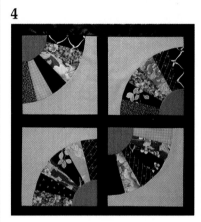

4

❖

---

1 To make templates for the Fan block, trace and cut a cardboard square the desired size of the finished block (12 inches, for quilt *at left*). Use a compass to trace an arc for the outer edge of the spokes. Place the point of the compass at one corner of the square, and trace a quarter-circle arc with the desired radius (10 inches). Then use the compass to trace a smaller quarter-circle (4-inch radius) for the base of the fan. Cut these shapes from cardboard.

Divide the middle arc into six equal wedges for spokes. First, fold the arc precisely in half, then pleat one of the halves into thirds, making pattern for spokes—each one-sixth of the total arc.

Make templates for the pattern pieces—the background fabric, fan spoke, and base of the fan.

For each fan block, cut one background piece, six fan spokes, and one quarter-circle fan base. Add ¼-inch seam allowances to each piece.

To assemble one block, sew six spokes together. Press seams in one direction. Baste under margins on quarter-circle base; lap this piece over raw edges of the pieced spokes. Pin, baste, and slip-stitch base in place.

Baste under seam allowance on outer edge of pieced fan. Pin, baste, and slip-stitch the fan shape to the curved edge of the background shape.

2 Arrange fan blocks as desired. Pictured here is the traditional Grandmother's Fan arrangement, with each block separated and framed with 2-inch-wide strips of black polished cotton.

3 and **4** Pattern variations.

Instructions for the coverlet are on page 174.

167

PIECING A DOUBLE WEDDING RING QUILT

The Double Wedding Ring pattern first gained popularity about the time of the Civil War, but did not reach all corners of the quilting community until the early decades of the twentieth century.

Symbolic of some of our most cherished sentiments, rituals, and traditions—friendship, love, marriage, eternal fidelity—the circle is one of the most common design motifs in every culture. When incorporated into the Double Wedding Ring Quilt, the circle is an integral part of one of the most beloved of all patchwork patterns.

Although the drafting, cutting, and piecing of the pattern demands great care and precision, it is no more difficult to piece than many apparently simpler patterns explored elsewhere in this book. Time, patience, and care are more important than skill or stitching experience.

Select 20 to 30 different print and solid-color fabrics for segments of the interlocked wedding bands. Repetition of solid-color spokes and consistency in corner diamonds and background fabric help to tie even the most disparate assortment of fabrics into a harmonious whole.

Though pieced here in a variety of sharp pastels, the design also looks elegant executed in various shades of a single color, or pieced in a variety of light-colored fabrics set against a darker background fabric.

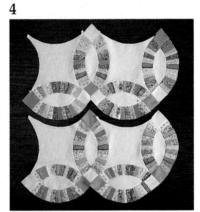

❖

1 Before beginning, examine the quilt design, *opposite,* to understand the structure. Each ring consists of four arcs; each arc crosses and meets with an arc from an overlapping ring to form a double arc. These double arcs, or ellipses, are the building blocks of the pattern.

Each ellipse consists of four pattern pieces: a shaped diamond at either end; an arc end (straight on one edge and curved to fit the diamond shape on the other); a spoke shape; and a center muslin ellipse.

For a block, cut 18 spokes (piece A), four arc ends (B), two shaped diamonds (C), and a muslin ellipse (D). (See page 175 for templates.) Add ¼ inch for margins.

2 To piece one block: Sew nine spokes (A) and two arc ends (B) together for one arc. For facing arc, sew nine spokes and two arc ends together and add one shaped diamond piece (C) to each end of the pieced strip. Press seams to one side on each strip.

3 Join each of the pieced arc strips to each side of a center muslin ellipse (D) to form a pattern block. Press. Cut one background shape (E) from muslin. Sew one pieced ellipse to the right side and another to the bottom of the background shape. Make enough blocks to complete top.

4 Join pieced blocks (each consisting of one center muslin shape with two pieced ellipses) together to form horizontal rows. Stitch rows together to form top. Piece top edge and left side of top with additional pieced arc blocks.

For complete instructions, see page 175.

169

INTRODUCTION TO APPLIQUÉ

A highly flexible form of patchwork, appliqué permits a spontaneity and a range of detail in figurative designs impossible to achieve in pieced work.

Almost any image—photographs, paintings, line drawings, or book illustrations—can be translated into appliqué successfully. Therein lies the charm and the challenge of this versatile technique.

In appliqué, various shapes are snipped from plain and print fabrics and *applied* to a background fabric to create a design. The shapes may be cut either freehand or following a pattern, and then sewn in place by hand or machine. The resulting image might be an abstract design, a strictly representational fabric painting, or a gently stylized arrangement of bird and flower motifs, like the traditional wreath design on the quilted fire screen, *opposite.*

This particular pattern is adapted from one of the blocks on a prizewinning nineteenth-century album quilt. (For details on the original quilt, see pages 286-289.)

❖

1 Make a master pattern for your design; lightly trace outlines onto background fabric. Number each shape on the master pattern. Cut out and number corresponding paper templates for each shape.

Trace pattern pieces onto right side of selected fabrics. Study the body of the robin, the butterfly wings, and some of the leaves and flower petals on the fire screen, *opposite,* to see how patterns and color variations in print fabrics can be used to subtly enhance selected appliqué shapes.

Cut fabric shapes, adding ¼-inch seams to all pieces. Stems, branches, and other narrow, curved shapes should always be cut on the bias so that the curves lie flat when stitched in place. Commercial bias binding can be trimmed to size for such pieces.

2 Refer to master pattern to determine the order in which shapes should be appliquéd to background fabric. Here, the bird's beak and the branch beneath his tail were stitched in place first, followed by the head and tail, the body, and finally the wing. When pattern pieces overlap, it is not necessary to turn under raw edges of the underlying piece.

To prepare pieces for appliqué, baste under raw edges as necessary. Clip angles and curves, using sharp scissors and taking tiny snips at right angles to the stitching line. Pin or baste shapes to the background; stitch in place. (For appliqué stitches, see page 178.)

Use the point of the needle to control the folded-under edge of each shape as you stitch. Aim for smooth, curved lines and crisp angles. On curved, bias-cut stems and branches, always stitch inner curves first, then stretch outer curves slightly as you stitch them in place to avoid puckers.

3 Add embroidery when appliqué is completed. (Instructions begin on page 174.)

1

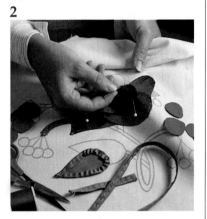

2

3

Whether you choose to copy a design exactly or adapt just a portion for a special project, antique quilts are a rich and varied source of appliqué designs.

The marvelously intricate appliquéd quilt, *opposite,* is one of several needlework treasures on display at Locust Grove, in Louisville, Kentucky. A restored Georgian mansion dating from the 1790s, Locust Grove was the last home of George Rogers Clark, known as the "Father of the American West" and founder of Louisville.

The Locust Grove Quilt consists of identically appliquéd quadrants and wide borders featuring bright-colored rose and grapevine motifs—a real challenge for accomplished quilters.

The folk art album cover, *left,* is an adaptation of a block from a famous appliquéd bride's quilt, pieced in Poughkeepsie, New York, in the 1850s. Make the cover as pictured, or take a drawing pad along on trips to museums and historical homes and sketch favorite sections of antique patchwork designs for inspiration.

DRUNKARD'S PATH WALL HANGING

PAGE 164

Finished size is 28½ x 28½ inches

Materials

⅜ yard *each* of dark and light print fabrics
⅝ yard of fabric for borders and bias binding
⅞ yard of fabric for backing
Batting

Instructions

The hanging consists of thirty-six 3½-inch-square blocks—20 with a dark background square and 16 with a light background square. The blocks are arranged in six rows of six blocks each and finished with 3¾-inch-wide borders and strips of bias binding.

To begin: First, cut four 4¼x30-inch strips of border fabric and set them aside. Also, cut and piece 3⅓ yards of matching bias binding (2 inches wide) and set it aside. To make templates, enlarge pattern block, *above right,* to size (3½ inches square) and cut out both pattern pieces. Trace and cut out the following fabric shapes, adding ¼-inch seams to each piece: 20 dark squares and 16 light squares, plus 20 light quarter-circles and 16 dark quarter-circles.

Piece blocks and assemble to form Love Ring or other variation of the Drunkard's Path design (refer to photographs on pages 164-165, and to pattern blocks on page 179). Follow basic piecing instructions on page 165. Add borders to sides and then to top and bottom, trimming length of border strips to size, as necessary.

To assemble wall hanging: Cut backing to size. Baste backing, batting, and top together; quilt as desired. Trim raw edges and finish with pieced bias strips.

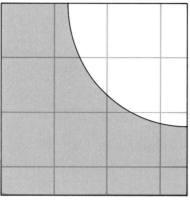

1 Square = 1 Inch

FAN COVERLET

PAGE 166

Finished size is 50x76 inches

Materials

6½ yards of black polished cotton (sashing, borders, and backing)
1¼ yards of yellow/gold background fabric (squares)
Scraps of red, yellow, orange, brown, and black prints, checks, and solids for fans
2½ yards of contrasting print fabric for borders
Batting

Instructions

The quilted coverlet consists of nine 12-inch-square fan blocks pieced together with 2-inch-wide black sashing strips, embellished at each end with large triangles of black fabric, and bordered with strips of a contrasting print.

Note: The fan blocks may be either machine-appliquéd or hand-pieced as described in the general instructions on page 167.

To assemble top: Cut black sashing strips: six 2½x12½-inch strips, four 2½x40½-inch strips, and two 2½x44½-inch strips. In addition, cut six black triangles, each 10½x10½x15 inches.

Enlarge pattern block, *above right,* to size (12 inches square) and make templates for all pattern pieces (background square, spoke of fan, and quarter-circle base).

Cut and piece nine fan blocks following directions on page 167.

Add rows of decorative machine stitching in black thread along inner and outer curves of pieced fan (see photograph).

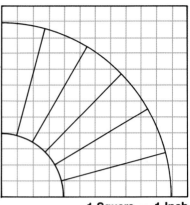

1 Square = 1 Inch

Using 2½-inch-wide black sashing strips and ¼-inch seams, sew pieced blocks together into three rows of three blocks each. Sew the three rows together with two 2½x40½-inch sashing strips between the rows and one to each end. (Trim sashing strips to size, if necessary.)

Sew one 2½x44½-inch strip to each side of pieced top; trim.

To piece the border: Cut two large black triangles in half to form four 7½x7½x10½-inch right-angle triangles. Baste two large triangles and two half-triangles to each end of fan block top to form border (see photograph).

Next, cut and piece 3-inch-wide strips of print border fabric to bottom edges of black triangles, mitering the edges of strips at corners and angles. Add 3-inch-wide strips of border fabric to long sides of pieced top.

To finish coverlet: Cut and piece backing to size. Baste backing, batting, and pieced top together; tuft or quilt. Trim raw edges; bind with black bias binding.

DOUBLE WEDDING RING QUILT

PAGE 168

Finished size is 60x74 inches

Materials

7 yards of muslin for background and backing fabric
½ yard of pink (corner diamonds)
4 yards (total) of assorted prints and solid pastel fabrics for segments of each ring
15 yards of bias binding

Full-Size Pattern

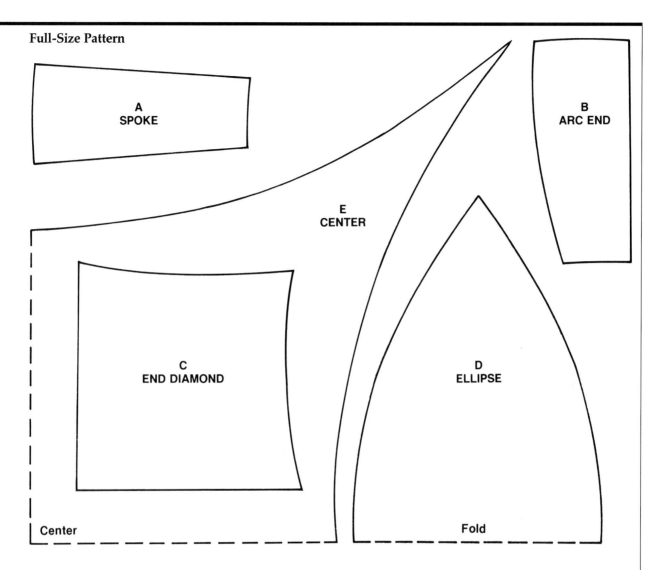

A
SPOKE

B
ARC END

E
CENTER

Center

C
END DIAMOND

D
ELLIPSE

Fold

Instructions

The quilt pictured on page 168 consists of four rows of four interlocking rings each (a total of 40 pieced ellipses). To increase the quilt size, increase the number of interlocking rings. Adjust fabric requirements accordingly.

Note: Because of the number of small pieces involved, precision marking, cutting, and piecing is essential. Replace templates as soon as they become worn. Use only a sharp pencil or water-erasable marking pen to mark each pattern piece.

To piece top: Trace full-size pattern pieces, *above,* and make templates for each of the five shapes. (Flop patterns D and E as required to make complete templates.)

Cut and piece 40 ellipses as described in basic piecing instructions on page 169. Make sure that

there is one pink and one muslin diamond shape on each arc end.

Cut 16 muslin center shapes. Assemble all pieces and center pieces to form four rows of four interlocked rings each, following instructions on page 169. *Note:* The bottom three rows will be unfinished along the top edge, as shown in illustration No. 4 on page 169. The fourth, top row will consist of four complete, interlocked rings. Sew these four rows together to complete quilt top.

To assemble quilt: Piece backing to size. Baste backing, batting, and quilt top together and quilt as desired (refer to photograph for suggested quilt motifs). Trim batting and backing to match scalloped edges of top. Bind raw edges with strips of bias binding.

LOCUST GROVE QUILT
PAGE 172
Finished size is 72x72 inches

Materials
4½ yards of muslin
3 yards of green fabric
1½ yards *each* of cranberry red and brown fabrics
¾ yard of red-and-white print
¼ yard of yellow fabric
4¼ yards of ecru backing fabric
5½ yards of green piping
Green embroidery floss
8 yards of green bias binding
Batting

Instructions
The quilt center consists of four 24-inch appliquéd blocks stitched into a square. The resulting 48-

(Continued)

Pattern A

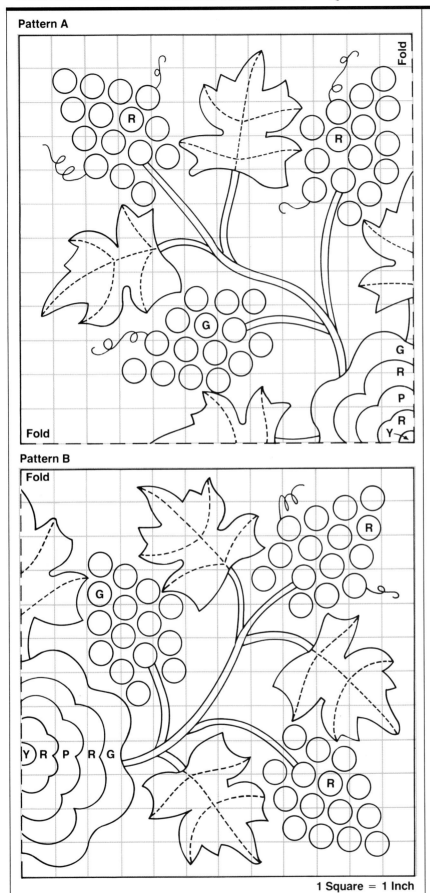

Fold

Pattern B

Fold

1 Square = 1 Inch

COLOR KEY
G Green   P Pink
R Red   Y Yellow

(Continued)

inch square is bordered by eight 12x24-inch blocks, two to a side. An appliquéd 12-inch square fills each corner.

For patterns and templates: Enlarge patterns A and B, *left,* to size, and transfer to tissue paper.

To make a master pattern for the symmetrical design layout for one 24-inch-square block, trace over the A pattern four times, flopping the pattern along fold lines to complete design.

For the border block, trace over pattern B twice, flopping the design along center fold line.

To make master pattern for corner blocks, trace over pattern A once; omit two half-leaves along fold lines and ignore fold lines.

Trace and cut out templates for the following pattern pieces: one grape leaf with stem, one grape, three parts of the vine (stem and branches), and each of the five separate layers of the flower, including the center circle.

To appliqué quilt top: Trace around templates onto appropriate fabrics, allowing for ¼-inch seams on appliqué pieces. From green fabric, cut 112 grape leaves, 112 stems, 540 grapes, and 14 outer flower shapes. From cranberry red fabric, cut 1,080 grapes and 14 of each of the second and fourth flower shapes (use pattern B).

From brown fabric, cut 36 of each of the three vine pieces. Cut 14 red-and-white print flower shapes and 14 yellow flower centers, also. Cut out all pieces, adding ¼-inch seam allowances.

From muslin, cut four 25-inch squares, eight 13x25-inch rectangles, and four 13-inch squares.

Use master patterns and marker to trace all designs onto appropriate pieces of muslin. Appliqué all of the shapes in place. Using three strands of green floss, work stem stitches for grape tendrils.

To assemble quilt: Construct the quilt top, using ½-inch seams. Join four 25-inch muslin blocks

1 Square = 1 Inch

together to form a 49-inch square. With raw edges matching, sew green piping around perimeter of large square.

To assemble borders, sew two rectangular appliquéd blocks together end to end and sew this border to one edge of large square. Repeat for opposite edge of square. For side borders, sew two rectangular blocks together. Add a 12-inch appliquéd corner square to each end of the pieced border. Sew side borders in place.

Press seams open and press entire quilt top on wrong side.

Piece backing to size. Layer the backing, batting, and pieced top and baste together. Outline-quilt around all appliqués and quilt along leaf veins. Then quilt in diagonal rows, spaced 1 inch apart, across all muslin background areas (see photograph on page 172).

Finish the edges with pieced or purchased green bias binding.

QUILT BLOCK ALBUM COVER
PAGE 173

Materials
½ yard of muslin
½ yard of calico for lining
Scraps of print and solid fabrics for appliqués
Scraps of embroidery floss for features and decorative details
Purchased photo album
Batting
Spray adhesive and fabric glue
Decorative gold cord
Water-erasable marker

Instructions
Enlarge pattern, *above*, to desired size and make a master pattern. (Adjust size of design to fit size of album cover, if necessary.)

Using pencil or water-erasable pen, sketch square or rectangular outline of the album cover on a piece of muslin. Then use the master pattern to center and trace the appliqué design within the muslin square (or rectangle).

Transfer elements of the pattern to appropriate fabrics. Trace

and cut out each appliqué shape, adding ¼-inch seam allowances to each piece. Turn and baste under seam allowances.

Position the shapes on muslin background; pin and appliqué in place. Add embroidered features and decorative details (buttons on dress, French knots around flower centers, and buttonhole stitches around petals, for example).

To complete album cover: Pad front of cover with quilt batting; secure with a light coat of spray glue. Wrap appliquéd muslin over batting, pull raw edges to back and secure with fabric glue. Clip and trim fabric as necessary.

Repeat with a plain piece of muslin to cover back of album.

Allow glue to dry. Cut two pieces of calico to size to line inside of back and front covers. Turn under raw edges and stitch or glue linings in place. Add decorative gold cording to completed album cover (see photograph).

ROBBING PETER TO PAY PAUL PATTERNED QUILT
PAGES 162-163
Finished size is 71x81 inches

Materials
4½ yards of blue fabric
3 yards of light print fabric
4½ yards of backing fabric
Batting
9 yards of bias binding

Instructions
The quilt pictured consists of 195 five-inch blocks with alternating blue and print centers. The blocks are arranged in 15 rows of 13 blocks each, and bordered with 3-inch-wide strips of blue fabric.

To begin: Cut two 3½x74-inch and two 3½x84-inch border strips from blue fabric and set them aside.

Enlarge block pattern on page 178. Make templates for center shape and for curved edge piece.

Trace and cut the following pattern pieces, adding ¼-inch

seam allowances to each piece: 98 blue centers and 97 light print centers, plus 388 blue curved edge pieces and 392 light print edge pieces.

Baste under seam allowances on all *blue* shapes, both centers and edge pieces. Clip curves as necessary. Pin and piece blue curved edge pieces on all four sides of light print centers to make 97 blocks. Then piece blue centers to light edging pieces to make 98 blocks. Follow basic curved piecing instructions on page 165.

Assemble blocks in 15 horizontal rows of 13 blocks each, alternating between blue and print centers. Add 3½-inch-wide blue border strips to top and bottom and then to each side of pieced top. Trim length of border strips to size, as required.

To assemble quilt: Piece backing to size. Layer backing, batting, and pieced top together and quilt as desired. Finish raw edges with contrasting bias binding.

APPLIQUÉD FIRE SCREEN
PAGE 163
Finished size is 19x19 inches

Materials
Muslin for background
Scraps of solid and print fabrics for appliqués
Scraps of embroidery floss for decorative details
Purchased or homemade fire screen frame
Plywood for backing, batting
Water-erasable pen

(Continued)

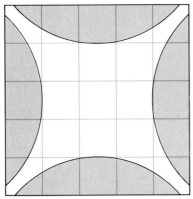

1 Square = 1 Inch

(Continued)

Instructions

The appliquéd design on the fire screen is an adaptation of one block from the Baltimore Album Quilt pictured on pages 286-289. For this and other album block patterns, see pages 304-305.

Enlarge album block pattern of your choice to desired size and transfer to tracing paper to make a master pattern. (Adjust size of design to fit screen, if necessary.)

Center and trace master pattern onto muslin with water-erasable pen.

Trace, cut out, and appliqué all shapes, following basic instructions on page 171. Add embroidered details. (Work eye of the bird in satin stitches, use stem stitches for vine tendrils, and add other details as desired.)

Cut plywood backing to size. Center appliquéd piece atop plywood; stretch fabric to back of plywood and staple excess fabric in place. Frame as desired.

Construct a pedestal for the frame, or mount the frame on a purchased pedestal.

BASIC APPLIQUÉ STITCHES

Three kinds of stitches are traditionally used for appliqué designs. Your choice of stitch will depend upon the effect desired, the fabric used, and your own personal preferences.

1 Running Stitch. Small, evenly spaced running stitches (about 1/8 inch long), worked close to the folded edge of the fabric, add a decorative touch and at the same time secure the appliqués to the background fabric. The running stitch adds a touch of texture, and it is a particularly appropriate choice for projects that are not going to be quilted.

Because running stitches are visible on the surface of the fabric, they are an integral part of the design, so thread should be selected to match or contrast with the appliqué fabric. Take care that stitches pierce *both* layers of the folded edge of the appliqué, as well as the background fabric, to keep raw edges from slipping free.

2 Whipstitch. Especially useful for securing points and sharp angles, the whipstitch creates a flat, crisp edge on appliquéd shapes. Draw needle up through background fabric, piercing both layers of the folded appliqué edge, and then reinsert into the background, making a series of small, slightly slanted stitches along the edge of the appliqué. Control your tension so that the edge of the appliqué remains smooth, not puckered by the stitches.

3 Blind Stitch. Done properly, the blind stitch is nearly invisible and gives the appliqué a soft, slightly rounded edge.

Using thread to match appliqué, bring needle up from wrong side of background fabric, just under folded edge of appliqué. Slip the needle in and out through the folded edge of the appliqué, then reinsert needle into the background fabric, next to point from which needle first emerged. Keep stitches tiny and spaced no more than 1/8 inch apart.

Decorative embroidery stitches also can be used for appliqué, particularly for Crazy Quilt projects (see page 248).

DOUBLE WEDDING RING

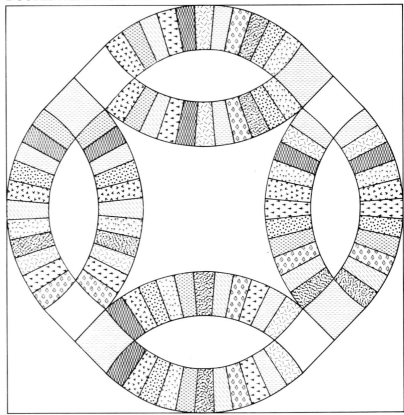

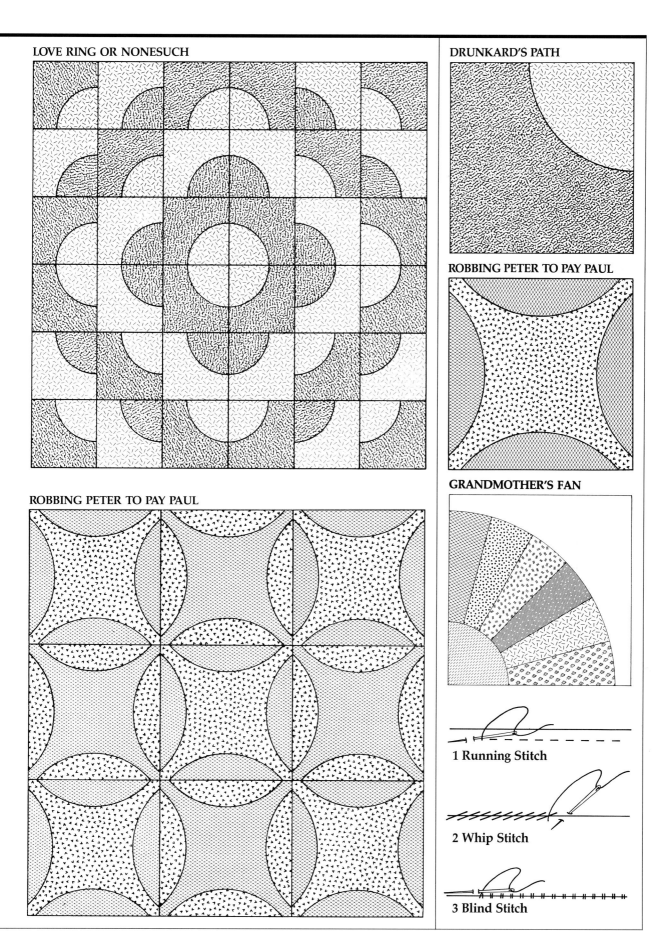

LOVE RING OR NONESUCH

DRUNKARD'S PATH

ROBBING PETER TO PAY PAUL

GRANDMOTHER'S FAN

ROBBING PETER TO PAY PAUL

1 Running Stitch

2 Whip Stitch

3 Blind Stitch

179

DECORATING
WITH PATCHWORK

Ⅰn recent decades, patchwork has graduated from its humble origins to near-preeminence among the decorative arts. And quilts and other patch-work creations have moved from bed to wall and back again in a re-markable show of versatility.

A GALLERY OF COLOR AND PATTERN FOR YOUR WALLS

Exquisite antique coverlets
and contemporary pieced quilts now
hang in museums, offices, and
public halls around the world. But
it was in the more modest setting
of the home that the art of
patchwork first flourished, and it is
here that patchwork is often
displayed to most striking advantage.

Wall-hung quilts have become a characteristic of country-style decorating in recent years. And what better way to bring the design impact of a patchwork masterpiece into play in your decorating scheme. Deciding where to hang a quilt so that it complements rather than competes with other elements in the room takes careful planning, however.

In the updated country setting, *right,* color, pattern, and prominent placement immediately establish the nine-patch quilt on the wall as the center of attention and point of departure for the mood of the entire room. Despite differences in period and style, folk art accessories and primitive American furnishings here mix comfortably with a vintage camelback sofa and a pair of contemporary wood and leather sling chairs.

The muted colors and natural materials of all these pieces take their cue from, and call attention to, the nineteenth-century quilt. Even the diamond pattern and soft red tones of the Oriental rug subtly echo the angled squares of the patchwork design, further unifying the room. (Directions begin on page 192.)

Antique or newly minted, a fine piece of patchwork can hold its own in any mix of design styles and periods.

It takes wit, confidence, and a well-developed sense of personal style to mix elements from widely different design periods. Selectivity is the key to success in this eclectic approach to decorating.

In each of the examples shown here, an outstanding contemporary piece is teamed with fine Americana, and the match seems tailor-made. Why? Because in both cases the *quality* of the designs and the *mood* of the pieces in each grouping are thoroughly compatible.

The bold design and somber colors of an Amish Diamond Quilt, *above,* offer a perfect complement to the clean lines of the Corbusier chaise and the formal mood of the room. In a more intimate setting, *opposite,* the pairing of old and new is reversed with equal success. Here, a strip-pieced wall hanging of very recent vintage seems right at home above a grouping of primitive furnishings. The symmetry of the quilt design is balanced by the symmetry of the furniture arrangement, yet the overall effect is one of cheerful informality.

If your favorite piece of patchwork is in less than perfect condition, or simply too small to build a room around, it can still win a place of honor in your decorating scheme.

Even when used only as a backdrop or as one element among many in a grouping, a strong patchwork piece can establish the design of a room or pull an eclectic collection together.

A beloved family heirloom, the vivid star-pattern design, *opposite,* had spots and tears along one side, and wouldn't stand up to the close scrutiny it would receive if displayed in solitary splendor on a wall. But when the quilt is hung as a sort of "wallpaper" panel behind the sofa, the damaged area is hidden and the part that shows serves as a perfect frame for the exuberant colors, patterns, and textures of the handcrafted pieces in the foreground.

Small patchwork pieces, such as the whimsical fabric still life,

above, can serve a similar role as color key and unifying backdrop for arrangements of knickknacks and collectibles. The wall hanging echoes the mix of colors and pattern-on-pattern feeling of the china collection beneath it. But the folk art quality of the hanging still offers a witty contrast to the more sophisticated design of the porcelain pieces on the shelf. Once again, it's the mix-and-match of moods and styles that produces interesting results in decorating.

For more tips on caring for and displaying quilts and other patchwork, turn to page 191.

When wall space is at a premium, hang a patchwork heirloom in a hallway, or tuck it into an otherwise underused corner.

Front and center display in the living room, family room, or other major traffic area is one way to guarantee a cherished quilt the attention it deserves. But contemporary houses often have little wide-open wall space, or homeowners need it for other purposes, such as storage. Alternative display areas do exist, however, as these two examples demonstrate.

A little-used corner becomes an inviting nook with the addition of this appliquéd Iris Quilt, *opposite,* made in North Carolina in the 1920s. When hanging your own quilt, look to the colors and rhythms of the pattern to establish a mood, then choose one or two items—whatever space allows—to reflect that mood and "frame" the quilt.

As commanding as a museum-size canvas, the Schoolhouse design, *above right,* transforms an awkward hallway into a miniature gallery. With the addition of an antique desk and chair, this carefully composed vignette takes on the appearance of a three-dimensional painting.

Stairways and landings are also excellent exhibit areas, especially for smaller quilts. Hunt through the house, and you're sure to discover other options for showcasing your prize piece of patchwork.

TIPS ON QUILT CARE AND DISPLAY

Whether your favorite quilt is a treasured antique or a newly minted beauty, careful handling will ensure many years of use and pleasure.

CHOOSING THE RIGHT DISPLAY SPACE

All textiles, but especially older ones, are sensitive to light, heat, and dampness. It is important to keep this sensitivity in mind when selecting a display spot.

Avoid hanging a quilt opposite a window that admits strong sunlight. Displayed in direct sunlight, colors are apt to fade and the quilt fibers will eventually weaken.

Artificial light (such as track lights) can have the same damaging effect on the colors and fibers of a quilt, so it's best to avoid training a strong spot directly on your quilt for long periods at a time.

Finally, avoid hanging a quilt near a radiator, directly over a hot air register, or in a damp environment (such as a bathroom).

Fragile antiques deserve tender loving care, because they were designed and stitched to be spread out on beds, rather than mounted on walls. The weight of hanging an old or especially delicate quilt may strain the fibers and stitching

beyond repair. Consequently, a fragile or damaged quilt, particularly if it is valuable, might be displayed best on a bed where it will not receive excessive handling (in a guest room, rather than in a child's room, for example).

Alternatively, old quilts might be folded and stacked in an attractive display cabinet, such as the nineteenth-century pie safe pictured *opposite*. The screened sides and front of the cupboard allow for ventilation while showing off the cheery mix of colors and fabrics in this particular quilt collection. Favorite quilts can be rotated into viewing position on the open cupboard door.

(The quilt hanging here is a Bow Tie pattern; for instructions, turn to page 196.)

HANGING QUILTS

For sturdy quilts, there are several simple methods for effective display that also provide adequate support for the fabric and stitches.

First, and simplest, is to hand-sew one side of a hook and loop fastening tape to the top back of the quilt. Staple the matching side of the tape to the wall or to a strip of pine or lath that has been positioned to receive the quilt and attached to the wall.

For more evenly distributed support, sew fastening tape to all sides of the quilt back. Stretch the quilt onto companion strips of fastening tape that have been stapled to the wall or to a made-to-measure wooden frame. This is an ideal method of mounting quilts, often used for museum displays.

A second hanging option is to hand-sew a muslin casing, about 4 inches wide, along the top back edge of the quilt. Slide a wooden lattice strip into the sleeve. Add screw eyes (for hanging wire) in the ends of the wooden strip, or rest the ends of the strip on support hooks or nails fixed in the wall at each end of the quilt.

For any of the display methods described above, you may need to

hand-sew a new lining to the back of the quilt if the original lining seems weak or damaged. Then sew the fastening or casing strip to the new backing.

Whatever method you select for hanging your quilt, it is best to take the quilt down periodically; either rotate it, or lay it out flat so the quilt isn't pulled out of shape by its own weight.

CLEANING QUILTS

Antique quilts are best cared for by professionals, and a valuable quilt that is in really poor condition probably should not be cleaned at all, because it might fall apart in the process.

Delicate quilts of materials other than cotton, such as silk, wool, or velvet, should be cleaned only if absolutely necessary, and then by a reputable firm experienced with antique fabrics.

Wash older quilts of cotton and linen by hand, but test them first for colorfastness. (If a quilt is colorfast, it is better to wash it than to have it dry-cleaned.)

Hand-wash old quilts in 3 to 4 inches of tepid water in a spotlessly clean bathtub. Use a mild, cold-water detergent or a laundry product specifically formulated for washing quilts.

Gently knead the quilt in water for three or four minutes, then soak it several minutes more. Repeat, being careful not to pull or wring the quilt. Rinse until the water runs clear. If possible, dry the quilt outdoors, on a clear, dry day. Spread it out flat, wrong side up, on clean sheets or towels.

Cotton quilts, made after 1910, can be machine-washed using a mild detergent and cool to lukewarm water. Rinse the quilts three or four times, and *never* dry them using a high heat setting. Machine washing is recommended *only* for quilts that are not considered valuable.

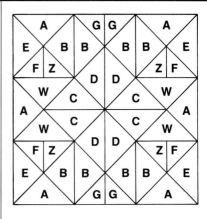

NINE-PATCH QUILT
PAGE 183
Finished size is 81x81 inches

Materials
3½ yards *each* of light and dark fabrics in assorted prints and solid colors
4½ yards of backing fabric
2½ yards of red fabric for borders and some blocks
9 yards of bias binding, batting

Instructions
The design consists of 4½-inch-square nine-patch blocks and plain blocks arranged in diagonal rows. Rows are pieced with triangles, and framed with a contrasting border of wide strips.

To make a similar quilt, follow instructions below. Refer to photograph for color and placement suggestions. Use ¼-inch seams.

To piece blocks: Cut two 5x74-inch and two 5x82-inch border strips of red fabric and set aside.

Cut and piece 121 nine-patch blocks. Piece each block, using four dark and five light 2-inch squares; measurements include seams. (To piece nine-patch blocks, see pages 28-29.) Cut 121 five-inch squares from solid colors, prints, stripes, and plaids.

To make triangle templates, cut a 4½-inch square in half diagonally; use one half for the border triangle template. Cut the remaining triangle in half again to make a template for the corner triangles. Trace and cut 22 border triangles and two corner triangles from dark fabrics, adding seams.

To assemble top: Begin with a pair of border triangles sewn together to form upper left corner of design. Lay the squares, pieced blocks, and triangles in diagonal rows, in a pleasing arrangement. Sew pieces together into rows; join rows together to form top.

To finish: Piece backing to size. Layer backing, batting, and top. Baste together; quilt. Bind edges.

STRIP-PIECED WALL HANGING
PAGE 184
Finished size is 48x48 inches

Materials
3 yards of green pindot fabric for strips and backing
1¼ yards of rust fabric
1½ yards of white fabric
¾ yard *each* of red fabric and black polished cotton
½ yard *each* of large floral print, taupe print, and light rose fabrics
⅜ yard of rose polished cotton
¼ yard *each* of brown, terra-cotta, and ecru fabrics
Batting

Instructions
The wall hanging is stitched entirely from two sizes of right-angle triangles. There are eight solid-color triangles in the design; the rest are machine-pieced from strips of fabric in varying widths.

To complete the hanging, piece from four to eight triangles in each fabric combination that are exact repeats or mirror images of each other. To ensure that the width of all stripes on each triangle in each set is the same, piece long strips of fabric together into rectangles of "new" fabric; cut matching or mirror-image shapes from this custom-stripe fabric.

Strip-piecing instructions: Always cut strips of fabric from selvage to selvage (44 to 45 inches wide). Sew two strips of each fabric together end to end to make 90-inch lengths. Repeat for strips in each fabric combination, using three strips for combination B.

When stitching strips together lengthwise to create pieced fabric, reverse the sewing direction each time you add a strip. This will help to maintain even tension on the strip-pieced cloth. Always press strips to one side as you work (toward darker side, wherever possible). Press on wrong side first, then on right side.

When cutting out repeat shapes from pieced cloth, be especially careful to position the template so that the fabric strips fall in exactly the same place on each pattern piece. For mirror-image shapes, be sure to flop the template and position it with care and accuracy.

Always stitch the strips together in the exact order in which they are listed under the instructions for each fabric combination.

Measurements and templates include seam allowances. Use ¼ inch for all seam allowances.

To piece triangles: To make templates for two triangular patterns, trace and cut out an 11½-inch square. Cut square in half diagonally. One half of the square is the template for the larger triangular shapes (pattern A).

Cut second triangle in half again to make template for smaller triangles (pattern B).

Refer to photograph and assembly diagram, *above,* when piecing the following combinations.

◆ For A, cut and piece four 2¼-inch-wide white strips and four 1½-inch-wide black strips in alternating sequence. Using template A, cut six triangles. The black strip should run along one short leg of the template; cut four triangles with stripes running in one direction and two with stripes running in the opposite direction.

◆ For B, cut and piece strips in the following colors and widths: red, 3½ inches; white, 1¾ inches; black, 1 inch; taupe print, 1¾ inches; rust, 2½ inches; floral print, 2¼ inches; and green dot, 1¾ inches. Using template A, cut eight triangles, four facing in each direction. Position template so that the green dot fabric runs along one short leg of the triangle.

Note: Fabric combination F, described below, will make use of template B and the strip-pieced fabric left over from B, above, so plan layout to allow for this.

♦ For C, cut and piece strips as follows: white, 3½ inches; rust, 2 inches; black, 1 inch; white, 2 inches; rust, 2 inches; taupe print, 1¾ inches; and green dot, 2¾ inches. Using template A, cut four triangles, two facing in each direction, with green dot strip running along one short leg of the triangle.

♦ For D, cut and piece strips as follows: rust, 2 inches; light rose, 1½ inches; red, 2 inches; floral print, 2½ inches; light rose, 1½ inches; rose polished cotton, 1½ inches; red, 2 inches; and black, 2 inches. Using template A, cut four triangles, two facing in each direction, with black strip running along one short leg of the triangle.

♦ For E, cut and piece strips as follows: taupe print, 1¾ inches; light rose, 1½ inches; rose polished cotton, 2 inches; brown, 1¼ inches; and rust, 3½ inches. Using template A, cut four triangles, with taupe stripe running along *long edge* of triangle.

♦ For F, use pieced fabric left over from combination B, above. Cut four triangles using template B. The red stripe should fall on *long* side of triangle on all four pieces.

♦ For G, cut and piece the strips as follows: brown, 1 inch; light rose, 1½ inches; terra-cotta, 1½ inches; rose polished cotton, 2 inches; and rust, 3 inches. Using template B, cut four triangles with brown stripe along long side of each triangle.

♦ Cut four white triangles using template A and four ecru triangles (Z on diagram) using template B.

To assemble wall hanging: Referring to assembly diagram, lay out all triangles in desired pattern. For best results, piece triangles into diagonal rows, beginning in the upper right corner and working toward the lower left corner. Stitch rows together to complete the top, carefully matching all strips and seams.

Piece the backing to size. Layer backing, batting, and pieced top; baste and quilt as desired. Turn under raw edges and slip-stitch front to back. Add a muslin casing to the back for a hanging rod.

AMISH DIAMOND-IN-SQUARE QUILT
PAGE 185
Finished size is 78x78 inches

Materials
3 yards of brown wool
1⅓ yards of turkey red fabric
1¾ yards of black fabric
4½ yards of backing fabric
9 yards of bias binding
Batting

Instructions
To make a quilt similar to the one shown, enlarge pattern, *below right,* and cut pieces from designated fabrics. Add ½-inch seam allowances to all pieces. Cut all straight edges on the grain of the fabric.

To piece the quilt top: Assemble pattern pieces from the center outward. Begin by stitching two short red strips to two opposite sides of center brown square. Add small brown squares to each end of remaining two short red strips, and join these strips to remaining two sides of center square.

Sew black triangles to each side of the square. Sew next red and black border in place, followed by outer border of brown strips and black corner squares.

To finish: Piece backing to size. Layer backing, batting, and pieced top; baste together. Quilt center square and borders as desired.

Elaborate quilting patterns stitched in threads to match fabrics are traditional on Diamond-in-Square quilts made by the Amish of eastern Pennsylvania, as this quilt may have been. The contrast between the lavish quilting and the almost Spartan simplicity of the pieced pattern is especially striking. However, this design also looks good quilted in a simple overall pattern.

Bind raw edges with pieced or purchased bias strips.

IRIS APPLIQUÉ QUILT
PAGE 188
Finished size is 86x89 inches

Materials
4 yards of white fabric for background
2½ yards *each* of blue, gold, red, and burgundy fabric
½ yard *each* of pink and deep rose fabric
2 yards of green fabric
5 yards of fabric for backing
Batting, water-erasable pen

Instructions
This quilt consists of 25 complete iris motifs in different color combinations, plus three clumps of

(Continued)

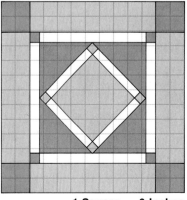

1 Square = 6 Inches
COLOR KEY
■ Black
▨ Brown
☐ Red

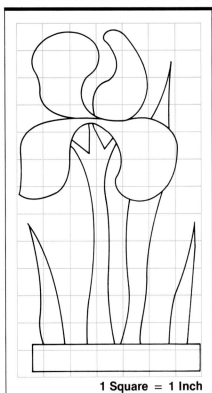

1 Square = 1 Inch

(Continued)

leaves, appliquéd onto seven vertical strips of background fabric. Strips are joined to form quilt top; top is framed with border strips in four of the petal colors.

To make a similar quilt, enlarge pattern, *above.* Make a master pattern. Cut templates for each appliqué shape (four different petals, stem, three leaves, and a base). Next, cut four 2½x92-inch border strips (blue, gold, red, and burgundy); set aside.

To prepare appliqués: Trace and cut each shape from appropriate fabrics (refer to photograph for color distribution on petals and flowers in each row). Add ¼-inch seam allowances to all of the pieces. Baste under raw edges.

Next, cut seven 10½x74-inch strips of white background fabric. Using master pattern, trace four irises onto each of four strips of fabric. Motifs should begin ½ inch from the bottom of the strip, and be evenly spaced, about 6 inches apart. Top flower on each strip should be about 7 inches

from the end of the strip. Moving from left to right on the quilt top, these will be the first, third, fifth, and seventh vertical rows of the quilt. Appliqué the four flowers to each strip.

For second, fourth, and sixth rows of the quilt, trace and appliqué three flowers and a single clump of three leaves at the top. The bottom motif should begin approximately 8½ inches above the edge of the strip. Again, the motifs should be evenly spaced, approximately 6 inches apart.

To assemble quilt: Stitch the seven appliquéd strips together and press. Stitch 2½-inch-wide border strips to sides, top, and bottom in the following order: blue, gold, red, and burgundy. Trim border strips as necessary.

Piece backing to size. Layer the backing, batting, and appliquéd top; baste and quilt as desired. Turn edges of outermost border strip to back of quilt and slipstitch in place.

SCHOOLHOUSE QUILT
PAGE 189
Finished size is 60x72 inches

Materials
8½ yards of white fabric for
   background and backing
4 yards of pink fabric(s)
8 yards of white bias binding
Batting, water-erasable pen

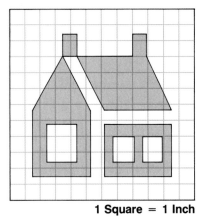

1 Square = 1 Inch

Instructions
The quilt consists of 30 appliquéd house blocks arranged in six vertical rows of five houses each.

This particular variation of the Schoolhouse block also is known as the Old Kentucky Home pattern. The block may be pieced or appliquéd. Directions for a quilt similar to the one pictured are given below.

For each block: Enlarge pattern, *below left,* and trace onto a 12-inch square of paper to make a master pattern. Next, make separate templates for each part of the house: roof, chimneys, front (single window), and side (double windows). Trace 30 of each shape onto right side of pink fabric(s) with water-erasable pen and cut out all pattern pieces. *Note:* Houses may be cut from the same or different pink fabrics, as desired. Add ¼-inch seam allowances to all pieces, including the window openings.

Trace the master pattern, centered, onto the right side of thirty 12½-inch white fabric squares.

Clip corners, and baste under seam allowance on all appliqué pieces. Stitch houses in place.

Note: One house in the bottom row of the quilt is flopped—an eye-catching design "error" that you may wish to adopt for your own quilt.

To assemble quilt: Join appliquéd squares into five horizontal rows of six blocks each; stitch rows together. Piece backing to size. Layer backing, batting, and appliquéd top together; baste and quilt as desired. Bind the raw edges with pieced or purchased bias strips.

SIX-POINT STAR QUILT
PAGE 186
Finished size is 70x80½ inches

Materials
6 yards total of assorted light and
   dark fabrics
5½ yards of backing fabric
8½ yards of bias binding
Quilt batting

Full-Size Pattern

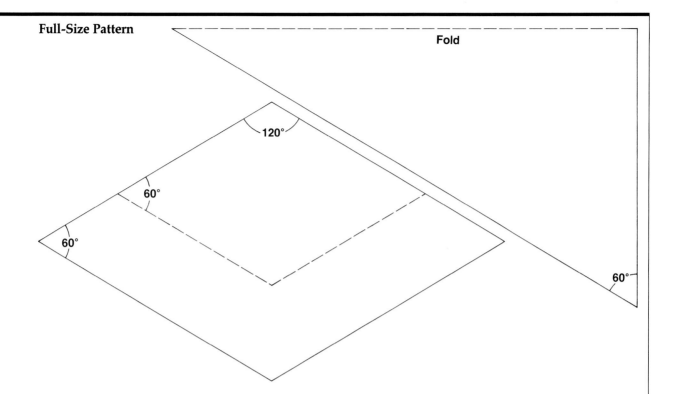

Fold

120°

60°

60°

60°

Instructions

For each block of the quilt, piece six diamonds into a star, then add six contrasting diamonds around the star to make a hexagon. Piece the hexagons and large triangles point to point and frame with right-angle triangles to form horizontal rows. Finish the ends of every alternate row with pieced diamonds so star blocks are staggered from row to row. (See piecing diagram, *right.*)

To complete the quilt pattern, stitch seven horizontal rows together. To adjust the size of the quilt, alter the number of blocks in each row or the number of rows in the quilt. To make a quilt similar to the one pictured, follow instructions below.

To piece a block: Enlarge patterns for *large* diamond only and equilateral triangle, *above right;* make templates. Cut one equilateral triangle in half to make a template for right-angle border triangles.

For each block, cut six diamonds from one fabric for center star and six diamonds from contrasting fabric to complete the hexagon. Add ¼-inch seams to

(Continued)

ROW 2

ROW 1

ROW 3

195

(Continued)

the pieces. Stitch and assemble a total of 45 star-filled hexagons.

For the border diamonds, piece together two of the light diamond shapes and two of the dark diamonds, as shown in the assembly diagram, to form a larger diamond. Make eight.

To assemble quilt top: Begin by piecing the center horizontal row of the top (Row 1). Cut four equilateral triangles from one fabric; join a pair of triangles to both sides of a pieced hexagon (see photograph). Repeat this procedure for two more hexagons, choosing different fabrics for the triangles stitched to each one.

Next, stitch plain hexagons *between* each of the three triangle-framed hexagons. Stitch plain hexagons to both ends of the row and finish each end with a pair of right-angle triangles, as shown in the assembly diagram.

For the rows above and below the center row (Rows 2 and 3),

piece five hexagons between equilateral triangles in such a way that the *bottom* triangles in Row 2 and the *top* triangles in Row 3 form a pattern of larger six-point stars.

(The *top* triangle in Row 2 and the *bottom* triangle in Row 3 are the beginnings of new star patterns to be formed by succeeding rows.)

Complete each end of Rows 2 and 3 with a pieced diamond and two right-angle triangles. For Rows 4–5, repeat Row 1. For Rows 6–7, repeat Rows 2 and 3.

To finish quilt: Stitch the horizontal rows together. Press seams carefully to one side.

Cut and piece the fabric for the back of the quilt. Then, lay out the backing fabric, smooth batting atop the backing, and position the quilt top in place.

Pin and baste the layers securely together. Quilt the design in the pattern of your choice. After quilting is complete, remove basting stitches and bind the edges of the quilt with bias strips.

APPLIQUÉD PAINTING
PAGE 187
Finished size is 21x26 inches

Materials
21x26 inches *each* of quilt batting, background, and backing fabrics
1½ yards of black ribbon
Scraps of brocades, damasks, velvets, linens, and satins
10 inches of fringe (for tapestry)
Black pearl cotton
Matching threads for appliqués
Dressmaker's carbon

Instructions
Enlarge the pattern, *below left,* to size; transfer it to paper to make a master pattern. Center and transfer the *outlines* of the pattern onto the right side of the background fabric, using dressmaker's carbon.

Next, make paper templates for each appliqué piece and cut the appliqués from appropriate fabrics. Do *not* add seam allowances to the pieces.

Pin the fabric shapes to the background fabric and machine-appliqué each one in place using matching threads. Sew fringe to the bottom of the tapestry.

Layer the backing, batting, and appliquéd picture. Pin the layers together, then baste around the sides. Bind the edges with 2-inch-wide bias-cut strips of contrasting fabric; sew narrow strips of black velvet ribbon between the fabric frame and the edge of the appliquéd picture.

To finish, use black pearl cotton to run wide quilting stitches along inside and outside edges of frame and along the edge of appliquéd tapestry on right side of picture.

Add a muslin casing for a hanging rod to back of picture.

1 Square = 1 Inch

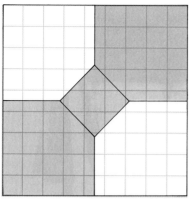

1 Square = ½ Inch

BOW-TIE QUILT
PAGE 190
Finished size is 72x72 inches

Materials
3 yards of red print for borders
  and solid squares
2 yards of assorted dark and light
  prints for bow ties
4½ yards of backing fabric
Quilt batting
8½ yards of bias binding
Cardboard or plastic for templates

Instructions
Four-inch bow-tie blocks alternate with solid squares in this simply pieced quilt. To make a similar quilt, follow instructions below.

To piece top: Cut two 2½x78-inch strips of red print for borders; set aside. Next, enlarge the pattern block, *above,* and cut out the cardboard or plastic templates for each pattern shape.

Adding ¼-inch seam allowances to all pieces, cut and stitch 162 bow-tie blocks. Use darker fabrics for the bow-tie shapes and lighter fabrics for the background pieces.

Next, cut 162 solid-red squares (each 4½x4½ inches, including seam allowances).

Piece the bow-tie blocks and solid squares into 18 rows of 18 squares each. Then piece the horizontal rows together to form the quilt top. Press all seams carefully.

To assemble quilt: Stitch borders to both sides of pieced top, trimming to fit. Piece backing to size. Layer backing, batting, and pieced top together and baste. Quilt as desired. Bind edges with pieced or purchased bias strips.

RED AND WHITE BASKET QUILT
PAGES 180-181
Finished size is 74x90 inches

Materials
8 yards of white fabric for background and backing
2½ yards of red fabric for baskets, borders, and bindings
Quilt batting
Cardboard or plastic lids for templates

Instructions
The quilt pictured consists of 20 pieced basket blocks and 16 plain white blocks set together on the diagonal in four rows of five patterned blocks each. The design is pieced out with half- and quarter-blocks (triangles) of white fabric

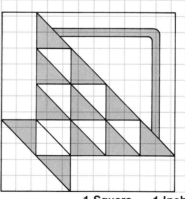

1 Square = 1 Inch

and then bordered with a 5-inch-wide strip of white fabric embellished with an appliquéd red chain design.

The finished quilt is bound in red (the border and binding are not pictured) and lavishly quilted.

Following are instructions for a single block. To make a quilt similar to the one shown, make 20 basket blocks and assemble with plain blocks and borders as described above. Quilt the design in the pattern shown in the photograph, or substitute the pattern of your choice.

To make one block: Enlarge the block pattern, *below left,* to size (11½ inches square), and transfer it to graph paper.

Note that this basket design is a combination of piecing and appliqué. The lower portion of the design is entirely pieced. The basket handle is appliquéd to a triangle of fabric to make the top portion of the block, and then the two sections are stitched together.

Cut cardboard or plastic templates for each pattern piece. Use ¼-inch-wide seam allowances throughout. For tips on piecing right-angle triangles, see pages 126–127.

First, cut 11 red and seven white triangles and piece them together to form the basket (see pattern for assembly). Add the bottom triangle and side rectangles to the basket to complete the lower portion of the block. Press all seams toward the darker fabric.

Next, cut out a red basket handle, baste under the seam allowance along the long sides, and appliqué the handle to the white triangle for the top of the block.

To complete the block, stitch the appliquéd triangle to the top of the basket.

197

PATCHWORK NATURALLY— QUILTS FOR EVERY BEDROOM

The magnificent heirloom quilts so highly prized today were designed first and foremost as functioning bedcovers, and only secondarily for show. Though contemporary collectors may reverse these concerns, the bedroom still offers a uniquely appropriate showcase for patchwork creations, antique or otherwise.

The opulent orchid and pinwheel coverlet and companion wall hangings, *right,* exemplify a thoroughly modern and wonderfully imaginative mix of different styles of patchwork.

The coverlet and hangings are pieced from scraps of velvet, brocades, and damasks—elegant fabrics reminiscent of the Victorian crazy-quilt era. But the border blocks of the quilt are variations of the formal pinwheel pattern, a design most often pieced in traditional calicoes and cotton prints.

The appliquéd vase of flowers on the center panel of the coverlet recalls the medallion quilts popular during the first half of the nineteenth century, many of which also featured appliquéd floral motifs. Yet spontaneity of design, choice of fabrics, and the no-nonsense, machine-appliqué approach are definitely new.

As with many of the most stunning patchwork designs of the past, this contemporary ensemble combines a variety of traditional elements in new ways to satisfy the maker's individual sense of color and design. The results are elegant, original, and an inspiration to patchworkers everywhere.

Instructions for these projects, and for other bedcovers shown in this section, begin on page 210.

Patchwork is a collection of skills and techniques— an art in and of itself, rather than a particular style. With imagination and ingenuity, you can fashion a patchwork bedcover to suit your own level of skill or manner of decorating.

Pictured here are two extremes in patchwork styling. *Opposite,* the traditionalist's fantasy: a scrolled iron bedstead topped with a lavish collection of country quilts. *Above left,* the minimalist's dream: an easy-to-piece duvet cover and pillow shams sewn from strips, rectangles, and squares.

Pattern and detail here are all. This plump duvet cover consists of a sophisticated palette of solid-color scraps in geometric shapes. Once pieced, the top is backed with fabric and slipped over a purchased comforter. Finished with a set of one-patch pillow shams, the bed is dressed with flair.

A color-coordinated set of antique quilts in traditional patterns graces the bed, *opposite.* By changing the arrangement of the quilts from time to time, you can create a rotating display for a rather extensive quilt collection.

To make the duvet cover, see the instructions that begin on page 210.

Unusual fabrics and unexpected colors can completely transform the look of even the most time-honored and traditional patchwork patterns.

To create the striking pair of Log Cabin coverlets pictured here, an innovative stitcher substituted glimmery satin fabrics in sherbet shades for the usual brightly colored calicoes and ginghams favored by quilters of the past.

Probably stitched in the early 1940s, these sumptuous spreads make inventive use of the reflective qualities of the satin weave. Each block is pieced from a single pastel shade of satin. But when the narrow strips are arranged in the Courthouse Steps pattern, the fabric subtly reflects the light in such a way that the squares seem to be pieced from a lighter and a darker shade of the same color.

The lightweight coverlets are lined but not quilted, as is often the case with Log Cabin patchwork. Satin piping and a graceful ruffle contribute to the overall effect of elegance.

Today, satin is available in a delectable range of colors, so you can choose your favorites to create a coverlet of your own. Consider a similar fabric switch or unusual color combination to update or enliven any traditional patchwork pattern.

Floral designs are a traditional favorite for patchwork quilts and coverlets, and the variety of pattern sources for both abstract and realistic flower motifs is vast and exciting.

The bedroom full of delight-fully fresh ideas, *right,* takes its design inspiration from the marvelous rose rug on the floor. A single full-blown blossom and a selection of stems, leaves, and buds were picked from the rug pattern and adapted for use as appliqué shapes.

By sizing the basic pattern from large to small, you can create the entire array of patchwork projects pictured here, plus others of your own design.

The coverlet, pillows, and table skirt all were appliquéd by hand and embellished with touches of hand embroidery, but the designs are equally suitable for machine appliqué, if you prefer.

The oversize scale of the appliqués on the coverlet and pillows, and the unexpected mix of contemporary fabrics used for the collection, keep the designs from appearing too fussy, and offer an interesting contrast to the ornate wallpaper, framed picture, and other furnishings in the room.

For suggestions on how to adapt designs for patchwork, and tips on enlarging and reducing patterns, turn to page 312.

Here's another idea for patch-work enthusiasts: Note the pretti-ly pieced and appliquéd skirt of the porcelain doll on the edge of the bed. Designing and stitching a more or less elaborate patchwork costume for a favorite doll is an excellent way to practice your piecing skills, use up the tiniest odds and ends of fabrics and laces, and create a one-of-a-kind heir-loom doll for a special child. Use silks, satins, and such to create an elegant patchwork overskirt for a purchased porcelain doll, as pictured here, or stitch colorful calico scraps into a patchwork pinafore for a new or antique rag doll from your own collection.

Lavishly embroidered crazy quilts and other museum-quality coverlets from the past are an especially rich source of design ideas for present-day patchwork artists. This bedroom ensemble, inspired by the Mittie Barrier farmyard quilt shown on page 299, is a case in point.

Stitched in the 1920s, the original Mittie Barrier quilt is an inspiring blend of imaginative design and impeccable workmanship. But, as illustrated in these projects, successful translation of the past into the present often depends on selective adaptation, rather than slavish imitation.

To catch the flavor of the original coverlet, while reducing the requisite handiwork to manageable proportions, only two of Mrs. Barrier's 25 designs were selected for the coverlet, bed skirt, headboard, valance, and pillows, *left.* Key elements from each of these two patterns were enlarged, simplified, and recombined in different ways for each project.

To make the coverlet, squares of soft woolens in muted shades were joined into strips and assembled on the diagonal. Machine-stitched seams were embellished with simple featherstitches, and an embroidered bunny, flowers, and a bird were scattered across the spread, to recall the more richly worked surface of the original quilt.

A stately procession of geese, adapted from one of the original pattern blocks, marches in rhythmic repeats around the bed skirt and across the window valance. From a second pattern block, a pastoral scene of bunnies, birds, and baby chicks was enlarged for the headboard.

Individual motifs from each of these block designs embellish the companion throw pillows on the bed and chair and complete this ensemble.

Keep the concept of selective adaptation in mind as you study other patchwork masterpieces in search of design ideas to use in your own home.

Repetition of a single motif on a coverlet and companion pillows offers a quick-to-stitch way to perk up a plain bedroom ensemble.

The fanciful flock of bluebirds gracing the pristine white quilt and collection of throw pillows shown here brings a refreshing breath of spring to a bedroom in any season. Simple bird shapes are machine-appliquéd across a sheet, embellished with satin-stitch details, and then outline-quilted for quick results. Machine stitching makes the crafting of this coverlet fast, but it could just as easily be stitched by hand.

As with the rose motifs that are pictured on pages 204-205, this bluebird design can be enlarged, reduced, or reversed to suit a variety of other patchwork projects—curtain borders, seat cushions, or a tablecloth, for example.

If birds or flowers don't suit your fancy, scout through magazines, children's coloring books, and other pattern sources for an easy-to-reproduce design with simple outlines that would work well as an appliqué motif. The diagonal flight of the bluebirds is part of the appeal of the quilt shown here, but the appliqué motifs you choose can be stitched in whatever arrangement you prefer.

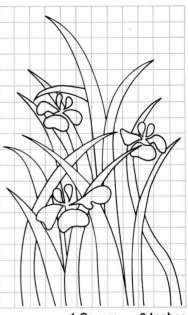

1 Square = 2 Inches

1 Square = 2 Inches

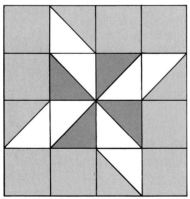

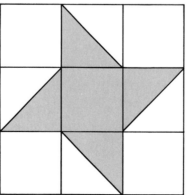

APPLIQUÉD ORCHID PANEL WALL HANGINGS
PAGE 199
Each panel is 26x60 inches

Materials
(for each panel)
27x61 inches of black velvet
27x61 inches of muslin (backing)
Scraps of melon and lavender
  velvet (flowers)
3 shades of green fabrics such as
  satin, damask, or linen (leaves)
4¼ yards of 1-inch-wide yellow
  ribbon
Black pearl cotton
White dressmaker's carbon

Instructions
Enlarge pattern, *above;* transfer to
tracing paper for a master pattern.
Transfer pattern to black velvet,
using carbon paper (see page 312
for transferring tips).

Make templates for each appliqué. Cut pieces from fabrics; do
not add seams. Pin, baste, and machine-appliqué shapes to velvet.

Frame design with strips of yellow ribbon; sew ribbon in place.

To complete panel: Layer backing, batting, and appliquéd panel;
pin and baste. Using black pearl
cotton, quilt around ribbon frame;
tie layers together at various

points. Sew front and backing together along edges. Add muslin sleeve or plastic rings for hanging.

For second panel (at right in the photograph): Rearrange design elements from the first panel to create a master pattern for the second. Trace templates for leaves and flowers used for the first panel. Study photograph for inspiration. Complete as described above.

PIECED AND APPLIQUÉD ORCHID QUILT
PAGES 198-199
Finished size is 91x103 inches

Materials
4½ yards of black velvet (center panel, sashing, and borders)
6 yards of backing fabric
Scraps of velvets, brocades, damasks, and prints (appliqués and border squares)
3 yards of 1-inch-wide yellow ribbon
Black pearl cotton
Lightweight batting

Instructions
This quilt consists of a 21x32-inch appliquéd center panel framed by an inner border of 9-inch-square Friendship Star blocks and an outer border of 12-inch-square Clay's Choice blocks. Blocks are separated by 2½- to 3-inch-wide black velvet sashing strips. (Width depends on placement of blocks.) Quilt is finished with a 7-inch-wide black velvet border.

For center panel: Enlarge pattern, *opposite, above left,* and make a master pattern. Transfer outlines to front of a 22x33-inch piece of black velvet. Make templates for appliqués; cut pieces from fabrics. Pin, baste, and machine-appliqué shapes to velvet. Sew yellow ribbon 2½ inches from edge.

To piece inner border: Cut a 3½-inch-square template. Cut a second 3½-inch square. Cut this square in half diagonally to make template for right-angle triangles. Trace and cut five squares and

eight triangles for each block (see photograph for color and pattern suggestions). Add ¼-inch seams.

Piece eight triangles into four squares. Assemble nine pieced and plain squares into Friendship Star blocks (see diagram, *opposite, below right*). Make 14 blocks.

Sew a 3-inch-wide sashing strip between two blocks. Sew pieced strip to top of appliquéd panel, using ¼-inch seams. Repeat for bottom of panel.

Sew six sashing strips between and to ends of five pieced blocks; sew this strip to one side of appliquéd panel, aligning seams. Repeat for other panel side.

To piece outer border: Using the same 3-inch-square and right-angle-triangle templates used for the inner border, cut eight squares and 16 triangles for each Clay's Choice block (see photograph for color and pattern suggestions).

Piece the 16 triangles into eight squares. Join the plain and pieced squares into a block (see diagram, *opposite, below left*). Make a total of 18 blocks.

Join four completed blocks using 3-inch-wide sashing strips. Stitch a 3-inch-wide sashing strip to the bottom of this pieced strip and stitch to one side of the quilt top. Repeat for the other side.

For the top and the bottom border, piece five blocks together with four 3½-inch-wide sashing strips. (For these outer borders, lay out blocks and sashing strips along top and bottom of quilt; adjust final width of sashing strips to make sure that borders meet evenly at outer edges and seams.)

When top and bottom borders are pieced, add a 2½-inch-wide sashing strip between outer and inner borders.

To complete quilt: Sew 7½-inch-wide border strips to top and bottom and then to sides of quilt.

Piece the backing to size; layer backing, batting, and pieced top; baste. Using black pearl cotton, tie through all three layers at various points across the top. Turn under raw edges; sew top to backing.

PATCHWORK DUVET
PAGE 200

Materials
White, rust, cream, light blue, and tan cotton fabrics
Backing fabric, graph paper
Two 24-inch-long zippers
8 inches of fastening tape

Instructions
Note: Duvet cover is designed to fit over a purchased down comforter. Because sizes of comforters vary, no fabric yardages are given. Refer to directions for designing pieced top and purchase fabrics accordingly. Carefully measure the comforter. Plan finished size of cover to these measurements.

Designing pieced top: The duvet cover is pieced in four sections (from foot of bed to the head) as follows: a checkerboard panel; a randomly striped panel; a blue-and-white striped panel; and a second checkerboard panel. Chart top to scale on graph paper before beginning. Add to or subtract from length and/or width of each panel for desired dimensions.

For first checkerboard panel, chart 5-inch squares across the width. Row 1 is blue and white. Row 2 is white and blue. Row 3 is blue and rust. Row 4 is rust and gray. Row 5 is gray and cream. Row 6 is cream and tan. Row 7 is blue and cream. Be sure to alternate colors to form a checkerboard pattern.

For randomly striped panel, chart four stripes as follows: a 4-inch-wide stripe; a 2-inch-wide stripe; a 6-inch-wide stripe; and a 3-inch-wide stripe. Piece stripes randomly from leftover fabrics.

For blue-and-white striped panel, alternate a 3x14-inch blue stripe with a 1½x14-inch white stripe.

For second checkerboard panel, chart four rows of 5-inch checks. Row 1 is gray and tan. Row 2 is cream and gray. Row 3 is gray and white. Row 4 is white and rust.

(Continued)

(Continued)

To piece top: Use ½-inch seams; press seams open after stitching.

For checkerboard panels, cut a 6-inch template. Draw pattern onto wrong side of fabric. Cut the number of squares needed. Lay squares in rows. Sew squares into rows. Sew rows together to form checked panels, matching corners.

For blue-and-white striped panels, cut 4x15-inch and 2½x15-inch templates. Cut out large light blue rectangles and small white rectangles. Aligning each long side, and alternating colors, sew rectangles together to desired width.

For randomly striped panels, cut 3-, 4-, 5-, and 7-inch-wide templates. Cut strips from fabric scraps. Matching widths of stripes, sew strips end to end to form patched lengths. Sew strips together.

Sew panels together as follows: large check, random-stripe, blue-and-white stripe, and small check.

To assemble duvet cover: Piece backing to size. Place backing and top right sides together. Position two zippers along bottom edge of cover so that the zippers, when closed, meet at the center. Sew in place. Sew remaining sides.

Cut fastening tape to 2-inch lengths. Sew a piece to corners of the comforter. Sew corresponding pieces to inside surface of backing fabric. This will prevent comforter from shifting. Turn to right side. Insert comforter; zip closed.

❖

CHECKERBOARD-PATTERN QUILT

PAGE 201
Finished size is 78x95 inches

Materials

3½ yards of light fabrics and 3 yards of dark fabrics in assorted solids, plaids, and stripes (checkerboard squares)
3 yards of rose fabric (borders)
2 yards of yellow fabric (sashing)
6 yards of backing fabric
11 yards of green bias binding
Quilt batting

Instructions

Quilt consists of twenty 15-inch-square checkerboard blocks arranged in five horizontal rows of four blocks each. Blocks consist of 25 alternating dark and light squares sewn into diagonal rows, pieced out with triangles, and bordered with 2-inch-wide sashing strips.

For each block: Cut a 2½-inch-square template. Cut a second 2½-inch square and cut it in half diagonally to make right-angle-triangle templates. Cut one triangle in half again to make the templates for corner triangles.

For one block, trace and cut 16 dark and nine light squares, 12 side triangles, and four corner triangles. Add ¼-inch margins.

Lay out squares and triangles as shown in the diagram, *right.* Beginning in upper left corner, sew a corner triangle to one edge of a dark square; sew two side triangles to sides of same square, forming first corner of the block. Piece a light square between two dark squares; add a side triangle to each end of the strip, forming the second row of the block. Continue until all rows of the block are pieced. Sew rows together following diagram. Make 20 blocks.

To assemble quilt top: From yellow fabric, cut 31 sashing strips, each 2½x15½ inches. Lay pieced blocks in five rows of four blocks each; sew sashing strips between blocks in each row, using ¼-inch seam allowances.

Cut and piece three 2½-inch squares between four sashing strips; sew strips between rows of blocks, matching seams. Repeat for sashing between all rows of blocks. Press quilt top; sew 6½-inch-wide borders to top and bottom, and then to sides of quilt.

To assemble quilt: Cut and piece backing to size. Layer backing, batting, and pieced top together; baste. Quilt and bind edges.

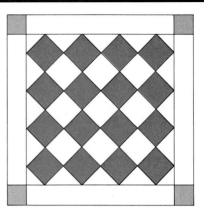

❖

COLONIAL FLOWER BASKET QUILT

PAGE 201
Finished size is 84x84 inches

Materials

6 yards of white fabric (background squares)
5½ yards of backing fabric
2 yards *each* of rose and yellow fabrics (baskets)
Quilt batting, water-erasable pen

Instructions

Quilt consists of 36 appliquéd blocks (six rows of six squares each). To alter quilt size, alter size or number (or both) of blocks used to piece the top.

To assemble blocks: Cut out 36 squares, each 14½x14½ inches, from white fabric; set aside.

Enlarge pattern, *opposite left,* and transfer to paper for a master pattern. Using water-erasable pen, trace outlines of basket and handle to center of each square.

Make templates for appliqués. For pieced basket, trace and cut out a 2-inch square. Trace a second 2-inch square and cut it in half diagonally to form template for the right-angle triangle. Cut a template for the basket handle.

For each block: Trace and cut out one yellow fabric square, five yellow triangles, 11 rose triangles, and one rose basket handle. Add ¼-inch seam allowances.

Piece square and triangles together to form basket, following diagram, *right.* (For easiest piecing, divide basket pattern into diagonal rows. Piece the triangles into squares, then assemble squares into rows to form basket, finishing rows with triangles.)

Baste under raw edges on basket. Clip curves on handle; baste under raw edges. Press.

Arrange handle and basket on background square; appliqué in place. Make 36 blocks.

To assemble quilt: Sew blocks into six rows of six blocks each. Cut and piece backing to size. Layer backing, batting, and pieced top together; baste. Quilt as desired, then bind the raw edges.

SATIN LOG CABIN QUILTS
PAGES 202-203
Finished size is 54x91 inches, excluding ruffle

Materials
(for each quilt)
8 yards of satin in shades of yellow, blue, copper, gray, and ecru
4½ yards of muslin (backing)
8½ yards of cable cord
3 yards of light green taffeta

Instructions
Each twin-size quilt contains 126 Log Cabin blocks (each 6¼ inches square) arranged in 14 rows of nine blocks each. To alter size, adjust number of blocks in the rows.

Cut 126 muslin blocks, each 6¾ inches square. Cut 1¾-inch squares for centers and 1-inch strips of satin for logs for each block. (Dimensions include ¼-inch seam margins.)

For each block: Baste satin square to center of muslin square. Piece five rounds of logs from the same-color satin around each center square. (Follow instructions on pages 83-85.) Use ¼-inch seam allowances. Make 126 blocks.

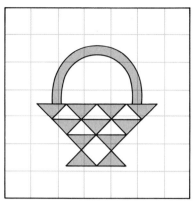

1 Square = 2 Inches

To assemble top: Sew completed blocks into 14 horizontal rows of nine blocks each.

Cut and piece 1½-inch-wide bias strips of green taffeta; cover cable cord. Baste cord around the edges of quilt top. Cut and piece remaining taffeta into a 6x480-inch strip. Narrowly hem long edge and short ends; gather remaining edge. Baste and sew ruffle to long sides and one short end of quilt (top edge has no ruffle).

To finish, cut and piece muslin backing to match quilt top. Sew backing to top along three sides, with right sides facing. Turn and press; stitch fourth side closed.

ROSE APPLIQUÉD QUILT AND PILLOWS
PAGES 204-205

Materials
2¼ yards of windowpane plaid fabric
2¼ yards of white backing fabric
1 yard *each* of light and dark rose; light, medium-, and dark green; and blue fabrics
½ yard of pink polka-dot fabric
3 yards of blue-and-white polka-dot fabric (for dust ruffle)
Quilt batting and thread
White pearl cotton floss

Instructions
Note: This quilt is designed to fit a standard twin-size bed. To adjust size, alter the scale of the rose patterns, the number of rose appliqués used, or the width of the border strips.

To begin, enlarge patterns, *right;* make master patterns. Number or letter the individual shapes in the

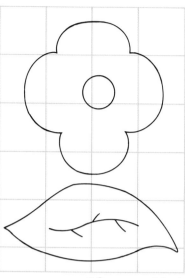

1 Square = 1 Inch

1 Square = 2 Inches

design and note how many of each shape you will need to cut. Cut out templates for each pattern piece.

Trace and cut out all fabric shapes, adding ¼-inch seam allowances. Turn under and baste raw edges of all appliqués.

To assemble quilt top: Pin and baste seven large rose appliqué designs to a 32x68-inch rectangle of windowpane plaid fabric. (See photograph on page 205 for colors and placement.) Sew designs in place. Trim overlapping fabric.

Cut and piece 1-inch-wide strips of blue fabric and sew to all four sides of top (mitering corners). Cut and piece 4-inch-wide

(Continued)

213

1 Square = 1 Inch

(Continued)

strips of white-and-pink polka-dot fabric and sew around all four sides of pieced top. Use ¼-inch seams and miter corners.

Pin and stitch the small rose and leaf motifs to the pink and white border strips. Embroider flowers and leaves as shown, using pearl cotton and stem stitches.

Cut backing fabric 1 inch larger than the pieced top. Place batting between backing and pieced top and baste layers together. Quilt around flowers, leaves, and stems.

To finish: Cut and piece a 22x108-inch strip of blue-and-white polka-dot fabric for the dust ruffle. Gather along one long edge. With *wrong* sides together, pin and sew dust ruffle along sides and bottom of quilt top. Conceal seam with a 1-inch-wide strip of blue fabric. Hem ruffle.

To make pillows: Appliqué one large rose to center of a 25x25-inch piece of plaid fabric.

For ruffles, cut strips of fabric twice the desired width of the ruffle and twice the circumference of the pillow. Baste long edges together, gather, and sew to pillow front. Cut blue backing fabric to size; sew back to front around three sides. Turn, press, stuff, and sew fourth side closed.

✦

APPLIQUÉD TABLECLOTH
PAGE 204

Materials
Pink-and-white polka-dot fabric (cloth)
Windowpane plaid fabric (ruffle)
Blue fabric (border stripes)
Dark, medium-, and light rose, and dark, medium-, and light green fabrics (appliqués)

Instructions
Note: The tablecloth can be sized to fit any round table. Simply measure the diameter and height of your table to make sure the tablecloth has adequate drop.

To make cloth: Cut and piece polka-dot fabric to make a circle with the desired diameter of the cloth. Enlarge large blossom and a single leaf of the rose pattern on page 213 (lower diagram) to size (use a scale of one square equals 1 inch for these smaller appliqués). Make a master pattern and templates, as described for quilt.

Cut out appliqués, adding ¼-inch margins. Position randomly on tablecloth top; sew in place.

Cut windowpane fabric to desired width for ruffle. The length should be twice the circumference of the tablecloth top. Border ruffle top and bottom with 2-inch-wide strips of blue fabric.

Enlarge entire design on page 213 (lower diagram). Cut and sew motifs along border. Hem cloth.

✦

EMBROIDERED HEADBOARD
PAGES 206-207

Materials
18x28-inch rectangle of solid-color wool fabric
Scraps of assorted wool fabrics for crazy quilt piecing
Batting, eyelet ruffle
Plywood for base of headboard
Crewel embroidery yarn in your choice of colors
2 skeins of gold embroidery floss
Cording or decorative braid
White dressmaker's carbon

Instructions
Enlarge bunnies, chicks, and grass from the pattern, *left,* and the tree of birds pattern on page 311 to size. Arrange elements from both patterns as pictured on pages 206-207; transfer the composite design to the center of the 18x28-inch rectangle of wool. Adapt the design elements to fill the space.

Work the embroidery with one strand of three-ply crewel yarn in colors and stitches of your choice. (Refer to photograph for inspiration, and see pages 310-311 for notes on suggested stitches.)

From plywood, cut a headboard to fit your bed. Cut a piece of muslin backing fabric to match the headboard shape, adding a 3-inch margin on all sides. Center and baste embroidered panel to this muslin backing piece.

Arrange wool fabrics around embroidered piece and cut fabrics accordingly; add ¼-inch seams. Working from the center of the design outward, begin stitching pieces of fabric to sides of the finished embroidery; continue adding pieces until the design covers the muslin backing piece. Press. Featherstitch along seam lines, using six strands of gold floss.

Place the batting between the headboard and the embroidered fabric; staple to back of board, pulling taut. Clip corners on back to ease curves. Cut a piece of fabric slightly larger than the headboard. Turn under raw edges; sew or staple to back of headboard.

Tack cording to headboard; attach headboard to bed frame.

❖

EMBROIDERED DUST RUFFLE
PAGES 206-207

Materials

3 yards of navy wool fabric
3-ply crewel yarn in your choice of colors
2½ yards of muslin
White dressmaker's carbon

Instructions

Note: Instructions are for a twin-size bed dust ruffle; adjust sizes and placement of motifs.

Select three geese from pattern on page 311; enlarge to desired size. Make a master pattern.

Cut two 16x86-inch strips and one 16x42-inch strip of navy wool fabric. Using dressmaker's carbon, transfer two sets of geese onto longer strips, spacing evenly, for sides; center one set of geese on shorter strip for end. Work embroidery as described in instructions for Mittie Barrier quilt on pages 310-311. Press gently on wrong side.

Cut muslin the same size as the top of box spring, adding ½-inch seam allowances. Sew end sections of embroidered fabric and two side sections together. Hem raw edges on two ends. Make a deep pleat in each corner of one end to fit foot of bed. Baste and press. With right sides together, baste embroidered strip to muslin, easing pleats around corners. Sew in place; hem bottom edge.

❖

EMBROIDERED PILLOWS
PAGES 206-207

Materials

Assorted wool fabrics
3-ply crewel embroidery yarns
Transfer pencil or dressmaker's carbon
Fiberfill or pillow forms

Instructions

Enlarge selected portions of the Mittie Barrier embroidery designs here and on page 311 and transfer to squares or rectangles of wool fabric. Embroider as described for other projects, above. Back with matching piece of fabric; stuff and sew opening closed.

❖

WOOL CRAZY QUILT
PAGES 206-207

Materials

Assorted wool fabrics, sufficient for fifty-eight 8½-inch squares and twenty-four 9x9x12¾-inch right-angle triangles for edges
5 skeins of gold embroidery floss
Blanket binding or strips of muslin to pleat for edging

Instructions

Cut fifty-eight 8½-inch squares from wool fabrics. Cut twenty-four 9x9x12¾-inch triangles for the borders. Stitch pieces together into diagonal strips. Then stitch strips together to form quilt top.

Press the quilt top. Using six strands of gold floss, featherstitch along all seam lines and then back with muslin or a lightweight blanket, if desired.

Bind edges of quilt with blanket binding, or turn raw edges under and add a pleated muslin border, as pictured.

❖

BLUEBIRD APPLIQUÉD QUILT AND PILLOWS
PAGES 208-209

Materials

2 white muslin sheets
2 yards *each* of light and dark blue fabrics
⅛ yard of gold fabric
Batting, eyelet ruffle
½ yard of matching or contrasting fabric for each pillow
Matching or contrasting piping
Matching threads for appliqué
Fiberfill or pillow forms
Water-erasable pen

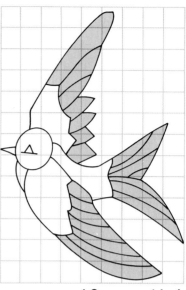

1 Square = 1 Inch

Instructions

Eighteen bluebirds are pieced and machine-appliquéd to a double-size muslin sheet. Adjust size of sheet and number of motifs to suit desired size of quilt.

To appliqué quilt top: Enlarge pattern, *above,* to size and make a paper master pattern.

Cut templates, then cut shapes from fabrics. Trace motifs in horizontal rows of three on quilt top, staggering position of birds so that they fall in diagonal lines across quilt. Machine-appliqué birds in place; embroider eyes.

To assemble quilt: Layer backing sheet, batting, and top; baste together. Hand- or machine-quilt ⅜ inch outside appliquéd edges of each motif. Turn under raw edges on top and bottom sheets. Insert and pin edge of eyelet ruffle in place; topstitch.

For matching pillows: Appliqué birds to squares or circles of white fabric, back each piece with batting and lining fabric; hand- or machine-quilt around each bird. Frame with a square or round of contrasting fabric, add piping, and use matching fabric to create a knife-edge or box pillow.

EXTRAORDINARY PATCHWORK ACCESSORIES

Attention to detail is as important
in decorating a home as it
is in piecing a prizewinning quilt.
And whether your taste runs
to country classic or urban eclectic,
whether you prefer a single,
grand decorating gesture or a
collection of whimsical accents,
patchwork is a wonderfully versatile
way to personalize your home.

If you think of patchwork as a form of soft architecture, the pillows, *left*, suggest all sorts of possibilities for constructing your own patchwork neighborhood for a sofa or settle.

Pieced and stitched to evoke the stately facades of a bygone era, pillows like these are easy to build from snippets of lace and fabric. The trick lies in the choice of textured fabrics and appliquéd details. Here, pretucked cotton fabrics call clapboards to mind,

and lace appliqués suggest the ornate carving of a stately door and a flower-filled window box.

If Victoriana isn't your style, design a dream house in the architectural idiom of your choice.

Urbanites might prefer a sofa full of pillows patterned after a favorite block of apartments or town houses. Or, you may wish to bring a touch of country to the city with a pieced and appliquéd cottage or two. Instructions for the projects in this section begin on page 224.

When you think of yourself as a patchwork architect, you needn't confine your dreams to single dwellings. For example, here is a deftly designed collection of country homes and gardens to piece and quilt, opposite, and an appliquéd cityscape, right, that pays tongue-in-cheek tribute to the urban scene.

The ten different house designs ranged across the colorful quilt, *opposite,* are a snap to piece from just two basic building blocks: squares and triangles. Each pieced block uses a clever arrangement of these two shapes in assorted colors to suggest houses in different styles and sizes.

Doors, windows, and chimneys are snipped from scraps of black bias binding. Appliquéd suns and moons and a touch or two of embroidery for the birds and television antennas complete each picture. You'll find each block as interesting to design as it is to construct.

The highly stylized garden blocks are even easier to piece. Each is a calico version of the four-patch Spirit of St. Louis pattern introduced on page 34. Each square of the block is pieced from a light-, medium-, and dark-colored rectangle in complementary shades. The four squares are then stitched together in a pinwheel arrangement to suggest the carefully planted rows of a tidy family garden.

Rome wasn't built in a day, but the patchwork cityscape, *right,* can be pieced together in next to no time. To build your own skyline wall hanging, adapt the design shown here, or select another city view from a postcard, photograph, or slide.

To make a pattern, just enlarge the scene, using graph paper or a projector. (For tips on enlarging patterns, turn to page 312.)

Cut buildings, sky, and other features of landscape from assorted print, plaid, and checkered fabrics and attach the shapes to a muslin background using fusible webbing. Glue decorative trim over all the raw edges, and border the picture with narrow bands of contrasting fabric.

If rolling hills or wide-open spaces are more to your taste, try this simple cut-and-paste technique with a rural landscape. But for best results, reduce the elements of the design to gentle curves and simple geometric shapes before you begin to stitch.

American folk arts—
particularly the stylized
motifs favored by the
Pennsylvania Dutch—
provide a rich source of
appliqué designs for these
two unusual projects.

In the traditional design vocabulary of the Pennsylvania Dutch, hearts bespeak brotherly love, tulips are symbols of faith, and pert little birds—called distelfinks—are harbingers of luck wherever they appear. Few motifs are more delightfully appropriate to patchwork projects for your home.

Stylized hearts and flowers and other mirror-image motifs are snipped from felt and machine-appliquéd to a felt background for the handsome hearth rug and oversize pillows pictured *opposite.*

For the hutch, *right,* similar shapes are cut from closely woven calicoes and glued directly onto the painted surface of the cabinet. The design is protected with several coats of polyurethane for a wipe-clean finish. You might wish to try this combination of fabric appliqué and decoupage techniques on a serving tray or other small item before tackling an entire piece of furniture.

For a touch of whimsy in the dining room, stitch up one of these made-to-measure wall hangings in colors and patterns to complement your favorite table settings.

If your china cupboard is a trifle bare, or absent altogether, the amusing bit of appliquéd trompe l'oeil, *above,* might be just the piece you need.

Patterns are provided in the instructions for each of the shapes pictured in the cupboard. Use these, and others of your own design, to fashion a set of fabric dishes in colors and patterns that coordinate with your existing china—or duplicate the dinner service of your dreams. Just cut out the dishes you want from floral prints and arrange them on fabric shelves sized to fit over an existing side table or buffet.

The nineteenth-century quilt pictured *opposite* makes a dramatic backdrop for any dining setting—from the most formal dining room to a cozy breakfast nook.

Striped, plaid, and floral fabrics cut on the bias and pieced into seemingly random geometric arrangements contribute to the vibrancy of this highly original design. The effect is startlingly contemporary, despite the fact that the quilt was pieced more than 100 years ago.

The pattern seems complex at first, yet the center is pieced entirely of right triangles that have been joined on the diagonal and sewn into squares. It can be pieced easily in a size and color combination to suit your own decor.

When planning either of the designs shown here, keep this tip in mind: If you routinely use more than one set of dishes—one for everyday and a second set for company, for example—be sure to mix and match fabrics for the wall hanging in colors that will complement both patterns.

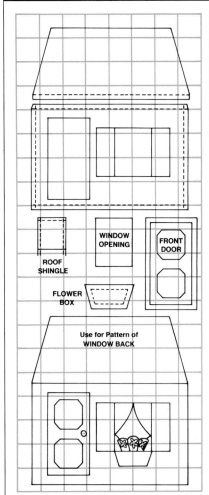

ROOF SHINGLE

WINDOW OPENING

FRONT DOOR

FLOWER BOX

Use for Pattern of WINDOW BACK

1 Square = 2½ Inches

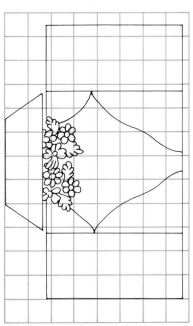

1 Square = 1 Inch

WINDOW BOX PILLOW
PAGE 216
Finished size is 14x14 inches

Materials
½ yard of pin-tuck fabric for house front
½ yard of muslin for backing
Square of windowpane-tuck fabric for window
Wide braid or trim for shutters
Scraps of lace for curtains
Bits of eyelet or white trim for flowers in window box
2½ yards of pregathered lace for ruffle
14-inch-square pillow form or fiberfill
Dressmaker's carbon or transfer pencil

Instructions
Note: Add ½-inch seam allowances to all appliqué pieces and use ½-inch seams throughout unless otherwise noted.

Cut a 15-inch square of pin-tuck fabric for pillow front (includes seam allowances).

Enlarge the window and shutter pattern, *above left;* transfer outlines of the window to the right side of the pin-tuck square with dressmaker's carbon or transfer pencil. Position the pattern so pin tucking runs horizontally, parallel to the bottom of the window. Stay-stitch along square outlines of the window frame.

Cut out the inside of the window, leaving ½-inch seam allowances all around. Slash corners and turn raw edges to the back; baste and press. Next, cut a 7-inch square of windowpane-tuck fabric for inside of window; cut scraps of lace for curtains. Baste window and curtains in place.

Cut pieces of trim for shutters and cut muslin shape for window box; turn under raw edges and baste in place. Snip flowers from eyelet and lace appliqués and position in window box. Hand- or machine-stitch pieces in place.

Baste and then machine-stitch preruffled lace in place ⅜ inch in from raw edges of pillow top. Cut

a 15-inch square of pin-tuck fabric for backing and, with right sides together, pin back to appliquéd front.

Stitch the pillow cover together around three sides (using ½-inch seams), being careful to catch edge of lace ruffle in seam. Turn cover right side out; press. Insert pillow form or stuff with fiberfill and slip-stitch fourth side closed.

HOUSE PILLOW
PAGE 216
Finished size is 17x17½ inches

Materials
½ yard of pin-tuck fabric for siding
½ yard of muslin for backing
Assorted scraps of eyelet and dotted swiss for shingles
Square of windowpane-tuck fabric for window
Wide braid or trim for shutters
Scraps of lace for curtains
Lace medallions (door appliqués)
Lace flowers for window box
Button for door handle
Fiberfill

Instructions
Note: Use ½-inch seam allowances unless otherwise noted.

Enlarge house pattern pieces, *below left,* and trace onto paper. Cut a rectangular piece for the house front from pin-tuck fabric (tucks should run horizontally), and cut roof section from plain muslin. Stitch house facade and roof section together.

Next, cut a total of 22 shingles from assorted scraps of eyelet and dotted swiss. Line each shingle with muslin, turn right side out, and press. Stitch shingles to roof in overlapping pattern (refer to photograph).

Fashion the window, curtains, shutters, flower box, and flowers as described for the Window Box Pillow, above.

Cut door from muslin. Machine-satin-stitch octagonal outlines for door panels, and then appliqué lace medallions to the center of each panel. Stitch the door in place on the house front, then add a small button for the doorknob.

For pillow back, cut a piece of muslin to match the shape of the pieced and appliquéd house front. With right sides facing, stitch the back to the front around three sides. Turn right side out, press, stuff, and stitch opening closed.

HOMES AND GARDENS QUILT
PAGE 218
Finished size is 78¾x94¼ inches

Materials
Scraps of calico in assorted colors
1¼ yards of dark green fabric for sashing
2⅔ yards of red calico for outside border and corners of sashing
6⅔ yards of pale yellow fabric for inner border and backing
Scraps of muslin and solid-color fabrics for sky, suns, and moons
1 package of black bias tape
Black embroidery floss
Quilt batting
10 yards of white bias tape for binding
Graph paper

Instructions
The quilt is composed of twenty 14-inch-square blocks. Half of the blocks are composed of a 16-patch arrangement of squares and triangles representing houses. The other 10 blocks, representing gardens, are pieced variations of the Spirit of St. Louis pattern.

To cut fabrics for sashing and borders, first cut 49 dark green sashing strips, each 2x14½ inches. Also cut thirty 2-inch squares from red calico for joinings between sashings.

Next, cut two 4½x96-inch and two 4½x80-inch outer borders from red calico. Then cut two 4x88½-inch and two 4x72½-inch inner borders from yellow fabric. Set the sashing and border strips aside.

For house blocks: On graph paper, sketch a series of 10 blocks, each divided into four rows of four squares each. Referring to the photograph on page 218, plan 10 different blocks of houses, using triangles to shape sloped roofs, and arranging smaller wings or buildings in the foreground. Use only squares and right-angle triangles to construct the simple house shapes. For best results, plan to use no more than three or four different fabrics for each collection of buildings.

Draw in windows, doors, suns, and moons, following placement suggested in the photograph. These details are appliquéd after blocks are pieced.

To make the templates for the squares and triangles used to piece each house block, first cut a 3½-inch square of cardboard for the square template. Then trace a second 3½-inch square and cut the square in half diagonally to form the template for the triangles.

Select fabrics for each house block. Trace squares and triangles onto the wrong side of fabrics and cut out pattern pieces for each block (adding ¼-inch seam allowances to each piece).

For each block, first piece triangles together into squares, wherever required. Next, beginning with the top row of squares for the block, stitch four squares together horizontally. Press seams to one side. Repeat for the remaining three rows. Stitch rows together to complete the block; press seams in one direction.

From black bias tape, cut 1½-inch-long rectangles for windows and chimneys, and 2-inch-long rectangles for doors. Pin, baste, and hand- or machine-appliqué these details in place.

Next, cut 2¾-inch circles of solid-color fabric for suns and moons. Turn under raw edges ¼ inch and baste. Appliqué circle shapes on house blocks, wherever appropriate (study photograph for suggested placement).

Use three strands of black embroidery floss and backstitches or stem stitches to embroider birds and television antennas on some of the house blocks.

For garden blocks: Use three coordinating print fabrics in graduated shades of the same color to piece each block.

For a single garden block, cut out four 2¾x7¼-inch rectangles from each of the three fabrics. Stitch three rectangles together along long edges to form a square; make four squares. Piece each of the squares in the same sequence, keeping the top, center, and bottom colors consistent.

Referring to the photograph on page 218, stitch four pieced squares together into the Spirit of St. Louis pattern to form each 14½-inch garden block. (For a drawing of the Spirit of St. Louis pattern, see page 39.)

To assemble the quilt top: Lay out the 20 blocks in five rows of four blocks each, alternating the home and garden blocks, and striving for a pleasing balance of color and type of house design.

Working with the top row of four blocks, stitch one dark green sashing strip between each block, and one to each end of the row. Repeat with the remaining four rows of blocks. Set aside.

To piece the horizontal sashing strips, stitch five red squares and four green sashing strips together. Repeat, to make a total of six horizontal sashing strips. Sew a horizontal sashing strip between each row of blocks and to the top and bottom of the pieced top.

To complete, trim 4-inch-wide yellow border strips to size; sew to top and bottom and then to sides of pieced top. Repeat with 4½-inch-wide red calico outer border strips. Use ¼-inch seams.

Cut and piece yellow backing fabric to size. Layer backing, batting, and pieced top together; pin and baste. Quilt ¼ inch from all seams. Quilt border areas as desired. Bind edges of completed quilt with white bias tape or with bias-cut strips of fabric.

(Continued)

CITYSCAPE WALL HANGING
PAGE 219

Materials

Square of muslin for backing
Scraps of prints, stripes, small plaids, and solids for appliqués
10 to 20 yards of upholstery gimp or decorative braid
Striped fabric for binding
Fusible webbing
Water-erasable pen, fabric glue

Instructions

Select a cityscape or other scenic view from a slide, postcard, book, or magazine illustration, and enlarge it to the size of your choice, using graph paper or a projector. (For hints on how to enlarge a design, see page 312.)

Trace the outlines of the design onto a large sheet of paper to use as a master pattern. Cut the muslin to the desired size (including an allowance for the frame). Trace the master pattern onto the muslin, using a water-erasable pen. Lay a piece (or pieces) of fusible webbing across the entire pattern and tack it in place.

Trace and cut out a paper pattern for each appliqué shape on the hanging. Cut shapes from fabric. Do *not* add seam allowances.

Working from the top of the design (background) toward the bottom (foreground), lay out all pieces on the webbing-covered muslin. (They should fit like pieces of a puzzle.) Using a warm iron, press the appliqués in place.

Next, cover the completed appliqué picture with a press cloth and press the entire hanging thoroughly on the right side to secure the pieces to the muslin. If you have used any pins, remove them and press the hanging again on both the front and back.

Again working from the top of the hanging, glue strips of upholstery gimp or decorative trim over all the raw edges of the appliqués.

To finish the hanging, glue 4-inch-wide strips of striped fabric to the outer 2 inches around the edges of the picture. Fold the raw edges of striped frame fabric to the back and glue in place. Attach fabric loops or a muslin sleeve to back of the picture for hanging.

APPLIQUÉD FOLK ART RUG AND PILLOWS
PAGE 220
Finished size of the rug is 32x47 inches; the smallest pillow is 16x16 inches

Materials

72-inch-wide felt in the following amounts and colors: 1⅔ yards of red, ½ yard of green, ¾ yard of yellow, ¼ yard of blue
Threads to match fabrics
Dressmaker's carbon
Paper for patterns
Fabric glue

Instructions

Enlarge the patterns for all six squares, *opposite,* to size. Center and trace each pattern onto a 13-inch square of brown paper. Flop each pattern to complete the design.

Cut six 13-inch squares of yellow felt. Center and transfer one pattern onto each of the six yellow squares, using dressmaker's carbon.

Referring to the photograph for color placement, cut individual pattern motifs from felt. Tack each motif in place with dabs of fabric glue, then topstitch the motifs to the yellow squares, using matching threads. Stitch as close as possible to the edges of each appliqué piece.

Cut a 32x47-inch rectangle of red felt. Spread the rectangle out on floor or table and position the appliquéd blocks on top, three blocks wide by two blocks deep.

Pin all squares in place, leaving 2 inches between squares and a 2-inch-wide border on all sides. Topstitch squares in place.

Enlarge the flower and leaf patterns for the center divider strips. Complete the patterns by adding stem and leaf motifs wherever indicated by dashed lines. Pin and topstitch the flower centers and leaves in place, using matching threads.

Cut a second piece of red felt 36½x51½ inches. Center and sew the appliquéd piece to this larger rectangle. Fold the border edges in half and pin them toward the center of the rug so that the finished border measures 2 inches wide. Trim, if necessary. Miter corners and topstitch along both the inner and outer edges of the border.

Enlarge the border patterns, *opposite,* extending the leaf and stem motifs until the desired length is reached. Finish the borders with a flower motif in each corner.

Cut the motifs from felt. Pin the floral and leaf borders in place and topstitch close to the edges, using matching threads.

For matching pillows: Enlarge the pattern for one square to the size of your choice. Cut all the pieces from felt and appliqué them to a square of yellow felt.

Cut 2-inch-wide borders from red felt and topstitch the border strips to the appliquéd square, mitering the corners. Appliqué a border of stems and leaves in the same manner as described for the rug border above, omitting the corner flower motifs.

Back the appliquéd pillow top with a matching square of felt, using ½-inch seams. Turn right side out, stuff with fiberfill, and slipstitch the opening closed.

1 Square = 1 Inch

FABRIC DECOUPAGE CABINET
PAGE 221

Materials
Closely woven calico print fabrics in red, yellow, and blue (or colors of your choice)
Spray starch
Spray glue
Clear acrylic finish or polyurethane, paintbrush
Purchased, painted cabinet

Instructions
Trace squares and rectangles on brown paper to duplicate the size and shape of each drawer and door on the cabinet you plan to appliqué. Design folk art motifs to fit these shapes, using heart, flower, and bird designs pictured on page 221 as inspiration.

Cut each appliqué shape from *stiffly starched* calico fabrics, being especially careful to avoid loose threads or ragged edges.

Use a *light* coat of spray glue to position each appliqué on the front of the cabinet. Protect the designs with several coats of clear acrylic or polyurethane applied with a brush.

APPLIQUÉD HUTCH
PAGE 222
Finished size is 28x44 inches

Materials
28x44 inches *each* of background fabric (brown), muslin, and quilt batting
1 yard of striped fabric for shelf, divider strips, and frame
Scraps of floral fabrics and other small prints for crockery

Instructions
Enlarge sample patterns, *opposite,* to size, or sketch crockery shapes of your own choice, based on photographs, illustrations, or available dishware. Make paper patterns

for each piece or portion of a piece of china (handles and lids, for example, are cut separately). Trace patterns onto assorted print and floral fabrics and cut out, adding ¼-inch seam allowances to all pieces. Cut multiples of some shapes (cups and saucers, small bowls), as pictured.

Turn under seam allowances on all pieces and baste. Then baste lids and handles to jars, pots, and cups. Press all pieces and set aside.

From striped fabric, cut a 2¾-inch-wide shelf and divider strips. Press under ¼-inch seam allowance on long sides of each strip and baste shelf and divider strips to background fabric, positioning strips to accommodate crockery shapes. Add similar strips to the sides, top, and bottom of the hutch. Turn raw edges of these border strips to the back of the hutch and whipstitch in place.

Position fabric crockery appliqués on background fabric and baste in place. Sandwich hutch, batting, and backing together; pin and baste through all layers. Machine-topstitch all appliqué pieces in place, stitching ⅛ inch from edges of shapes. Add fabric loops or a muslin sleeve for hanging.

GEOMETRIC-DESIGN WALL HANGING
PAGE 223
Finished size is 61x75 inches

Materials
4½ yards (total) of blue, brown, and beige fabrics in prints, solids, small plaids, and stripes
4 yards of contrasting fabric for backing
Quilt batting

Instructions
The quilted wall hanging is pieced from right-angle triangles that are cut on the bias and pieced together along the diagonal. The 2½-inch-wide border consists of narrow strips of fabric set perpendicular to each side of the quilt.

To create a template for the triangles, cut a 7-inch square from

cardboard and then cut the square in half along the diagonal.

Trace this right-angle triangle onto the wrong side of the fabric scraps, taking care to position the *diagonal of the template* along the *straight* grain of the fabric. This is especially important when cutting shapes from plaids and stripes, because the direction in which the lines on the fabric run contributes considerably to the dynamism of the design.

Note: Right-angle triangles that are to be pieced on the diagonal, as these are, usually are cut so that the sides are on the straight grain, rather than on the bias, as here. For more on working with triangles, see pages 126-131.

Cut 160 triangles, adding ¼-inch seam allowances to all pieces.

To begin piecing, stitch together two triangles along the diagonal, to form a square. Make 80 squares. Press the seams toward the darker of the triangular pieces.

Referring to the color photograph for inspiration, arrange the squares into 10 horizontal rows of eight squares each, altering the direction of the center seams at random. Stitch squares into rows and press seams to one side. Then stitch rows together to form the quilt top. Press all the seams in one direction.

To make borders, stitch narrow, 3-inch-long pieces of fabric together into long strips. (The width of these pieces can be uniform or varied, depending on your supply of fabrics.) Press all seams in one direction. Stitch borders to the top and bottom of the quilt top and then to the sides.

Cut and piece backing to size. Layer backing, batting, and pieced top together; pin and baste. Quilt as desired.

Turn under the edges of the top and backing ¼ inch and slip-stitch the top to the backing.

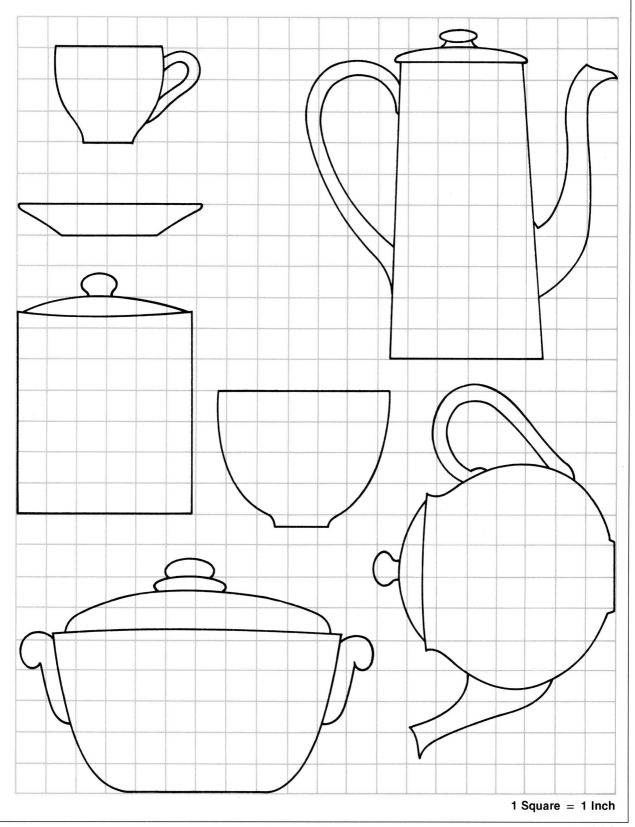

1 Square = 1 Inch

QUILTING AND FINISHING YOUR PATCHWORK PROJECTS

Even the most pedestrian patchwork takes on an elegant air when embellished with fine quilting or embroidery, as shown on the following pages.

OVERALL QUILTING PATTERNS

Quilting, a decorative pattern of tiny stitches, is the traditional way to secure patchwork top, batting, and backing fabric together.

The small, regular stitches of quilting designs actually serve a dual purpose. They strengthen the fabric sandwich (top, batting, and backing) and keep the three layers from shifting or stretching out of shape. They also add a subtle surface texture that can greatly enhance the design impact of the finished patchwork.

Stitched onto the coverlet and pillow pictured here is a sampling of several "filler" patterns used to quilt large areas, such as plain blocks and borders, or to cover the entire surface of a project.

❖

1 It is easiest to trace a quilting pattern onto a plain or patchwork surface *before* joining the fabric to batting and backing.

Linear designs—parallel diagonal lines or a simple diamond pattern—can be measured with a ruler. For intricate designs use a purchased template or one you create from cardboard or plastic.

Plot the design on paper to be sure it suits the size and shape of the surface you plan to stitch. Transfer design to fabric with *light* pencil strokes or an erasable dressmaker's pencil (pictured).

2 After pattern is marked on fabric, pin and baste top, batting, and backing together. Run basting stitches from center of design out to edges, as shown, to minimize bunching and wrinkling.

3 Baste 3-inch-wide strips of muslin to edges of a small project, such as this pillow top, so that the project can be held securely in quilting hoop or frame as you quilt. Quilt from the center of the pattern out toward the edges, catching all three layers with each stitch. (See pages 242-249 for quilting tips and instructions to make these projects.)

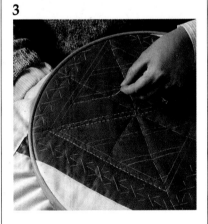

In addition to the comparatively limited number of overall quilting patterns described on the preceding pages, a wide range of individual motifs in various shapes and sizes can be used as quilting designs for plain blocks and other open spaces.

When plain blocks are combined with pieced or appliquéd blocks for traditional patchwork projects, quilting on the plain blocks often repeats the stitched designs on the patchwork blocks. But frequently a different, self-contained, design is used for the plain blocks.

Five of the most popular of these traditional block motifs—feathered wreath, tulips, fan, scallop shell, and a graceful heart shape—are quilted on the throw pillows pictured here. These and other traditional motifs can be mixed and matched with each other and with a variety of overall quilting patterns to create surface textures that will complement any pieced or appliquéd design.

Traditionally, quilting stitches are worked with white thread or in colors to match the fabric against which the stitches are laid. Using colored threads against a plain white background for the pillows shown here is one way of emphasizing the decorative charm of these designs, over and above their original and primary function of holding the three layers of backing, batting, and patchwork top together.

Small projects like these are an excellent way to practice your quilting skills before tackling a major piece of patchwork, such as an entire quilt. Using colored threads against a light background (or vice versa) enables you to keep track of the size, evenness, and regularity of your stitches.

Sized to fit a specific space, any one of these motifs makes an intriguing embellishment for other small projects as well. Choose one to grace a jacket, tote bag, or hem of a skirt, for example.

If traditional motifs are not your style, remember that almost any line drawing or design can be translated into a quilting pattern. Geometric, figurative, or wholly abstract doodlings are equally appropriate and offer exciting alternatives to the more traditional quilting motifs.

On this superbly stitched tulip quilt, three different styles of quilting—an overall pattern, individual motifs, and outline stitching—are combined to stunning effect.

The time and attention lavished on the finishing steps of a patchwork project often mark the difference between a merely pretty piece and a masterpiece.

For example, elegant white-on-white quilting in an overall diamond pattern and in feather and medallion motifs is skillfully combined with outline quilting to enrich the surface texture of the tulip quilt, *above* and *opposite*. Imaginative use of quilting patterns, plus exceptionally fine stitching, turn this charming but rather ordinary design into a quilt of heirloom quality.

Outline quilting, used here to enhance the appliquéd leaves and flowers (see the detail, *opposite*), is perhaps the most common solution to the problem of matching the quilt design to the patchwork pattern. In this approach, the quilting stitches follow the shape of each pattern piece, running about ⅛ to ¼ inch from the seam line and around the edges of each shape. Outline quilting is especially effective on appliquéd designs, but is an easy way to quilt patchwork designs as well.

The quilting designs you select for any given project will depend on the size and complexity of the pieced or appliquéd pattern, the weight of the fabrics, the kind of batting used, and—most importantly—your own preferences.

APPLIQUÉD PLACE MATS

A traditional and pleasingly decorative finish for appliqué shapes is the simple blanket stitch, worked in matching or contrasting embroidery floss.

On appliquéd coverlets and other projects that were not designed to be quilted, traditional needlecrafters often embellished the designs with a tidy edging of blanket or buttonhole stitches.

Taken with a single strand of matching thread, the blanket stitches served to further secure the appliqués to the background fabric, while remaining nearly invisible. Alternatively, when stitched with two or three strands of floss in a contrasting color, the blanket stitches became an integral part of the patchwork design, as in the colorful '30s-vintage appliquéd squares, *left.*

Blanket stitches, and their cousins, more closely spaced buttonhole stitches, are particularly effective in securing raw-edge appliqués, or fabric shapes on which the turned-under edges are not easily or successfully concealed with regular whipstitches or slip stitches (see the work-in-progress photograph, *above right*).

The raw edges of the flower and petals, appliquéd onto the square place mats, *left,* have not been turned under, but are neatly concealed by the ridge of stitches laid down to protect and highlight the outline of each shape.

Although first-class antique patchwork quilts are increasingly difficult to come by, quilt remnants and individual pieced or appliquéd blocks are still relatively easy and inexpensive to acquire at tag sales and thrift shops around the country.

As the place mat samples at left so charmingly illustrate, such in-progress or incomplete patchwork pieces have exciting potential for projects that aren't quilt size. Pieced or appliquéd squares can be parlayed into any number of decorative projects for your home or for gift giving, including place mats such as these, pillow tops, pot holders, and clothing insets (from jacket backs to pockets and tote bags).

To make your own set of place mats, back patchwork squares with a double layer of batting, then border each square with wide strips of contrasting fabric. Or, you might stitch together four patchwork squares and add backing and borders to make a small table mat, or assemble 16 or more squares for a tablecloth. If you don't have enough matching blocks to piece a large project, such as a tablecloth, alternate the patchwork squares with squares of solid-color or print fabric.

239

For a touch of Victorian opulence, beaded motifs and lavish rows of embroidery accent each scrap of fabric pieced into the Crazy Quilt pattern of this heart-shape pillow.

The mania for Crazy Quilt designs—a form of patchwork in which small bits of fabric in widely varying colors, textures, shapes, and sizes are pieced together in an entirely random design—reached its height during the last quarter of the nineteenth century.

In 1876 the Centennial Exhibition in Philadelphia introduced many Americans to Japanese art and culture for the very first time. Undoubtedly, the subsequent national fascination with things Oriental and the popularity of asymmetrical designs in the decorative arts of the period received added impetus from this and other cross-cultural events of the day.

This passion for exotica, plus the Victorians' penchant for "fancywork" projects that made practical and decorative use of scraps and remnants, combined to make Crazy Quilt patchwork the needle arts fad of the 1880s.

Crazy Quilt designs are actually a form of appliqué. Scraps of fabric in various colors and textures and in irregular shapes and sizes are appliquéd onto a muslin or other background fabric in an overlapping pattern. The entire background is eventually completely covered—just as it is in a Log Cabin pattern.

The elegant fabrics and extravagant embroidery on the pillow, *right,* are similar to those on Crazy Quilt designs of the Victorian era. But simpler versions of these designs—pieced from humbler cottons, linens, or woolens, and often embellished only with simple rows of featherstitching along the seams—also have been popular with needle artists, off and on, from that day to this.

Whether you prefer the plain or fancy version, the Crazy Quilt technique adapts wonderfully to all sorts of small projects, including clothing and accessories. For more on Crazy Quilt piecing and embroidery stitches, please turn to page 247.

FINISHING TIPS AND TECHNIQUES

Choosing the right materials for filling and backing a patchwork project and the best method of finishing the edges and joining the layers together is just as important as the initial selection of fabric for the patchwork itself. All affect the appearance of the finished design, its durability, and the way it is cleaned and cared for.

The tips that follow are for finishing a quilt, but you'll find them equally useful for any patchwork project.

BATTING

Although many cotton, wool, silk, down, and synthetic fillers are available to serious quilters, an 80% cotton/20% polyester blend and several varieties of 100% glazed and bonded polyester batting are what you will find in most quilt shops. These two types of batting are more than sufficient for most patchwork projects.

Both cotton-blend and all-polyester battings are sold in pre-packaged sheets in standard quilt sizes (crib—45x60 inches; twin—72x90 inches; full—81x96 inches; queen—90x108 inches; and king—120x120 inches).

Cotton-blend battings are generally thin, low-loft, soft, and drapable. Because they contain natural fibers, they breathe well and are absorbent and comfortable at most temperatures.

For best results, this batting should be quilted with lines of stitching no more than 4 inches apart to keep the batting from shifting with use. Quilting on a cotton-blend batting gives a flat, smooth "heirloom" look that most closely resembles the feel and appearance of antique quilts.

All-polyester battings, unlike blends, come in lofts (or heights) from ¼ inch to 3 inches high and in varying degrees of density. Low- to medium-loft weights are excellent for beginning quilters. The material is easy to handle, need not be quilted too closely to prevent shifting, and retains its shape and springiness even after repeated washings.

Before selecting a batting, determine how you want the finished quilted item to look. High-loft polyester battings are somewhat difficult for a novice to handle, but give a quilted vest or comforter a fat, cushiony look. Low-loft cotton-blend batting, on the other hand, is perfect for fine, intricate quilting, and lends the finished project a more supple, traditional look.

In addition to appearance, keep in mind the end use of the project. Quilts that are intended only for decorative use—to be hung on the wall, for example—can be filled with any variety of batting that suits your design purposes. But projects that are destined to receive considerable wear and tear (quilts for kids' rooms, or a quilted tote bag, for example) require easy-care battings. As a general rule, the batting should have the same care requirements as the outer fabrics.

Selecting a batting is a matter of personal preference. However, experience does lead to more informed—and often more successful—choices. Take time, if possible, to experiment with quilting on different types and weights of batting to get a feeling for how each handles.

BACKING

For the back of a patchwork project, select a lightweight to medium-weight fabric of the same or similar fiber content as the quilt top. If you are planning to hand-quilt a project, choose a backing fabric that a quilting needle can slip through easily. A percale sheet, for example, is so closely woven that it is a poor choice for backing a hand-stitched quilt.

Keep in mind that intricate quilting patterns will show to best advantage against a backing of solid-color or muted print fabric. However, if the quilt is tufted, or quilted in relatively simple geometric patterns, you may want to be more adventuresome in your selection of a backing fabric.

For large quilts, it is necessary to seam together several fabric lengths. Piece the backing in any fashion that makes good use of the available fabric. Sew seams carefully; press open and flat.

The size of the backing is governed by the method you've selected for finishing the edges of your quilt. If you are using separate binding strips (see below), cut batting and backing the same size as the patchwork top.

If the backing will be folded over the top of the quilt to serve as a binding, cut it 1 to 2 inches larger than the top on all sides. And, if the top is to be used as self-binding, cut the backing and batting correspondingly smaller.

Finally, if you plan to omit binding altogether, cut the edges of the quilt top and back to match, then turn under the seam allowance and slip-stitch the top and back together.

Whatever method you use, be sure to purchase an appropriate amount of fabric for the backing, plus a little more. *Do not* cut backing or batting to size until quilting is completed, because quilting tends to shrink the fabric surface.

BINDINGS

Bindings finish and protect the raw edges of a quilt or other patchwork project. (The edges are usually where a quilt wears fastest.) However, the color and width of the bindings become an integral part of the final quilt design, and the decision about how to bind a quilt should be made with aesthetic, as well as practical, considerations in mind.

As mentioned above, a quilt is either self-bound, using a fold of the top or backing fabric, or it is bound with separate strips, either wide or narrow, and of matching or contrasting fabric.

Binding with a separate strip offers better protection than self-binding, and when worn it is replaced easily without affecting the body of the quilt.

Cut binding strips on the bias and at least 1½ inches wide (wider for a more substantial edging). Cut strips to the desired length and piece on the diagonal, with all seams pressed open.

After the design is quilted and the edges are trimmed to size, press under the raw edges of the bias strips ⅜ inch on each side and hand- or machine-stitch one fold along all four sides on the top side of the quilt, right sides together. Ease or miter binding at the corners. Fold binding to the back of the quilt and slip-stitch remaining edge in place. (Use purchased bias binding if desired.)

TUFTING

Patchwork projects don't have to be quilted. But, if a large patchwork quilt, layered with batting and backing, is *not* quilted, the batting tends to droop and shift, and the backing sags and wrinkles alarmingly. So if you lack the time or inclination to quilt an entire piece, consider tufting (or tying) the piece instead.

Less elegant than rows of fine quilting, tufting is, nevertheless, a time-honored (and fast and effective) method of holding quilt layers together. It also is suitable for high-loft comforters, log cabin patterns, and wool or velvet quilts in which thick batting, layered fabrics, or heavy materials make quilting difficult or impractical.

To tuft a quilt, thread a needle with one or two strands of pearl cotton or cotton crochet thread. Avoid using synthetic thread; it does not hold a knot well. Use wool yarn for tufting a quilt that will be dry cleaned.

To begin, take a single running stitch, about ¼ inch long, through all three quilt layers. Backstitch in exactly the same spot, reinserting the needle and bringing it back out through the same holes. Tie the thread ends in a tight square knot; cut ends to desired length. (The ends may be left on the top or the back of the quilt.)

It is generally best to tuft in a symmetrical pattern, about every 4 to 6 inches across the surface, or at conveniently spaced pattern points or seam junctures across the quilt top.

MACHINE QUILTING

Quilting by machine is increasingly the choice of many contemporary quilters because it is faster than hand quilting and creates a different surface texture.

If you opt for machine quilting, work with a batting that is not too thick. It is essential to baste all the layers together securely, without any bunching or buckling.

Select a cotton/polyester or an all-cotton thread in a matching or contrasting color for stitching. Use a needle that is slightly larger than the one normally called for, so the thread enters the fabric smoothly, without pulling or puckering.

To discover the proper tension and stitch length settings for the materials used, experiment, quilting on a small, basted-together, sandwich of top fabric, batting, and backing.

When you end lines of stitching, avoid the temptation to backstitch. Snip and tie off threads as neatly as possible.

Do not try to duplicate hand quilting with the machine. Instead, choose quilting patterns that complement the design of the patchwork top and make the most of the smooth regularity of machine quilting. A diamond grid or other overall pattern, simple outline or echo quilting, free-form quilting designs, and "stitching in ditch" (along the seam lines) are appropriate choices for machine quilting.

Adapt your method of machine quilting to the design. For example, long straight or gently curving lines are best stitched with the presser foot on, but intricate and free-form designs are best worked with the presser foot removed.

With experimentation, you'll discover that the sewing machine actually expands your repertoire of quilting designs and techniques in exciting new directions.

TIPS ON QUILTING

All it takes to perfect your quilting skill is careful attention to the tips below—and practice, practice, practice! Keep in mind that there are as many ways of quilting as there are practitioners of the art, and that there is no indisputably *right* way to quilt. Whatever feels comfortable and produces the desired results is the best way for you to quilt.

Needles: Most quilters find that a Size 7 or 8 *between*—a short, slender needle—is ideal for quilting. Although initially it may seem a bit awkward to those accustomed to working with longer needles for other forms of needlework, the size and shape of this needle make it easier to control the up-and-down motion of quilting, and hence the size and evenness of your stitches.

Always wear a thimble to protect your finger and to help in pushing the needle through all three layers of fabric.

Thread: Waxed or specially processed quilting threads are stronger, smoother, and less likely to tangle than conventional sewing threads. However, cotton or polyester thread may be used to quilt small projects that will not be subjected to repeated washings or excessive wear and tear.

Quilt with either matching or contrasting color thread, but be aware that irregularities in stitching are more apparent when quilting is done in a contrasting thread.

Keep your quilting thread relatively short—between 12 and 18 inches is a workable length—to reduce snarls, tangles, and breakage as you stitch.

Quilting frame: Since today's homes rarely have sufficient floor space to accommodate a full-size, freestanding quilting frame, most quilters happily make do with a large round or oval quilting hoop. A smaller embroidery hoop is per-

fect for stretching small projects. It can be held in a stand or propped against a table or other support, freeing both hands for quilting.

Although not absolutely essential, a hoop reduces the risk of stitching in wrinkles or stretching fabric out of shape, and encourages uniformity in size, spacing, and tension of your stitches.

The quilting stitch: Although the size of quilting stitches is important (they should be as small as possible), uniformity of size and regularity of spacing and tension are actually more important to the overall appearance of the design.

Most professionals quilt with a two-hand up-and-down motion, passing the needle vertically down through the layers of the quilt with one hand, and directing the needle back up from underneath with the other. This method enables the quilter to make stitches of the same size on both the top and back of the quilt. Although this method may feel a bit awkward until you become accustomed to it, it should develop into a natural (and comfortable) rhythm with practice.

Some quilters prefer a regular, one-hand running stitch, gathering two or three stitches at a time on the needle before pulling the thread through. Whichever method you choose, remember that every stitch *must* go through all three quilt layers.

Beginning and ending stitches: The start and finish of each line of quilting should be as inconspicuous as possible. Bury small knots at the beginning and end of each line of quilting so that they are caught *between* the layers of fabric and do not show on either the quilt front or back. Avoid backstitches if possible, but if there is a seam near the start or finish of your quilting line, anchor the thread there for extra security.

Whatever methods of quilting you adopt, remember that neatness and uniformity of stitching are always your prime objectives.

QUILTED SAMPLER COVERLET
PAGE 232
Finished size is 39x43 inches

Materials
2½ yards of rose chintz
1 yard of ecru chintz for bias binding
1½ yards *each* of lightweight batting and lightweight muslin
Ecru embroidery floss

Instructions
Three strands of floss are used on this coverlet, so each stitch is visible as part of a decorative pattern. The same designs, stitched with regular quilting thread in a color matched to the quilt top, create a more subtly textured surface.

Each of the five center panels and four border panels is quilted separately. Panels and borders are then assembled with strips of ecru piping. The coverlet is backed with rose chintz, and edges are bound with ecru bias binding.

To begin: Cut a 40x44-inch rectangle of rose fabric for backing; set aside. Cut five 6x30-inch strips of rose chintz (center panels), two 8x26-inch strips (top borders), and two 8x44-inch strips (side borders). Mark panels and borders with ½-inch seams.

Use graph paper, ruler, and compass to enlarge a selection of patterns on page 249 to desired size for panels and border strips.

To establish scale: The diamond pattern on the center panel consists of ⅝-inch squares; diagonal lines on the chevron panel are slanted at 45-degree angles and are ½ inch apart; each clamshell measures 1⅛ inches tall from point to curved peak, and 1¼ inches wide. Quilted lines on the chain border at the top of the quilt are 1 inch apart, and the curved designs on the side borders measure ¾ inch between rows of stitches. Adjust the size of other patterns accordingly.

Note: You may substitute a selection of purchased template patterns or other quilting designs for the patterns used here. Templates are available at most quilting supply shops.

To trace designs onto fabric, use a tracing wheel and dressmaker's carbon and a No. 3 lead pencil, water-erasable pen, or tailor's chalk.

Cut matching strips of batting and muslin and baste to each panel and border strip. Prepare pieces for quilting (see page 233).

Use quilting hoop and three strands of ecru embroidery floss to quilt designs. Remember that evenness and regular spacing of stitches is more important than actual size of stitches.

To assemble coverlet: When quilting is completed, set panels aside. Cut and piece about 13 yards of ecru chintz bias strips. Cover eight yards of cording with bias strips; use the remaining bias strips to bind edges of coverlet.

Baste a length of ecru piping along one long edge of each of four center panels, then stitch all five panels together, using ½-inch seams. Press seams open.

Sew piping to one long edge of top and bottom border strips; join borders to center panels. Press seams. Repeat for side borders.

Trim raw edges of quilt top to 39x43 inches. Bind edges with ecru bias strips. Turn under raw edges of rose backing piece; sew to back of coverlet.

RUFFLED PILLOW
PAGE 233
Finished size is 16x16 inches

Materials
1 yard of rose chintz
13-inch square *each* of batting and muslin, 1⅓ yards of ecru piping
Ecru embroidery floss
Fiberfill or 12-inch pillow form

Instructions
Trace a quilting design of your choice on a 13-inch square of rose chintz (measurements include ½-inch seam allowance). Baste matching squares of batting and muslin backing to wrong side of pillow top and prepare for quilting as shown on page 233. Insert top in hoop and quilt designs.

Baste ecru piping around seam lines. Piece a 5x96-inch strip of rose fabric for ruffle. Fold strip in half, wrong sides together; gather and sew ruffle to pillow top.

Cut a 13-inch square of rose chintz for pillow back. Sew back to front, turn, and stuff. Sew fourth side closed.

QUILTED PILLOWS
PAGES 234-235

Materials
Off-white cotton for pillow tops and backs
Lightweight muslin for backing quilt designs
Polyester fleece or lightweight batting
Embroidery floss or crochet cotton in assorted colors
Piping to match floss
Fiberfill

Instructions
Enlarge quilting motifs of your choice to desired size and transfer to pieces of white fabric (see patterns, page 249).

Cut batting and backing to size and baste all three layers together. Prepare tops for quilting, as described on page 233. Stitch designs in colors of your choice, using three to five strands of floss or a single strand of crochet cotton, depending on desired effect.

Baste matching piping along seam lines of each pillow shape. Cut backing fabric to size. Stitch backs to fronts; turn and stuff. Slip-stitch openings closed.

TULIP QUILT
PAGES 236-237
Finished size is 88x88 inches

Materials
¼ yard *each* of light and dark pinks, light and dark purples, light and dark golds, light and dark blues, and light and dark red fabrics for flowers
1½ yards of gray-green fabric for leaves and stems
10 yards of white fabric for background and backing
Batting

Instructions
Quilt consists of nine 22-inch blocks arranged in three rows of three blocks each. Five appliquéd blocks alternate with four plain blocks. Each appliquéd block features a pattern of 16 tulips and eight leaves arranged in a circular design. Leaves and tulips are appliquéd at regular intervals around an 11-inch-wide border.

To begin: Cut two 12x67-inch top borders and two 12x89-inch side borders from white fabric; set aside. Cut nine 22½-inch squares of white; set squares aside.

Enlarge the tulip, leaf, and curved stem patterns on page 246 to size and make templates for each shape. Trace and cut the following pattern pieces, adding ¼-inch seam allowances to each piece: 16 *each* light gold, dark gold, and light red tulips; 12 tulips from *each* of the remaining flower colors; and 64 leaves and 40 curved stems from gray-green fabric. Also cut forty-four 1x3¾-inch straight stems from green fabric (measurements include ¼-inch seam allowances).

Sort pattern pieces by color and shape. Clip curves and angles as necessary and baste under raw edges on all appliqués (except on portions of leaves and stems that will be overlapped by other shapes, as indicated by dotted lines on patterns).

(Continued)

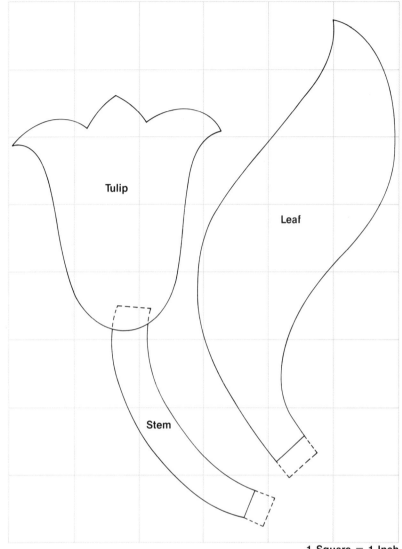

Tulip

Leaf

Stem

1 Square = 1 Inch

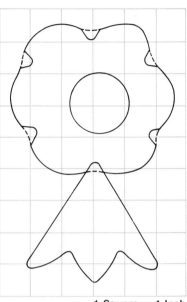

1 Square = 1 Inch

feather motifs. The entire surface is quilted with a diamond filler pattern. See photograph.)

❖

APPLIQUÉD PLACE MATS
PAGES 238-239
Finished size is 14x14 inches

Materials
1 yard of muslin
1½ yards of print fabric for backing and borders
Scraps of solid, print, plaid, and striped fabrics for flowers
Scraps of cotton embroidery floss in assorted colors
Fusible webbing and polyester fleece (optional)

Instructions
Enlarge pattern, *above,* to size and make templates for flower, center circle, and petal shapes. For a set of four place mats, cut a total of 4 blossoms, 4 circles, and 24 petals from assorted fabrics.

Cut four 14-inch squares of muslin; arrange one flower, one center circle, and six assorted petals in the middle of each square. Pin and baste shapes in place.

On the vintage place mats in the picture, raw edges of appliqué shapes are simply covered with rows of blanket (buttonhole) stitches. To help keep raw edges from raveling, secure appliqué shapes to background fabric with

(Continued)

To appliqué one block: Mark center point of block and arrange four straight stems so that they form eight equal spokes in the center of the block. Refer to close-up of design on page 237. Alternating light and dark red tulips, arrange a center wreath of eight flowers and an outer ring of eight stemmed tulips and eight leaves, as shown.

Pin, baste, and appliqué all pieces in place. Repeat for each of the four remaining blocks (make one *each* with pink, blue, gold, and purple tulips). Press carefully.

To assemble the quilt: Arrange the nine white squares in three rows of three blocks each, alter-

nating pieced and unpieced blocks. Stitch blocks together (¼-inch seams). Stitch top, bottom, and side borders to appliquéd top.

For borders, pin and baste leaves alternating with straight stemmed tulips along all four borders. Position leaves and tulips at right angles to edges of quilt, spaced about 5 inches apart. Alternate colors of tulips at random.

For each corner of borders, arrange a dark red tulip on a 5½-inch straight stem at a 45-degree angle, with two light red tulips on curved stems on each side. Appliqué all border designs in place.

Piece backing to size. Baste backing, batting, and appliquéd top together; quilt. (On this quilt, appliqués are outline quilted; plain blocks are embellished with cut-to-size pieces of fusible webbing before embroidering.

For an even neater finish, add seam allowances to fabric pieces, baste under raw edges, and appliqué shapes in place with invisible slip stitches before embellishing with buttonhole stitches.

To finish mats: Baste one appliquéd square in the center of the wrong side of an 18-inch square of print fabric. Fold raw edges of backing fabric to front of muslin square to form borders. Turn under raw edges, miter corners, and slip-stitch or topstitch borders in place. To provide extra protection for your table, line each appliquéd square with a layer of polyester fleece or batting before backing.

CRAZY QUILT HEART PILLOW
PAGE 241
Finished size is 15x15 inches

Materials
13-inch square of muslin
½ yard of burgundy fabric for backing and ruffle
Scraps of velvet, silk, satins, ribbon, and trim for patches
Scraps of cotton and metallic embroidery threads in assorted colors
Small glass and metallic beads
1⅛ yards of satin piping
2 yards of 2-inch-wide crocheted edging for ruffle
Polyester fiberfill

Instructions
To make heart pattern, fold a 13-inch square of paper in half lengthwise. Sketch a half heart on the paper; cut out heart pattern.

Trace pattern onto muslin square and cut out heart shape, marking ½-inch seam allowances on all sides.

Beginning in upper right-hand corner of heart shape, pin small, irregularly shaped pieces of fabric to muslin background, turning under raw edges and overlapping

shapes until entire heart shape is covered. Blindstitch fabric appliqués to background and to each other, trimming away excess fabric where pieces overlap. Press completed heart.

Embellish all seams between fabric shapes with a variety of embroidery stitches worked in assorted colors. Study the stitch diagrams on page 248 and the color photograph on page 241 for ways to combine various stitches in border patterns along seams. Add touches of beading and embroider simple motifs in the center of selected patches, if desired.

To complete pillow, baste piping along seam line of appliquéd heart shape. Next, cut and piece a 4½x72½-inch strip of burgundy fabric for ruffle.

Fold strip in half and baste crocheted edging to front of strip, matching raw edges.

Gather basting stitches and pin ruffle to pieced pillow top, aligning raw edges.

Using heart-shape pattern, cut a piece of burgundy fabric for pillow back. Pin back and pieced top together, right sides facing (be sure to keep ruffle tucked to inside). Sew around heart, leaving a 5-inch opening along one side for turning. Turn pillow to the right side, stuff, and sew opening.

CHECKERED PATTERN QUILT
PAGES 230-231
Finished size is 72x90 inches

Materials
2½ yards of assorted print fabrics for pieced blocks and bindings
7½ yards of white fabric for top and backing
½ yard of red plaid fabric for border triangles on blocks
Batting

Instructions
Quilt consists of 20 pieced and 14 plain blocks set together on the diagonal; pattern is completed with white triangles along borders and at corners.

Each pieced block measures 12¾ inches square and is composed of 25 print and 36 white 1½-inch squares set together on the diagonal; block is pieced out with triangles of red plaid fabric.

To make one block: Trace and cut 25 print and 36 white 2-inch squares (dimensions include ¼-inch seam allowances). Next, to make templates for border and corner triangles, draw a 1½-inch square, cut it in half diagonally, and cut one of the resulting triangles in half again. Use larger triangular template to cut 20 triangles for border of each block, and use smaller triangle to cut four corners for each block (add ¼-inch seams to each of these triangles).

Assemble squares and triangles as shown on pattern block (see photograph). Make 20 blocks.

To assemble quilt: First cut two 12¾-inch squares as templates for solid blocks. Cut one square in half diagonally and cut resulting triangle in half again, to make templates for border and corner triangles. Now cut 16 white squares, 14 white border triangles, and 4 white corner triangles, adding ¼-inch seams.

Assemble squares and triangles to complete quilt top. Stitch pieces together (¼-inch seam allowances). Layer and baste backing, batting, and pieced top together and quilt as desired. (On the quilt pictured, pieced blocks are quilted with closely spaced parallel lines, and solid white blocks are quilted with a feathered wreath combined with an overall diamond pattern.)

Trim quilt edges; bind with bias strips of contrasting fabric.

OCEAN WAVES PATTERN QUILT
PAGE 231

Refer to pattern and instructions for similar quilt on page 52.

(Continued)

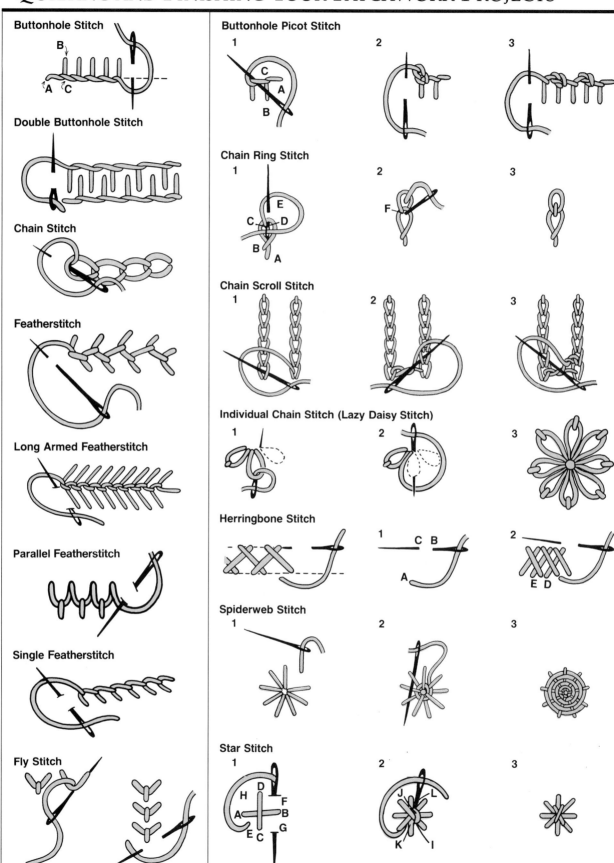

Buttonhole Stitch

Double Buttonhole Stitch

Chain Stitch

Featherstitch

Long Armed Featherstitch

Parallel Featherstitch

Single Featherstitch

Fly Stitch

Buttonhole Picot Stitch

Chain Ring Stitch

Chain Scroll Stitch

Individual Chain Stitch (Lazy Daisy Stitch)

Herringbone Stitch

Spiderweb Stitch

Star Stitch

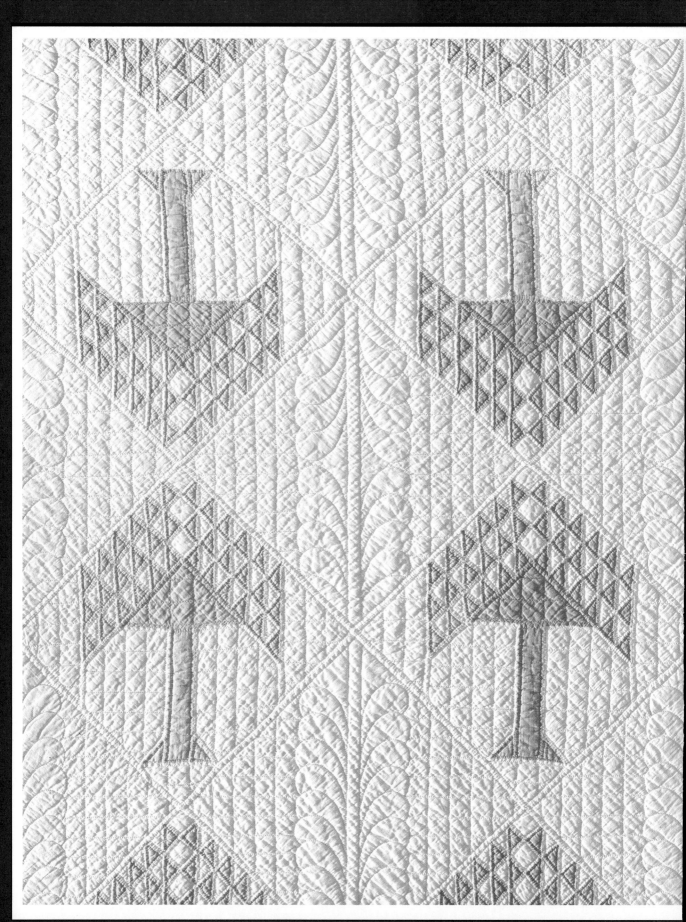

LIVING WITH PATCHWORK

The enduring
appeal of many a patchwork piece
is to the heart as well as the eye.
An antique family quilt is a
cherished link to generations past,
while a contemporary design may
speak just as eloquently of hearth
and home.

PERSONALIZING YOUR HOME

A lively imagination—yours and your family's—plus a few needlecraft skills are all you need to make your home distinctively your own. In this section you'll see how designer Rebecca Jerdee combines an artist's eye and a sophisticated flair for patchwork and color to create a warmly personal environment for her family.

Among Becky's most imaginative projects are these handsome appliquéd portraits of her children, Adam and Amy, *left*. A unique alternative to the traditional family album, this patchwork gallery is all the more precious because each portrait is lovingly handcrafted by Mom.

To make patterns for your own family portraits, you'll need photographic slides to work from. Spend an afternoon photographing your subject (aim for shots that look spontaneous and natural). Or, look through family slides for an appropriate pose. Project the chosen slide onto a sheet of paper taped to the wall. Then carefully trace the outlines of the figure to make a master pattern.

If time is of the essence, you'll want to stitch your portrait entirely by machine. However, pretty trimmings, laces, and simple touches of hand embroidery also make nice additions.

For tips on composing a portrait, selecting fabrics, and stitching your own designs, turn to page 260.

Children's original artwork is one of Becky's favorite sources of design ideas, and drawings by Amy and Adam (her two young artists-in-residence) have inspired some wonderfully whimsical projects over the years.

The backyard in summer, *opposite,* provides a place for all the Jerdees to pursue their individual interests and still spend time together. While Becky catches up on some hand stitching, her husband, Allen, enjoys tending the garden with Adam and Amy.

"I'm very proud of my wife's designs and I have a special appreciation of her work because I know what goes into each project," says Allen.

Two of the family's favorite creations are the cheerful sun screen Becky stitched for the backyard fence and a Martianlike scarecrow that Adam plants each spring to protect their garden. Both are fabric adaptations of the kids' early drawings.

Becky translated more of the children's artwork into appliqués for a set of appliance covers, *above right,* and to embellish the one-of-a-kind apron that Adam dons for kitchen duty, *below right.*

For hints on how to adapt your own kids' drawings for various patchwork projects, see page 261.

"Using Adam's and Amy's
drawings in my designs,"
says Becky, "helps
me preserve each stage of
their childhood."

Adam's room, *left,* boasts a colorful profusion of transportation motifs. For the bedspread, Becky personalized an inexpensive ready-made with appliqués adapted from Adam's original car drawings. To create instant patchwork pictures for the walls, she enlarged some of Adam's favorite drawings and appliquéd cutout shapes to background fabric with fusible webbing.

Amy's room, *opposite,* you'd never mistake for anyone else's. Her unique quilt features pieced and embroidered adaptations of grammar school artwork. A matching pillow was inspired by a prize-winning drawing Amy did to promote fire prevention.

In addition to the place of honor over Amy's bed, Becky's patchwork portraits turn up in more unexpected corners of the house—like the delightfully informal family portrait stitched on the shower curtain, *above.*

"I wanted to quilt a marriage certificate for our bed that would be a living heirloom, not just a piece of paper tucked away in some filing cabinet."

Becky's pride and joy is this anniversary quilt she made to commemorate her marriage to Allen. The embroidered verse on the center of the quilt, *right,* which the couple finds especially meaningful, is taken from a Pennsylvania Dutch marriage certificate.

The addition of the children's names and birth dates makes the quilt like a family tree—a unique record of special occasions that are important to the entire family.

Becky used contemporary folk art designs for both the quilt and the appliquéd pictures that hang on the wall above the bed. Although the designs are traditional folkloric motifs, Becky made changes and modifications to create these updated versions.

The 14-inch-square wall hangings are some of the experimental designs Becky came up with before she started the quilt. They represent love, fertility, and happiness—symbols that relate to the earth and celebrate human relationships. The heart, leaf, and flower motifs selected for the quilt "grow" out of the urn, symbolizing good luck and prosperity.

Directions and patterns for the quilt and wall hangings are included in the how-to instructions.

APPLIQUÉD PORTRAITS
PAGES 252-253

Materials

Unbleached muslin (background)
Fabric scraps (appliqués)
Iron-on interfacing
Fusible webbing
Two sets of fabric stretchers
Water-erasable pen
Camera and slide projector

Instructions

Note: The appliquéd portraits shown on pages 252-253 are intended as inspiration only. To design and make a pattern for your own portrait, you'll need a slide projector and a clear (sharply focused) color slide of your subject.

After selecting an appropriate slide, decide on the size you want the finished portrait to be. Mark the dimensions on a large sheet of plain newsprint or brown wrapping paper to establish the portrait's boundaries.

Tape the paper to a wall and project the chosen slide onto the paper, positioning the subject of the portrait within the marked outlines. Now is the time to make minor changes in the original composition to refine the overall design. Some general rules:

Make the face the focal point by placing it either to the left or right of center in the upper half of the composition. (When the face is centered, the composition becomes too formal.) Be sure the face isn't positioned too close to the picture's edge.

Keep the background simple to avoid distraction. The subject's face should be the most important element; the body, second.

Tracing the pattern: Once the image is positioned within the frame, use a fine-tip felt pen to trace the composition onto the paper. *Draw only what you plan to sew.*

Begin by drawing embroidery details, such as facial features, hands, and hairlines. Keep the hair simple, concentrating on shapes rather than individual

strands. (Plan to use different fabrics for separate hair sections.)

Continue drawing in the remaining shapes until you have captured the basic outline of your picture. (You should feel as if you could cut each shape of your composition from fabric.) Add more embroidery lines for detail.

Make a copy of the original drawing on tissue paper; use this tracing to cut out the pattern pieces and use the original drawing for reference. It is not necessary to include the embroidery lines on the tissue paper patterns because these will be drawn and stitched directly onto the larger appliquéd pieces and the muslin background fabric.

Selecting the fabrics: After tracing the portrait onto paper, estimate the amounts of fabric you will need. Plan to purchase enough unbleached muslin to cover the entire portrait, adding at least 2 inches on all sides to pull around the stretcher frames. You also will need about ½ yard each of medium-weight, iron-on interfacing and fusible webbing.

Fabric selection is a key step in creating a successful portrait. Because every appliquéd portrait is a one-of-a-kind design, you will have your own unique reasons for selecting certain fabrics, colors, and textures. Here are some general guidelines:

Choose one printed fabric to play a major part in the composition, then select a variety of complementary prints and solids. Avoid excessively bold prints that compete with the overall design.

Position light and dark fabrics so that each shape is easily distinguishable. Place light colors next to dark ones so the shapes are clearly defined. As you work, look at your composition from a distance to make sure the fabrics "read" well. Use subtle fabrics for the background and scatter darker colors throughout.

For subtle arrangement of fabrics, limit your colors to a fairly small range; for a more intense composition, choose fabrics that range from unbleached muslin to navy blue, dark brown, and black.

Appliquéing the portrait: First, lay the muslin atop the original drawing. Trace embroidery lines onto the muslin with a water-erasable pen. Outline face, hands, and other flesh-tone shapes.

Iron pieces of interfacing to the back of the portrait, positioned beneath each flesh-colored shape, to make the muslin stiff enough to embroider without a hoop.

Work the embroidery lines by hand in stem stitches, using ecru, black, and pink floss as required. Do not pull the stitches too tightly. Press the muslin gently after you have finished stitching.

Next, place the muslin over the original drawing again and trace the remaining shapes onto the fabric. Cut fabric shapes to match each pattern piece exactly. (Add a 2-inch stretching allowance to each fabric piece that falls along the edge of the portrait.)

Cut out each fabric appliqué piece together with a layer of fusible webbing. *Precise cutting of each shape is essential.*

To appliqué the portrait, begin working from the subject's face and gradually move to the background. Position the fusible webbing atop the muslin, then add the fabric pieces, aligning edges and filling in the entire composition.

To fuse the pieces in place, cover the fabric with paper towels and press for 12 seconds, using a "wool" or "permanent press" setting. *Do not slide the iron.* (Practice the procedure before you begin, to make sure the temperature setting is correct.)

Baste, rather than fuse, large pieces of fabric to the background. (Large pieces of fusible webbing may cause the fabric to buckle or crack.)

Once the pieces are fused or basted in place, zigzag-stitch around all raw edges with matching or contrasting thread. Stitch over any small gaps between the fabric pieces. If desired, define the edges of some or all of the shapes in the design by positioning embroidery floss on the fabric and zigzag-stitching over it with a narrow, loose stitch.

Finishing: Purchase two pairs of wooden stretchers (available at art stores) to match the size of the portrait. Assemble the frame and stretch the fabric portrait in place, using ¾-inch nails or industrial staples. Frame as desired.

KIDS' ART PATCHWORK PROJECTS
PAGES 254-257

Instructions

Note: Patterns for the sun screen, scarecrow, apron, kitchen accessories, quilts, and wall hangings shown on pages 254-257 are all based on original children's drawings. Some of the designs, such as the blender and toaster covers, were drawn with specific projects in mind; others, such as the designs for Amy's quilt, were adapted from doodles, sketches, and school artwork collected over the years. Specific instructions for these projects follow.

For helpful hints on how to select and adapt your own children's drawings for similar projects, see "Adapting Kids' Art for Appliqué," *right.*

◆ SUN SCREEN: Finished size is 33x51 inches.

Cut and hem a piece of natural-colored canvas to fit a purchased or preexisting wooden frame. Cut a cheerful sun shape from yellow canvas and machine-appliqué to the background. Use machine couching (zigzag stitching over black floss) to outline the sun shape and make the sun's rays. Add metal grommets along each side; lace with cord to hang.

◆ SCARECROW: Finished size is 36 inches tall, excluding the post.

Ask your child to design a scarecrow figure for the project or adapt any suitable "scary" figure from existing artwork. Enlarge the figure to about 36 inches high and make a paper pattern.

Cut matching front and back shapes for the figure from sturdy canvas. Next, cut out fabric pieces for costume and features and machine-appliqué them to the front. With right sides facing, stitch front and back together, leaving bottom open. Turn, press, stuff with fiberfill or rags, and stick one end of a stake or broom handle inside the figure for support. Gather raw edges at bottom of figure around stake and tie off.

◆ APPLIANCE COVERS: For kitchen designs like these, provide your youngster with a selection of objects to draw. You might start with a few simple objects—an apple, a banana, grapes, and a pear (use these drawings to make appliquéd pot holders). After a few drawings are finished, invite the child to draw your toaster or blender or other kitchen appliances. Then, if necessary, enlarge the drawings to an appropriate size and make tissue paper patterns for the appliqués.

From quilted fabric, cut fronts, backs, and side strips to fit your toaster and blender. Cut fruit or appliance shapes from decorative fabrics, using paper patterns.

Attach appliqués to fronts of appliance covers, using fabric glue or fusible webbing, and machine-appliqué in place, using a medium-width zigzag stitch. For narrow lines and details (stems, cords), use lines of satin stitching.

Next, stitch contrasting piping around raw edges of front and back pieces of appliance covers. With right sides facing, sew fronts and backs to side strips, sewing along previous stitching lines. Trim seams, clip curves, and turn the covers right-side out. Finish bottoms with narrow hems or additional piping.

(Continued)

ADAPTING KIDS' ART FOR APPLIQUÉ

If you don't already have artwork on hand, or if you want to collect drawings on a specific theme for use with a particular project, here are several techniques you might use to guide your children in making drawings that will translate effectively into fabric.

Provide young artists with a good selection of crayons and wide-tip felt pens. Suggest that they use black or dark colors for outlines and lighter, more vibrant colors for filling in the designs. This will encourage strong, well-defined shapes that are easy to reproduce in fabric appliqué.

If you have a particular project in mind (squares for a quilt, for example, or a collection of pillows), suggest that the kids work to the scale that suits your project. You might give them sheets of paper to work on that are the size and shape of the designs you require. But also remember that enlarging all or just a portion of any picture can produce wonderfully dramatic results.

If drawings are too small as they are, enlarge them for use as patchwork patterns (see suggestions for enlarging patterns, page 312). If necessary, when making a pattern from original artwork, eliminate extraneous details for the sake of balance or composition, or pull out and focus on one single element in a drawing to be enlarged, reduced, or repeated.

Once you've refined the design to your satisfaction, cut the basic shapes from fabric and use fabric glue or fusible webbing to position them on background fabric. Add details and embellishments with hand or machine embroidery, and finish with a touch or two of embroidery.

(Continued)

◆ APRON: Using the photograph on page 255 for inspiration, cut and appliqué simple food or utensil shapes to a purchased apron (or make your own chef's apron from striped fabric, using an existing apron as a pattern).

◆ ADAM'S WALL HANGINGS AND PILLOWS: Following suggestions for enlarging and adapting children's drawings, on page 261, make paper patterns from a few of your child's drawings. Cut each design piece from fabric and iron the appliqués onto a fabric background, using fusible webbing. Frame or mount as desired.

To make matching pillows, follow instructions for assembling the wall hangings, *above,* then cut around the outside edges of the design, leaving an additional ½ inch all around for seam allowances. Cut a matching-size piece of fabric for backing. With right sides facing, stitch fronts to backs. Clip curves, turn, press, stuff, and slip-stitch openings closed.

◆ ADAM'S QUILT: To make a child's quilt similar to the one shown on page 256, start with a purchased, prequilted bedspread. Then cut and piece a sheet of green fabric the size of the quilt and appliqué designs made from children's drawings along the bottom edges of the fabric.

Lay the appliquéd fabric atop the purchased spread and pin in place. Join the two layers together by tufting every 6 inches with black yarn. Use the spread's quilting pattern to determine placement of tufts. (For tips on how to tuft a quilt, turn to page 243.) Use contrasting hem tape to bind edges.

◆ AMY'S QUILT: The quilt measures 76x96 inches.

To make a quilt similar to the one shown on page 257, refer to

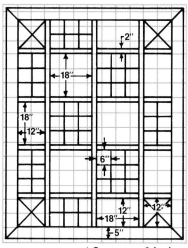

1 Square = 6 Inches

the diagram, *above,* for sizes and placement of squares. The finished quilt consists of 20 quilt blocks in three different sizes, and is constructed using ¼-inch seams throughout.

First, adapt eight of your child's drawings to fabric appliqué patterns, following suggestions on page 261. Size each fabric drawing according to the diagram, *above,* adding ¼-inch seam allowances.

When appliquéd pictures are completed, piece scrap fabric squares together to make three 9-patch quilt blocks and five 6-patch quilt blocks. (Refer to diagram for sizes and placement.) Cut four corner pieces from fabric; add ¼-inch seam allowances.

To assemble the quilt top, stitch the blocks together following the diagram and using 2-inch-wide sashing strips. Back the quilt with batting and a sheet or backing fabric pieced to size. Quilt as desired. Finish with a 5-inch-wide fabric border.

FAMILY PORTRAIT SHOWER CURTAIN
PAGE 256

Materials
Purchased solid-color cotton or cotton-blend shower curtain (or fabric cut and pieced to size—72x72 inches)
Color slide of family
Slide projector
Assorted fabrics for appliqués
Fusible webbing or fabric glue

Instructions
Following general instructions for "Appliquéd Portraits," on page 260, project the slide picture against a sheet of paper taped to the wall. Trace outlines of picture onto paper to make the master pattern.

Cut, fuse, and machine-appliqué pieces of fabric to background to complete the family portrait. Hem shower curtain, and add grommets, if necessary.

FOLK ART WALL HANGINGS
PAGE 258
Finished size of each: 14x14 inches

Materials
18-inch squares of fabric for backgrounds
Scraps of print and solid fabrics for appliqués
Scraps of fusible webbing

Instructions
Enlarge the folk art patterns, *opposite.* Cut all pattern pieces from fabric, referring to the photograph for colors.

Cut an 18-inch square of background fabric for each design; center and iron the pattern pieces in place, using fusible webbing. Machine-appliqué around the edges of each piece, using matching or contrasting thread.

Cut and baste a matching-size piece of quilt batting to the back of each appliquéd square; quilt the designs as desired.

To finish, wrap the background fabric around a 14-inch square of cardboard or hardboard, securing the edges to the back. Frame as desired.

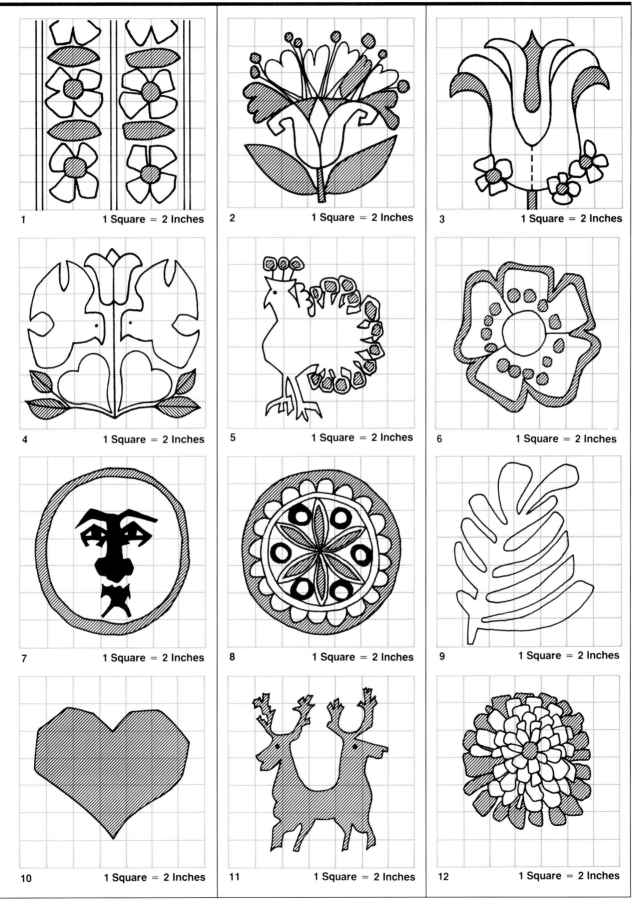

1   1 Square = 2 Inches

2   1 Square = 2 Inches

3   1 Square = 2 Inches

4   1 Square = 2 Inches

5   1 Square = 2 Inches

6   1 Square = 2 Inches

7   1 Square = 2 Inches

8   1 Square = 2 Inches

9   1 Square = 2 Inches

10   1 Square = 2 Inches

11   1 Square = 2 Inches

12   1 Square = 2 Inches

MARRIAGE QUILT
PAGES 258-259
*Finished size is 84x98 inches,
excluding eyelet trim.*

Materials

3 yards of off-white prequilted
  fabric
4 yards *each* of muslin and batting
1 yard *each* of black and brown
  polka-dot fabric and red fabric
½ yard *each* of lime green, blue-
  green, avocado green, and pink
  fabrics
Scraps of gold, pink, and purple
  fabric
12 yards of 8-inch-wide eyelet
8 yards of red bias hem tape
3 yards of fusible webbing
14 skeins of black embroidery
  floss
White quilting thread
Red, black, and green sewing
  thread
5½ yards of backing fabric
Water-erasable marking pen

Instructions

Refer to diagram, *below right,* for
size and placement of appliqués
and patterned squares. Enlarge
pattern Nos. 2, 9, and 10, on page
263, plus dove pattern, *above right.*
Cut pattern pieces from fabric, referring to photograph for colors.

Cut forty-two 15-inch squares
for the quilt—14 from prequilted
fabric and 28 from muslin.

Embellish 14 prequilted squares
with machine couching lines, using a narrow machine-zigzag setting to anchor black floss along
each line of quilting.

Machine-appliqué the dove design to one prequilted square. Reverse the pattern and appliqué to
a second prequilted square.

Iron five leaf designs (No. 9) to
plain muslin squares; reverse the
pattern and iron the mirror-image
patterns to another five squares.
Machine-appliqué around edges
of each design. Baste batting to
backs of squares; quilt as desired.

Using fusible webbing and following instructions for the leaf
designs, iron two hearts (No. 10)
to two muslin squares.

1 Square = 2 Inches

Center of Quilt ⟶

1 Square = 3 Inches

Repeat this procedure for six
flower designs (No. 2), reversing
pattern on half of the squares. Position flowers diagonally on
squares (see pattern).

Enlarge urn (see diagram); cut
from black and brown dotted fabric. Sew four plain muslin squares
into one large square; iron urn in
place using fusible webbing. Machine-appliqué design, back
square with batting, and quilt.

Use a water-erasable marker to
write your wedding date, children's names, and other personal
information on the plain muslin
squares, allowing for ½-inch
seams on squares. Embroider with
stem stitches using three strands
of black floss. Back embroidered
squares with batting and quilt.

Assemble quilt as shown at left
using ½-inch seams. Sew two
center vertical strips together; machine-appliqué stem and curved
vines in place. Sew remaining four
vertical strips together; stitch to
each side of the center panel.

To complete the top, fuse small
branches in place, connecting design elements to the urn. Machine-appliqué around all edges.
Trim two bottom corner squares
as shown in the pattern to curve
the outside edges. Back quilt, and
bind edges with red hem tape.
Add ruffled eyelet edging to two
sides and bottom of quilt.

For pillow shams, add machine
couching to leftover scraps of prequilted fabric, back with muslin,
and trim with eyelet.

TREE OF LIFE
QUILT PATTERN
PAGES 250-251
Finished size is about 69x79 inches.

Materials
Muslin (background and backing)
Gold fabric (pieced trees)

Instructions
Quilt consists of sixteen 12-inch
pieced blocks set together on the
diagonal with nine plain background squares. Pieced blocks are
arranged in four rows of four

1 Square = 1 Inch

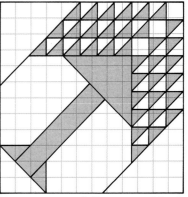

1 Square = 1 Inch

blocks each, with tops of blocks (tree tops) facing toward center. Top is pieced out with 12 half-squares along the sides and four smaller triangles at corners.

The quilt is finished at each end with 5-inch-wide borders (not shown) pieced from gold and muslin triangles and bound with gold bias binding.

Instructions below are for one block. Sew as many blocks as necessary to complete quilt.

To begin: Enlarge pattern, *above right;* make templates for pattern pieces. For each block, trace and cut out (add ¼ inch for seams) 38 small gold triangles (leaves and base of tree) and 30 small muslin squares (crown of tree). Cut two large and one medium muslin triangle (background at sides and base of tree). Cut one large gold triangle and one rectangular gold strip (trunk). Cut two irregularly shaped muslin pieces to complete block background.

To piece block: Sew small triangles together into strips; join the strips; to complete a square, add remaining fabric shapes. Press between each step. Make sixteen blocks (or as many blocks as desired). Assemble and finish quilt.

APPLIQUÉD ROCKER
PAGE 251

Materials
Slide, line drawing, or illustration
Muslin for backing
Fabric scraps, matching threads

Instructions
Enlarge, transfer, and complete appliquéd picture of your choice, using instructions for Appliquéd Portraits (from photographs) on page 260, or for Folk Art Fabric Pictures (from drawings), below.

FABRIC FOLK ART
(COFFEETIME)
PAGES 14-15
Finished size is 14x17 inches.

Materials
14x17-inch stretcher strips
17x20 inches *each* of fabric (background) and prequilted muslin (backing)
Assorted fabric scraps (appliqués)
Beads, buttons, and scraps of lace
Fusible webbing, thread

Instructions
Enlarge pattern, *above,* onto paper for a master pattern. Transfer pattern pieces to appropriate fabrics; cut out. (Do *not* add seam allowances.) Baste background and backing fabrics together.

Pin and baste pattern pieces to background fabric, referring to master pattern and to photograph on page 15 for placement. *Note:* Fusible webbing is helpful for holding small shapes in place while you're basting.

Using satin stitch (or closely spaced zigzag stitch) on your sewing machine, appliqué around fabric shapes using a coordinating thread color. For best results, use even hand tension on the fabric; guide, do not push or pull, fabric through the machine. Adjust the machine tension so that fabric doesn't gather or pucker as you stitch. Lightweight fabrics and small pieces may draw during machine stitching and may need to be lined with iron-on interfacing for support.

To sew sharp corners, stitch up to the corner and leave needle in fabric at outside of the line of stitches. Lift presser foot and start stitching so the first stitch goes toward the inside of the design, overlapping the stitch just made; continue stitching.

Once machine stitching is completed, pull threads to back of fabric and trim. Remove basting. Embroider the facial features by hand, using one strand of sewing thread or a single strand of embroidery floss; add beads and lace trims (refer to photograph).

Press piece on wrong side. Stretch over assembled stretcher frames; staple in place on back side. Trim excess fabric; frame.

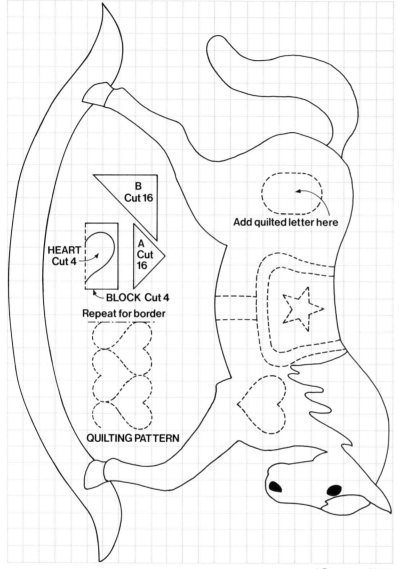

B
Cut 16

HEART
Cut 4

A
Cut
16

Add quilted letter here

← BLOCK Cut 4
Repeat for border

QUILTING PATTERN

1 Square = 1 Inch

❖

ROCKING HORSE CRIB QUILT
PAGE 9
Finished size is 56x60 inches

Materials
(Fabrics are 44 to 45 inches wide.)
3⅝ yards of calico for quilt back, border, and A triangles
1⅞ yards of calico fabric for horse body, border strips, hearts, and B triangles

1⅓ yards of calico fabric for background
¼ yard of solid-color fabric for mane, forelock, tail, and corner squares
¼ yard of calico fabric for rocker
⅛ yard of calico fabric for hooves, eye, and nostril
Quilt batting
6¾ yards purchased binding (or ½ yard of fabric to make strips for binding)

Instructions
To cut out fabric pieces: Enlarge patterns, *left,* onto paper. Trace outlines of patterns onto the right side of assorted calico fabrics and cut out, adding ¼-inch seam allowances to all pieces.

From the largest piece of fabric (3⅝ yards), cut and piece a 61x65-inch rectangle for the quilt back. Cut two 4½x44½-inch strips and two 4½x40½-inch strips (these dimensions include seam allowances). Cut 16 A triangles (add seam allowances).

From the 1⅞-yard piece of fabric, cut two 2½x44½-inch strips and two 2½x40½-inch strips (dimensions include seam margins). Also cut out four hearts and 16 B triangles; add seam allowances.

From the 1⅓-yard length of background fabric cut a rectangle 40½x44½ inches. From solid-color fabric cut four 4-inch corner squares; add seam margins.

To assemble quilt top: Turn under seam allowances on rocking horse pieces; baste. Clip curves before basting so turned edges lie flat and smooth. Do not turn under seam allowance where two or more shapes are layered together (lower shape will be covered by upper shape). Pin and baste appliqués in place; whipstitch all pieces securely.

Appliqué a heart to the center of a 4-inch square. Stitch longest side of four triangle A pieces to each side of the 4-inch square (right sides facing) to form a second square. In the same manner, sew four triangle B pieces in place to make an 8-inch corner square. Repeat for all four corner blocks. See photograph for guidance.

With right sides facing, sew one 2½-inch border strip to one 4½-inch border strip along one long side. (*Note:* The 2½-inch strip will always be against the quilt center.) Repeat for all four sides of border. With right sides facing, stitch long borders to long sides of quilt top. Stitch a corner block to each end of the short border; stitch to quilt top.

To finish quilt: Assemble quilt by laying out backing fabric, facedown. Place a layer of quilt batting on top and add quilt top, faceup. Pin and baste the layers together, starting in center and working toward outside edges.

Quilt around horse, rocker, and hearts in corner blocks. Then quilt pieced blocks and narrow border strip ¼ inch from all seams. Quilt wide border using heart pattern shown on diagram. If desired, quilt entire background in diagonal lines 1¼ inches apart.

Personalize the quilt by "branding" the horse with a quilted initial (see pattern).

Trim edges of quilt and stitch binding in place to outside edges.

❖

PAINTED PATCHWORK PICTURE
PAGE 20
Finished size is 24x28 inches

Materials
Two 30x34-inch pieces of
   unbleached cotton muslin
30x34 inches of quilt batting
Textile paints in the colors of your
   choice
Paintbrush
Dressmaker's carbon paper
Black, No. 8 pearl cotton thread
Embroidery needle
24x28-inch artist's stretcher
   strips or curtain rod or dowel

Instructions
Enlarge pattern, *above right.* Transfer the design, centered, onto a piece of preshrunk unbleached muslin, using dressmaker's carbon and a tracing wheel.

To paint design: Using the photograph as a guide (or your own color preferences), paint the design with textile paints, following the manufacturer's instructions. Allow each color to dry thoroughly before painting the next color.

To dilute paint, *do not* add water; thinning paints with water causes the colors to run beyond the edges of the design. Lighten paint by

1 Square = 2 Inches

adding a small amount of clear medium textile paint to the color.

Before painting the design, practice painting on scrap fabric to determine how close to pattern lines you can paint without colors bleeding together. Paint up to but not over the pattern lines. Do not place too much paint on the brush at one time. Thoroughly clean and dry brushes between each use.

When all painting is completed and fabric is dry, set the paint by carefully pressing the back of the painted muslin using a warm iron.

To quilt design: Sandwich batting between painted muslin and remaining piece of muslin; pin and baste all layers together.

Using black pearl cotton thread and small evenly spaced running stitches, quilt around the edges of all painted areas (see photograph).

To finish picture: Assemble stretcher strips; stabilize with glue and nails. Mount quilted muslin on stretcher-strip frame, stapling raw edges to the back. Frame as desired.

Or, trim edges of quilted piece close to the design, turn under raw edges ¼ inch, and slip-stitch front to back. Add a casing along the top edge and mount the picture on the wall, using a curtain rod or dowel for hanging.

267

CLASSIC CLOTHES FOR EVERY SEASON

Just as patchwork projects add a
uniquely personal touch to
your home, a favorite appliqué
motif or an imaginative bit of
piecing can turn off-the-rack
clothing into one-of-a-kind designs.
Here and on the following pages
you'll find delightful ideas for
transforming wardrobe basics into
wearable art for every member
of the family.

It takes almost no time at all to
turn thrifty mail-order sweaters
and caps, *left,* into folk art weara-
bles with colorful felt appliqués.
Just snip a selection of heart and
flower motifs from washable felt
and stitch the cutouts in place.
Add a touch or two of embroidery
for embellishment, and the trans-
formation is complete.

Other warmers that might benefit from the same buy-basic-
and-embellish treatment include
heavyweight ski or skating socks
(add trims around the cuffs or up
the sides) and gloves or mittens.
Just adapt your favorite motifs to
suit the size and shape of the item,
or use all or part of the simple
heart and flower design pictured
here. (For patterns, see page 278.)

Keep in mind that the appliqués should be made from fabrics
that require the same cleaning
methods as the background fabric. If you plan to wash your appliquéd sweater in cold water, for
example, be sure to prewash both
sweater and felt before beginning
to stitch. And when appliquéing
sweaters or other knitted items,
take care to stitch loosely enough
to allow for the natural give and
stretch of the garment.

Imagination and careful cutting and piecing are all you need to make pretty patchwork clothing from still-usable scraps of a treasured quilt.

Although old or valuable quilts always should be treated with respect and preserved whenever possible, quilted coverlets that have truly passed their prime can be recycled into strikingly original clothing and accessories.

To create your own version of the quilted jacket, *opposite,* select a jacket pattern with simple lines and minimal detail. If you're unable to salvage sufficient material from a single quilt for an entire jacket, cut only the fronts or the back—or just the collar, cuffs, and placket—from quilt scraps. Cut the remaining pattern pieces from contrasting fabric, or combine scraps from two different quilts to make one garment.

Arrange pattern pieces to avoid badly damaged areas of the quilt and to make the most of the patchwork design. Worn spots can be darned for strength (by weaving yarns over damaged areas) or concealed beneath decorative embroidery.

A simple circle skirt design, *right,* makes maximum use of a quilt with large undamaged areas at the center, but badly worn borders. Accessories, such as vests, belts, and purses, can be pieced from smaller quilt scraps.

Ready-made patches such as plaid hankies, small doilies, and embroidered napkins, plus ribbons, laces, and edgings, make it extra easy to piece a flirty skirt or a showstopper vest like those pictured here.

If you want a patchwork effect without the effort of piecing individual blocks, try these ideas for working with substitutes.

Horizontal bands sewn from border-striped men's hankies are pieced into an intriguing pattern of horizontal and vertical bars on the quick-to-stitch cotton skirt, *opposite.* Plaid or floral print handkerchiefs or assorted bandannas are other patch possibilities for similar projects.

The skirt pictured requires thirty 15-inch-square handkerchiefs. For a matching summer shawl, join four handkerchiefs into a square, then border with 10 more hankies snipped in half, stitched together, and gathered into a ruffled flounce. Loose-fitting peasant blouses and simple sundress patterns also are appropriate for this kind of patchwork.

The vest, *above,* makes the most of elegant odds and ends. Floral-pattern ribbons and delicate, scalloped laces are layered against a foundation of embroidered doilies and fancy fabric scraps to create an appliqué collage.

Try the same collage technique on the collar and cuffs of a jacket, the yoke of a blouse, or a single patch pocket for an evening skirt.

As you browse through yard sales and thrift shops, be alert for other "instant patch" possibilities.

Rich plaids, velvety corduroys, and subtly flecked tweeds bring an interesting combination of color and texture into play for this trio of winter-weight patchwork garments.

Illustrated here are two more contemporary approaches to traditional pieced patchwork.

For the sporty pair, *above,* each pattern piece of his windbreaker and her wraparound, shawl-collar jacket is cut from a different fabric. For the sake of symmetry, right and left sides of the jackets are pieced to match.

One satin lapel of the woman's jacket is embellished with oversize embroidered paisley motifs. But purchased appliqués or fabric cutouts could be used instead.

Fabric for the fashionably full wool skirt, *opposite,* is machine-pieced from large, randomly sized triangles of plaid, solid-color, and tweed wools. Solid-color waistband and flounce complete the look.

Try the same crazy-patch technique for other skirt shapes, jumper patterns, and loose-fitting dress designs. It's an imaginative and practical way to make the most of your fabric remnants.

For high fashion impact, piece this richly textured, folk art coat from an imaginative mix of new and antique fabrics, or stitch a pretty pair of patchwork mittens for winter evenings on the town.

Lovingly hoarded scraps of wool and velveteen fabrics—plaids, tweeds, paisleys, stripes, and solids—were artfully pieced together to create this colorful cossack-style coat, *opposite* and *right.*

To make your own version of this design, use a commercial pattern of your choice for the basic form. The coat pictured was fashioned from a pattern for a reversible coat, and is lined with dark print velveteen and trimmed with bias-cut strips of velveteen in a contrasting solid color. Any similar pattern will work equally well, but look for simple seaming, straight lines, and a minimum of darts.

In selecting fabrics for your coat, collect closely woven, light- to medium-weight woolens, velveteens, and other compatible materials. All fabrics should be of similar weight and fiber content, to equalize wear and tear and to facilitate cleaning.

Fragile scraps of antique fabric can be backed with lightweight iron-on interfacing for added stability, if necessary.

The coat pictured here has been machine-quilted "in the ditch," along seam lines between patches. But it could just as easily have been hand-quilted or even tufted, if desired.

For a spectacular evening version of this one-of-a-kind coat, create a similar random patch design using lightweight velvet, silk, and satin upholstery scraps.

The patchwork party mittens, *right,* are stitched from multicolored scraps of washable velveteen, pieced in a herringbone pattern and embellished with gold featherstitching. Washable acrylic fleece lining makes them extra warm.

You might try using the same techniques and materials to stitch a glamorous patchwork muff—or piece a tiny velveteen evening bag and line it with satin.

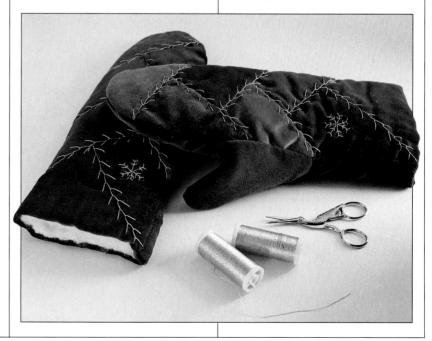

APPLIQUÉD SWEATER AND ACCESSORIES
PAGES 268-269

Materials
Purchased woolen sweater and cap (or socks, mittens, and other accessories)
Scraps of felt in red, orange, and green, or colors of your choice
Matching wool crewel yarns
Matching sewing threads
Scraps of fusible webbing
Water-soluble marker

Instructions
Pattern pieces are cut from scraps of felt (do not add seam allowances), and appliquéd to sweater or other garment or accessory first with tiny straight stitches worked in sewing thread and then with whipstitches taken with a single strand of matching or contrasting crewel yarn. Join appliqué motifs with stem stitches in green crewel yarn and add French knot accents (refer to photograph).

For the sweater: Enlarge the motif pattern, *above right,* and cut out pattern pieces from appropriate colors of felt. (Refer to photograph for color suggestions, or cut designs from felt in colors that complement those in the sweater.)

Cut two central heart pieces and stack one atop the other. Also cut double-leaf pieces for next-to-outer bud and layer leaves atop bud. Secure overlapping pieces to each other with scraps of fusible webbing tucked in between and ironed in place.

Pin all felt shapes to the sweater and appliqué them in place, using small, straight stitches taken with matching sewing thread. As you stitch, allow for ease and the natural stretch of the garment.

Embellish edges of appliqués with buttonhole stitches worked in matching or contrasting crewel yarn. Add embroidered accents in stem stitches and French knots, as indicated on pattern.

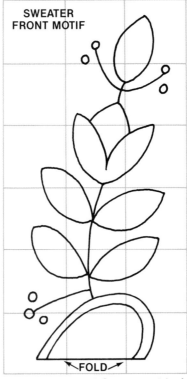

SWEATER FRONT MOTIF

FOLD

1 Square = 1 Inch

Next, add a row of purchased rya fringe around collar, accented by a row of chain stitches in contrasting yarn (see detail of pattern, *below*). Then add rows of red and green chain stitches along sleeves and cuffs, if desired.

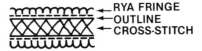

RYA FRINGE
OUTLINE
CROSS-STITCH

For caps, mittens, or socks: Adapt the pattern, *above,* or *above right.* (You may wish to eliminate some leaves or rearrange elements in the design to fit your garment.)

For knitted mittens or socks, stitch the appliqués following directions for the sweater.

For the cap or any other woven wool garment, transfer design to cap with water-soluble marker. Cut pattern pieces from felt and sew to cap with matching threads. Embellish projects with embroidery stitches, as described above.

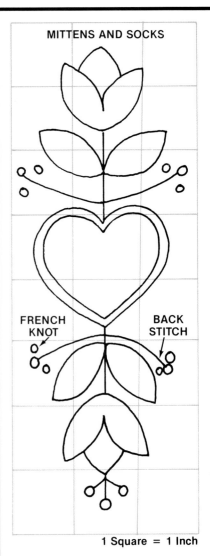

MITTENS AND SOCKS

FRENCH KNOT

BACK STITCH

1 Square = 1 Inch

QUILTED JACKET
PAGE 270

Materials
Jacket pattern of your choice
Worn quilt (or quilts)
Notions (as pattern requires)
Lining fabric (optional)
Various colors of 3-ply crewel yarn or cotton embroidery floss
Embroidery hoop and needles
Water-soluble marking pen

Instructions
Select a jacket pattern with simple lines and few or no darts.

Cut out pattern pieces and arrange on quilt fabric to make best use of quilt pattern and to avoid badly damaged areas. If available quilt pieces are insufficient for an entire jacket, just cut sleeves, fronts, or back from old quilt. If desired, piece and quilt new fabric in traditional patterns for remainder of garment.

Using water-soluble pen, trace pattern shapes onto quilted fabric and mark all seam allowances, but *do not* cut out pattern pieces yet.

Using a single ply of crewel yarn or three strands of cotton embroidery floss, use decorative embroidery stitches to darn any damaged areas on pattern pieces and to embellish seams or other areas of quilted fabric. Stitches used on jacket shown include satin, straight, outline, French knots, bullion knots, lazy daisy, chain, cross, buttonhole, feather, and simple running stitches. Use as few or as many stitches as desired; vary size and colors of stitches for contrast.

When embroidery is complete, press pattern pieces and cut out. Assemble jacket according to pattern instructions. Line jacket, if desired, or finish seams with overcast stitches or bias bindings.

QUILT SKIRT
PAGE 271

Materials
Purchased pattern of your choice for flared bias skirt (without darts or pockets)
Worn or damaged quilt with sufficient good areas to cut out pattern
Scrap of calico to line waistband
Notions (as pattern requires)

Instructions
Note: As for the jacket above, this project is designed to make use of worn and damaged quilts. If you do not have worn or damaged quilted fabric, use commercially quilted fabric or piece and quilt fabric of your own design, rather than cutting up new or antique quilts in good condition.

Clean and repair quilt, if necessary. Plan placement of pattern pieces to make best use of quilt motifs. Cut out pattern pieces and assemble skirt according to pattern directions, lining waistband. Machine-hem skirt, to keep fabric bulk to a minimum.

HANDKERCHIEF SKIRT
PAGE 272

Materials
Thirty 15-inch-square plaid handkerchiefs
Button, snap, or hook and eye
Scrap of iron-on interfacing for waistband

Instructions
First stitch six handkerchiefs together side by side to make the top tier of the skirt. (Before stitching, lay hankies out on a table or floor and arrange the plaids into a pleasing design.) Next, trim a 3-inch-wide strip from one long edge of this tier to use for the waistband; set aside.

Next, stitch 12 handkerchiefs together, edge to edge, to make the second tier of the skirt. Gather one long edge of the strip, then pin and stitch the gathered edge to the long (uncut) edge of the first tier.

For the bottom ruffle, cut remaining 12 handkerchiefs in half and stitch them together edge to edge, aligning bottom (hemmed) edges. Gather along the raw edge, then pin and stitch this ruffle to the second tier.

For the waistband, trim the 3-inch-wide strip to equal the waist measurement plus 3 inches (for the overlap and seam allowances). Reinforce the waistband with a matching strip of lightweight iron-on interfacing applied to the underside.

Mark the waist measurement on the inside edge of the waistband, leaving a ½-inch seam allowance on one end and a 2½-inch seam allowance and overlap on the other end.

Next, fold under all four edges of the waistband ½ inch and press. Gather the top tier of the skirt to fit the waistband (excluding seam allowances and overlap); pin in place. (Adjust the length of the skirt, as desired, by adjusting depth of the first tier.)

Make sure that all gathers are securely tucked into the folded waistband. Topstitch around all four sides of the waistband, using matching or contrasting thread.

Finish the waistband with snap, button and buttonhole, or hook-and-eye fastener, as desired.

Pin and stitch the back seam of the skirt to within 5 inches of the waistband. Press seam open. (If desired, add hook-and-eye fasteners along this edge.)

SAMPLER VEST
PAGE 273

Materials
Commercial pattern for simple, straight-line vest, without tucks or darts
1¾ yards *each* of lightweight muslin and print lining fabric
Assorted scraps of lace edgings, embroidered ribbons, small doilies, silk, satin, and other elegant fabrics
Scraps of fusible webbing or fabric glue
Pieced or purchased bias binding
Buttons as required for pattern (optional)

Instructions
Cut all pattern pieces except facings from lightweight muslin. (Because the vest will be lined, facings are unnecessary.) Muslin pieces will serve as backing for appliquéd bits of lace, ribbon, and fabric.

(Continued)

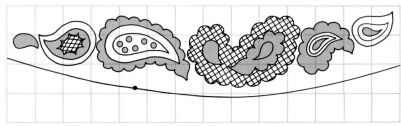

1 Square = 1 Inch

(Continued)

Lay muslin vest fronts faceup and cover each side with a collage arrangement of lace doilies, appliqués, or scraps; fabrics; and plain and fancy ribbons.

Assemble the design from the shoulders down, making both vest fronts match, if possible, or at least balance (in terms of intricacy of detail and intensity of color, for example). Tack the pieces in place using pins, scraps of fusible webbing, or dots of fabric glue.

When you have a pleasing arrangement of scraps, turn under raw edges, overlapping the pieces from shoulders down toward bottom edge of vest (refer to photograph). Pin, baste, and slip-stitch all pieces in place. Repeat for back of vest.

Cut patch pockets from muslin and embellish them following the same procedure used for the vest fronts and back. Cut a matching piece of lining fabric for each pocket. With right sides facing, stitch the lining to the pocket front around three sides. Turn right side out, press, and slip-stitch fourth side closed. Position pockets on vest fronts as shown on pattern and stitch in place.

Stitch appliquéd front and back pieces together at shoulder and side seams and press seams open. Press vest on wrong side.

Next, cut the front and back pattern pieces from lining fabric. With right sides facing, join lining pieces at side and shoulder seams. Press seams open.

With *wrong* sides facing, pin and baste lining inside vest, matching seams. Trim armholes and outside edges of vest back to about $\frac{1}{16}$ inch from stitching line.

To finish edges, piece 1½-inch-wide bias strips from matching or contrasting print. Fold under raw edges of bias strips ¼ inch; press. Pin and slip-stitch bias binding around the armholes and edges of vest. Add buttons and buttonholes, if desired.

MAN'S PATCHWORK JACKET
PAGE 274

Materials
Commercial jacket pattern of your choice
Wool and corduroy fabric scraps equivalent to pattern yardage requirements
Fabric for lining

Instructions
Cut and stitch jacket, following pattern directions and using a different fabric for each pattern piece (fronts, sides, back, sleeves, collar, and cuffs).

PAISLEY PATCHWORK JACKET
PAGE 274

Materials
Commercial pattern for wrap jacket with shawl collar
Wool and satin fabric scraps equivalent to pattern yardage requirements
Fabric for lining
3-ply crewel yarn in coordinating colors
Embroidery hoop and needle
Dressmaker's carbon

Instructions
Using dressmaker's carbon paper or basting stitches, transfer outline of upper collar and front facing pattern onto satin fabric.

Enlarge embroidery pattern, *above,* onto tissue paper. Transfer design to left front collar, adapting positions of motifs to suit the collar pattern. Do *not* cut out collar until embroidery is completed.

Separate the three-ply yarn; use a single strand for embroidery. Embroider design, working satin stitches on shaded areas, couched filling stitches on areas with grids, and outline stitches on remaining areas. For best results, use embroidery hoop to keep fabric taut while stitching.

Lay a damp cloth over finished embroidery and press. Cut out embroidered collar piece.

Complete jacket according to pattern directions, using different wool fabrics for each pattern piece.

PATCHWORK SKIRT
PAGE 275

Materials
Commercial pattern of your choice
Plaid, tweed, and solid-color closely woven wool fabric scraps and remnants
Pinking shears

Instructions
Using pinking shears, cut wool scraps and remnants into triangles of various shapes and sizes (see photograph for ideas). On table or floor, arrange shapes to create fabric yardage from which to cut skirt pattern pieces. (Don't worry about overlapping the pieces; the thickness of the layers will be trimmed away later.)

Carefully pin the pieces in place. Join pieces by topstitching ¼ inch in from pinked edges, using color-coordinated thread.

Turn pieced fabric to wrong side and clip away excess overlapping fabric. Turn back to right side and lay out pattern pieces. Cut out and assemble skirt following pattern instructions.

Cut ruffle from solid or plaid fabric. Ruffle can be any width desired and should be pieced lengthwise to measure twice the circumference of the bottom of the skirt.

Hem one long edge of ruffle. Gather remaining edge; pin and stitch to bottom of skirt.

❖

FULL-LENGTH PATCHWORK COAT
PAGE 276

Materials
Full-length reversible coat pattern of your choice with simple, straight lines and no darts
Wool and velveteen fabric scraps equivalent to approximately 1¼ times the pattern yardage requirements (to allow for piecing) for the patchwork side of the coat
Lightweight batting and lightweight wool or printed velveteen for lining
Approximately 2 yards of solid-color wool or velveteen for bias binding

Instructions
Cut all pattern pieces from batting and lining fabric, adding ½ inch to all seam allowances to compensate for shrinkage when fabric is quilted.

Baste batting to wrong side of each lining piece. Then, beginning with back of coat, lay batting/lining piece, batting side up, on a work surface. This piece will serve as a guide in constructing patchwork for back of coat.

To construct patchwork fabric, cut and piece randomly sized squares and rectangles of various fabrics into horizontal strips. Cut squares and rectangles on the true grain of the fabric. Strips should be 4 to 10 inches wide and long enough to extend across the back of the coat, including seam allowances. Press seams open. Clip corners; trim excess fabric.

Join these horizontal strips to construct a piece of fabric long enough and wide enough to accommodate the pattern piece for coat back. Position pieced fabric right side up atop batting/lining piece; baste layers together.

Then, machine- or hand-quilt through all three layers of fabric, following seam lines of patchwork. Reposition paper pattern on top of quilted shape and trim away excess fabric. Repeat for all pattern pieces.

Important note: Trim front and bottom edges of coat, top edges of collar, and edges of cuffs to *actual* seam lines, because all raw edges will be bound with bias strips. Leave seam allowances at sides, shoulder, and along sleeves.

Construct coat, following pattern directions. Press the side and shoulder seams open.

Grade seams, trimming away excess batting and lining fabric. Conceal all seams on lining side with 2-inch-wide strips of bias-cut, solid-color wool or velveteen. Turn under raw edges of bias strips ⅜ inch and slip-stitch in place over seams.

Cut and piece additional bias strips and bind all raw edges of coat, including front edges, collar, bottom edges, and cuffs.

❖

VELVETEEN PATCHWORK MITTENS
PAGE 277

Materials
½ yard (total) of assorted solid-color washable velveteen (or other napped) fabrics
⅜ yard washable fake fur for lining; gold embroidery floss

Instructions
Enlarge patterns, *right,* to size and cut from tissue paper.

Cut two thumbs and two palms from solid-color velveteen, flopping each pattern piece for right- and left-hand mittens. (Add ¼-inch seam margins to all pieces.)

Piece herringbone pattern for right and left mitten top, follow-

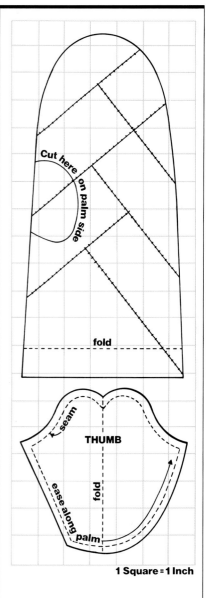

1 Square = 1 Inch

ing pattern. Press all seams in one direction, and embroider feather-stitches along all seams with gold floss. Add other touches of embroidery if desired (see photograph for inspiration).

Stitch pieced tops to palms, right sides together; use ¼-inch seams. Seam thumbs, then pin and stitch the thumbs to the mittens. Turn right side out.

Next, cut and stitch the linings from fake fur (use ⅜-inch seams). Slip velveteen mittens over fur linings (with wrong sides together). Turn under raw edges of cuffs and linings ⅝ inch; slip-stitch lining to mitten. Topstitch ½ inch above cuff of each mitten.

Our Patchwork Heritage— The Quilt Show

Museums, galleries, and local quilt shows offer excellent opportunities to study the best in patchwork. Constant exposure to first-class design and technique is the surest way to refine your appreciation for the finer points of the art.

THE
QUILT SHOW

A blue-ribbon sampling
of patchwork past and present was
assembled from museums and
private collections and displayed in
an elegant mansion for the "World
of Quilts" show at Meadow Brook
Hall in Rochester, Michigan.
The unusual setting enabled visitors
to view these outstanding examples of the quiltmaker's art as they
were intended to be enjoyed—in a
home and, often, on beds.

Meadow Brook Hall was once the home of automobile heiress Matilda Dodge Wilson. Built by American craftsmen and almost entirely of American materials, it was a most appropriate site for a major exhibition of exceptional American patchwork.

In the ballroom, *right,* superb examples of contemporary and antique quilts were shown side by side. The handsome Schoolhouse Quilt is a modern adaptation of a traditional pattern. The bold color scheme, strip-pieced center motif, and simple channel quilting update this ever-popular house and picket fence design. The Mosaic Quilt, *near right, background,* is a striking example of pieced artistry. Stitched in the 1840s, it contains thousands of tiny hexagons.

The Cross-in-Square design, page 283, is an Amish quilt pieced about 1900. Rich gemstone colors lend this quilt an air of modernity that belies its age.

Instructions for making quilts similar to some of those shown begin on page 304.

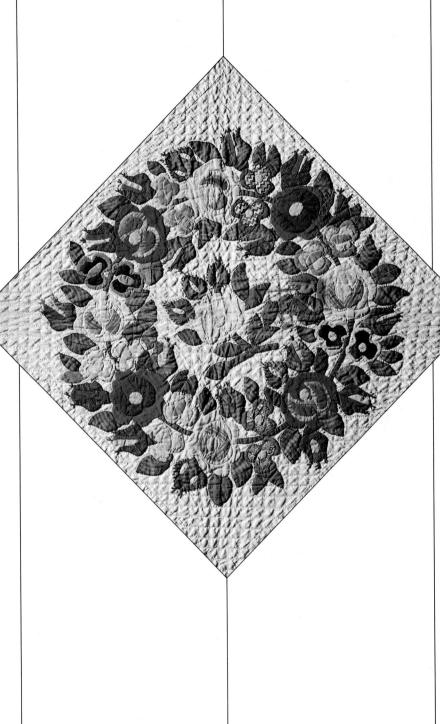

The Baltimore Album Quilt was a popular showcase for intricate floral appliqué and exquisite stitchery in the mid-nineteenth century.

A winner of many blue ribbons, this outstanding quilt, *opposite,* had never been publicly exhibited before the Meadow Brook show. It is a treasured family heirloom, stitched about 1850 by Eleanor Gorsuch and her sister Elizabeth and handed down from generation to generation through the "Eleanors" in the family.

The elaborate floral detail, skillful appliqué work, fine quilting, and trapunto make this an exceptional example of the American quiltmaker's art. Typically, none of the 25 blocks in the quilt are alike. The center block, *left,* is an example of the elaborate wreath designs that were staple motifs of Baltimore Album quilts.

Directions and a pattern for appliquéing this block are included in the instructions. For a closer look at two more of the blocks in this remarkable quilt, please turn the page.

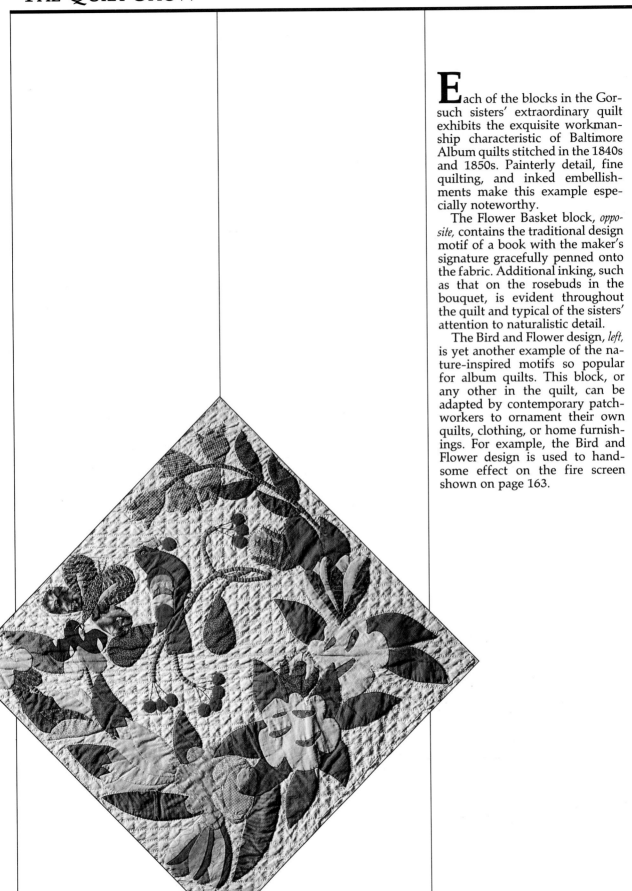

Each of the blocks in the Gorsuch sisters' extraordinary quilt exhibits the exquisite workmanship characteristic of Baltimore Album quilts stitched in the 1840s and 1850s. Painterly detail, fine quilting, and inked embellishments make this example especially noteworthy.

The Flower Basket block, *opposite,* contains the traditional design motif of a book with the maker's signature gracefully penned onto the fabric. Additional inking, such as that on the rosebuds in the bouquet, is evident throughout the quilt and typical of the sisters' attention to naturalistic detail.

The Bird and Flower design, *left,* is yet another example of the nature-inspired motifs so popular for album quilts. This block, or any other in the quilt, can be adapted by contemporary patchworkers to ornament their own quilts, clothing, or home furnishings. For example, the Bird and Flower design is used to handsome effect on the fire screen shown on page 163.

Experienced collectors and novices alike are attracted to the traditional red, white, and green fabrics found in many antique quilts. Long popular with patchworkers, this color scheme enlivens even the simplest patterns.

The Strawberry Wreath design, *foreground*, illustrates the charm of a single Baltimore quilt motif repeated across an entire bedcover. Exquisite quilting enhances the design, as do the minute buttonhole stitches used to attach the appliqués.

The Rose Tree Quilt on the bed, *opposite*, features a center medallion different from the surrounding blocks. Stitched about 1870, this design is complemented by unusual quilting—tiny stitches are clustered in parallel rows that run diagonally across the coverlet.

On the sofa, *left*, is a Coxcomb or Lotus Flower pattern made about 1850. The coverlet features hand-dyed green and red fabrics stitched onto a homespun background. Graceful feather motifs were incorporated into the dense quilting on this elegant bedcover, and almost invisible blindstitches were used to attach the appliqués.

The Eight-Petal Flower design on the chair, *opposite*, is thought to be a pattern that originated with the unknown quiltmaker. Superior patchwork and masterful quilting make it a treasured memento of times past.

291

Intricacy of piecing and quilting, artistry of design and color selection, and the age and condition of a quilt are all important considerations when choosing a quilt for your collection or for an exhibition.

The splendid Mariner's Compass Quilt, *opposite,* stitched about 1830, is a complex design in which the maker could show off her remarkable piecing skills. Each 24-inch block consists of 72 shaped curves or diamonds that must be pieced with precision. Hand-dyed fabrics and closely spaced rows of small quilting stitches add to the beauty of this design.

A quilter's skill at stitching decorative patterns was frequently more highly regarded than artful piecing, and solid-color quilts with fine stitches or intricately worked patterns are often of great value. The white-on-white, trapunto crib quilt, *above,* is such an example. Plain white fabric was layered with batting and backing and then meticulously quilted and stuffed to create a remarkably three-dimensional design.

Directions for the Mariner's Compass Quilt are included in the instructions.

This Flower Basket Petit Point design is perhaps the best known quilt stitched by the "Quilt Lady of Nebraska."

Grace Snyder, a master twentieth-century quilter, had the patience, skill, and love of detail that enabled her to complete several quilts of equally astonishing complexity in her lifetime.

The Flower Basket Quilt, *opposite,* is made from 87,789 tiny triangles. The intricate piecing leads viewers to believe they are looking at an example of needlepoint rather than pieced work.

The inspiration for magnificent quilt patterns often comes from unexpected sources. In this case, a motif found on a set of dishes given to Mrs. Snyder by her daughter Nellie Yost provided the basis for the design.

Directions and a pattern for the Flower Basket design are included in the instructions. You may wish to needlepoint the design for a pillow or rug. Or, piece it using larger triangles than those shown here, to make a single center medallion for a quilt of your own.

A quilt makes a wonderful canvas for exhibiting decorative embroidery skills and other embellishments.

The Music Quilt, *below,* is a contemporary example of superb embroidery skills devoted to a special interest. Blocks consist of music scores and composers' signatures lovingly stitched in great detail. A quilted lyre design continues the theme in this music lover's patchwork. A gracefully curved pattern quilted into the border sets off the design.

During the nineteenth century, scraps of elegant fabrics were frequently pieced into "crazy" patterns, making a background for lavish embellishment. The quilt, *opposite below,* made about 1890, is an outstanding example of such a Victorian crazy quilt. Randomly shaped pieces of silk, satin, and velvet are combined and decorated with profuse embroidery. A sampling of stitches, beadwork, and carefully embroidered pictorial details typify this creative form of quilting.

The Bible Sayings Quilt, *top right,* also made about 1890, is another fine example of crazy quilting. Pieced from a variety of wool fabrics, it is embroidered with cross-stitched Bible verses, Victorian pieties, and carefully rendered floral motifs.

A similar quilt is well-suited to contemporary patchwork. You may wish to adapt the idea for use with favorite nursery rhymes, poetry, or sayings that reflect your own special interests.

The charm of folk art is that the artist, often unknowingly, gives us a record of local history or a representation of daily life that otherwise might have gone unnoticed.

The Mittie Barrier Quilt, *opposite,* is just such a record. An accomplished embroiderer, Mittie Barrier was a plain South Carolina farm wife. But with this quilt, completed in 1920 and handed down to her daughter, she left us an imaginative and colorful record of her simple life and the beauty of the farmyard around her.

Essentially crafted from scraps of wool, silk, velvet, and brocade, this delightful crazy quilt is a unique example of American folk art, with its lovingly rendered scenes of animal life stitched on each 14-inch pieced square.

The viewer is introduced to an appealing cast of farmyard characters—hens and chicks, horses, rabbits with wildflowers, birds and their nests, even a few predatory alligators (see center quilt square, *opposite*)—an ever-present danger for Southern farmers.

The birds and flowering tree motif, *left,* shows the embroiderer's skill with a variety of stitches. Yet, the most remarkable feature of the pictorial detail is the skillful rendering of the designs using easy-to-work straight stitches.

For a closer look at two other blocks from this unusual masterpiece, please turn the page.

The delightfully intricate details embroidered into each chick and flower suggest that Mittie Barrier enjoyed both her life and her stitchery.

The parading geese and the hens and roosters on the quilt squares, *right*, are worked with abundant texture and realistic detail. Straight stitches make up each body, and a unique darning stitch that interweaves the embroidery threads suggests feather detail. Decorative flower and grass stitches add further pattern and interest to these quaint needle paintings.

Mittie Barrier's designs, and many others in this book, may be adapted for your own use. See the child's bedroom on pages 206-207 for one creative use of stitched scenes from this quilt. The how-to instructions for this chapter include directions and patterns for duplicating three of the blocks.

JUDGING AND PIECING A PRIZE-WINNING QUILT

Though you may never be involved in a quilt show as a participant, knowing what the experts look for in a master quilt will help you evaluate your own work—and others'—with a more critical eye.

In the past several decades, museums and collectors around the world have come to share the quilters' enthusiasm for the quilt as an art form. Antique quilts are valued for a variety of reasons—historical and sentimental, as well as aesthetic. And the selection of master quilts displayed at Meadow Brook Hall and pictured on the preceding pages are among the finest examples of the quilt-makers' art.

But when it comes to judging a freshly stitched piece of patchwork, how do you spot a prizewinner? What artful combination of color, line, and technical skill earns a blue ribbon at the county fair or a "Best-in-Show" award in a national competition? Despite the proliferation of local, state, and national quilt shows in recent years, there are, as yet, no nationally accepted standards for judging quilts.

As in any arts competition, the judge's personal taste invariably has some bearing on the outcome. But subjective considerations aside, quilts are evaluated on the basis of the general appearance, the design, and the quality of workmanship. Knowing what the experts look for in each of these areas will help you assess the prizewinning potential of a quilt with a fair degree of accuracy—whether it's one you see in a show, or the very first quilt you've stitched on your own.

GENERAL APPEARANCE

First of all, *never* underestimate the importance of first impressions. Whatever its age, origin, or supposed value, a quilt submitted for entry in a show should always be clean, neat, and tidy.

Although any quilt undoubtedly represents a labor of love, that labor should be evident only in the fine workmanship, and not as careless spots and smudges, food stains, or unpleasant (smoky) odors! If necessary, the quilt should be hand washed or professionally cleaned before being exhibited. (For hints on how to care for quilts, see page 191.)

All signs of construction (such as basting threads and quilting or appliqué lines made with pencil, chalk, or water-soluble markers) should be removed. No knots or loose threads should be visible on either the front or the back of the quilt.

In addition, the quilt should be squared: The sides should be perfectly parallel and at right angles to the top and bottom edges. And there should be no obvious technical errors in either construction or execution, such as a block set in upside down, or wildly irregular quilting stitches.

In terms of overall impact, a prizewinning quilt must be both visually pleasing and functionally sound.

DESIGN

Even if the quilt pattern is strictly traditional, rather than an original design, there are many areas in which the quilter makes design decisions that are wholly her own. Even with a tried and true design like the Blazing Star or a simple Log Cabin, the selection of colors, patterns, materials, and quilting designs has a significant effect on the ultimate success or failure of the finished quilt.

Color and pattern: The overall surface design should have a pleasing rhythm and balance, with an effective distribution of lights and darks, prints and solids.

All the elements of the design should appear to be part of a unified whole, and the relative proportions of the various design elements should be harmonious. (For example, if prints are used, the scale of the prints should be in keeping with the size of the pieces for which they are being used.)

Colors throughout the quilt should be appropriate for the pattern and work well together. Skillful use of accent colors also can lend movement and interest to a design. (For example, a warm, red center patch draws the eye toward the center of a predominantly somber Log Cabin block.)

Colors for the borders, bindings, and backing also should be selected to complement, contrast, or otherwise harmonize with other colors in the quilt.

Inventive use of patterned fabric is another attribute of a well-designed quilt. As with color, stripes and plaids or directional prints also can be used most effectively to add punch to quilt pattern repeats, or to unify disparate elements of an overall design. Patterned fabrics also can be used to develop intriguing secondary patterns within the basic design of the quilt top.

(Continued)

(Continued)

Finally, the number, size, and placement of the blocks or pattern repeats should be planned so the design will be displayed to advantage when the quilt is spread on a bed (if that is its ultimate destination). And whether the quilt is destined for a bed or a wall, the design should be "framed" with well-proportioned sashes or borders so it does not "bleed" visually off the edges of the quilt.

Materials: In addition to the aesthetic considerations of color and pattern described above, materials used for a well-designed quilt also will have been selected with practicality and function in mind.

Fabrics should be similar in weight and texture, as well as in the way they will wear and the kind of care they require. For example, it is inadvisable (not to mention unwieldy) to mix corduroys, wools, silks, and cottons in the same quilt top.

Such practical considerations are of less importance in a wall hanging or a quilt that is intended primarily for display, rather than for daily use. But compatibility of fabrics usually contributes to the aesthetic appeal of a quilt, whatever the intended use of the piece.

The filler or batting is also an integral part of the quilt and will be judged as such. A well-chosen filler will be compatible with surface textiles used in the quilt, and should meet the special requirements of the quilt design. For example, a thick, high-loft polyester batt is appropriate for a tied comforter or when a soft, sculptured look is desired. Cotton batting, which is thinner than polyester, might be more effective if the design calls for a densely quilted, highly textured surface. (For more on fillers, see page 242.)

Quilting pattern: As discussed in Chapter Ten, quilting stitches do far more than just hold the three layers of a quilt together. The artistry and originality with which the quilting pattern is integrated with the patchwork design is one of the hallmarks of a master quilt.

Whether it's a simple diamond "filler" pattern or an intricate tracery of garlands, wreaths, or other motifs, the quilting pattern should be carefully planned to fit gracefully into the spaces it is intended to embellish.

Ideally, the quilting pattern should enrich the surface texture and enhance the overall appearance of the quilt, without fighting the patchwork design in any way. As a general rule, the more complex the patchwork design, the simpler the quilting pattern should be, and vice versa.

Originality: Here, we encounter one of the more subjective criteria on a judge's scorecard. Some quilt shows, particularly in recent years, focus primarily on the expressive potential, rather than the technical aspects, of patchwork.

In many shows that specialize in contemporary quilt design, the innovative use of materials and techniques, or experimentation with new shapes, patterns, and subject matter may be more highly prized than the mastery of the traditional arts of piecing and stitching a quilt. In other quilt competitions, meticulous workmanship is regularly rewarded over originality of design.

But unless the invitation or entry form stipulates that *only* traditional or contemporary quilts will be considered, any well-designed and well-made quilt will surely be a welcome addition to the show. In the final analysis, originality of concept will generally receive high marks from a judge—though originality by itself is seldom enough to excuse poor design or careless craftsmanship.

WORKMANSHIP

Excellence of design is but half the key to a prizewinning quilt. Meticulous care in the cutting, piecing, and stitching of the design is every bit as important to the ultimate success of the quilt, both aesthetically and practically.

Construction: Whether stitched by hand or machine (or a combination of both), precision piecing is essential.

In critiquing a pieced design, the judge will check first to see that all blocks are of uniform size, and that all corners and points meet precisely and lie perfectly flat. Pieced curves must be even and flowing. The direction of the grain on all fabrics should be consistent throughout the quilt and, wherever possible, should run either parallel with or at right angles to the sides of the quilt blocks.

Stitching—by hand or machine—should be even, regular, and sturdy enough to last the life of the quilt. No stitching should be visible along any seams (such as light thread used to seam dark fabrics, or vice versa).

In a well-crafted appliquéd quilt, there should be no raw edges showing, and all edges should be fastened securely to the background fabric. Curves must be smooth and even, and there should be no unsightly lumps or bumps along turned-under seam allowances. If lighter fabrics have been appliquéd atop darker ones, the lighter pieces should be lined to prevent underlying colors from showing through.

Stitches used for applying fabric pieces should be either a decorative complement to the design (such as buttonhole stitches) or unnoticeable (such as slip stitches or blind stitches). They should be worked in threads that match the appliqués.

As in pieced tops, appliquéd designs should make effective use of fabric grain or print pattern, where appropriate.

"Set" of the quilt: If used, sashing strips between blocks should be consistent in grain line, width, and placement. At intersections, seams should be neatly and precisely matched.

Block-to-block sets (such as the Ocean Waves pattern on page 43) often have a secondary pattern, and, here again, all blocks should be the same size, with all corners and points meeting exactly and lying perfectly flat.

If pieced or appliquéd blocks alternate with plain blocks in the design, the plain blocks also must be accurately sized, with consistent placement of grain lines. Borders should be as carefully pieced and stitched as the rest of the quilt, and squared-off or mitered corners must lie smooth and flat.

Quilting: High quality quilting stitches are characteristically even and regular. In other words, the stitches are all the same length and uniformly spaced along each and every row of quilting.

The actual length of the stitches (the number of stitches per inch) is less important than this evenness and regularity—although the smaller the stitches, the more highly prized the quilting.

An expertly quilted piece will have uniform stitches on the back as well as the front of the quilt, and there should never be any missed stitches or loose fabric on either the back or the front.

The surface of the quilt should lie smooth and not puff up too much. Tension should be even along the lines of quilting; the stitches should show a slight depression but no gathers or puckers. There should be no pleats or gathers quilted into either the front or the back of the quilt.

Throughout the quilt, stitching should be uniform. Quilting lines should be straight or smoothly and gracefully rounded. Rows of quilting stitches should be evenly spaced from each other and from the seams of the pieced top or the edges of the appliqués.

The stitches should be sufficiently fine, and the pattern of the stitches should be sufficiently distributed across the surface of the quilt that all the layers (top, batting, and backing) are held securely together, with no slipping, shifting, or buckling of the filler.

Quilting guidelines marked with pencil, chalk, or water-soluble pen should have been removed or covered with stitches. There should not be an obvious beginning or end to the quilting lines—no knots or backstitches should be visible anywhere on the front or the back of the quilt.

If the quilt is tied or tufted (rather than quilted), the knots should be secure and evenly distributed across the surface of the quilt in a pleasing pattern.

Finishing: When the edges of the quilt are bound off, round or square corners should be turned precisely and stitched invisibly. Stitches should be unobtrusive but secure, and the binding should be uniformly filled with all three layers of the quilt (top, filler, and backing).

ENTERING A QUILT SHOW

Above all else, entering a quilt show should be fun—a sharing and learning experience. Take time to study other entries to learn new ways of handling design problems, explore new color and fabric combinations, and pick up tips on new techniques.

Look at each quilt as an individual piece and let it open your eyes to new and exciting possibilities. Whether or not a particular quilt *pleases* you is only one of the ways in which you can be stimulated to learn from it.

Whether you are a traditionalist or an innovator at heart, a champion stitcher or a beginner, any well-made quilt will have something to teach you.

CROSS-IN-SQUARE QUILT
PAGES 282-283
Finished size is 68½x83¼ inches

Materials
5 yards of solid-color cottons in assorted shades for pieced top
1¾ yards of gray fabric for borders
4 yards of fabric for backing
Batting

Instructions
Each finished block is 11¼ inches square.

To make a quilt similar to the one pictured, cut seventeen 2¾-inch squares and four 2¾x5-inch rectangles for each block. (See photograph for color suggestions.)

Assemble the block, following the Cross-in-Square pattern on page 39. Use ¼-inch seams.

Piece a total of 20 blocks. Using 4x11¾-inch sashing strips, assemble the blocks into five rows of four blocks each. (Do not join rows yet.)

Next, cut 24 black and 24 light-colored 2¼-inch squares and sew them into 12 four-patch blocks for the intersections of the sashing strips (see the photograph).

Piece together four 4x11¾-inch sashing strips and three of the small, four-patch blocks for each of four long sashing strips.

Finally, stitch these pieced sashing strips between the rows of blocks to form the quilt top. Border the top with 7-inch-wide strips of gray fabric, using ¼-inch seams.

Piece backing to size. Baste the top, batting, and backing together. Quilt and finish the coverlet.

Quilting motifs: Use a 10-inch-diameter Dresden Plate pattern on each block, feather patterns along each sashing strip, and triple rows of diagonal quilting around the borders. Bind the edges with light gray bias binding.

BALTIMORE ALBUM QUILT
PAGES 286-289

Materials
7½ yards of muslin for top
Scraps of cotton fabrics in a wide range of colors, including ombré shades and subtle prints for appliqué designs
7½ yards of fabric for backing
Water-soluble marking pen
Fine-point permanent marker

Instructions
Each finished block is 15½ inches square. Twenty-five full blocks are set together on the diagonal, and the pattern is pieced with triangles (half-blocks) embellished with sprays of flowers and greenery. The 8¼-inch-wide border also is appliquéd with elaborate garlands of fruit and flowers.

Patterns are given here (*left* and *opposite*) for three of the blocks in the Gorsuch sisters' quilt. You can use these three designs for the first blocks in your own album quilt, and adapt additional motifs from the quilt or invent designs of your own. Album quilts of this type traditionally featured lavish depictions of nature's bounty, but any appliqué design that can be adapted to a 15½-inch square is suitable. Choose patterns and subjects that reflect your own interests and enthusiasms or those of your family and friends.

If an entire album quilt seems too large an undertaking, any one of these appliqué patterns would make a handsome pillow top or album cover.

To make one block: Enlarge one of the patterns to size and trace it onto a 16-inch square of brown paper to use as a master pattern.

1 Square = 1 Inch

Center the master pattern under a 16-inch square of muslin and carefully trace the entire appliqué pattern onto the fabric, using a water-soluble pen.

Next, use the master pattern to trace individual paper patterns for each piece of the appliqué design. Working on background pieces first (vines and leaves on the wreaths, or the red basket in the pattern, *below right*), cut out a few paper patterns at a time and trace them onto the *right* side of selected fabrics with the water-soluble pen or with a fine, light pencil. These lines will be stitching lines.

Cut out the fabric pieces ⅛ inch outside the stitching lines; baste under the seam allowance, making sure that traced stitching lines are just barely concealed. Appliqué pieces in place on the muslin square. (For more detailed how-to on appliqué techniques, see Chapter 8.)

Study the album blocks pictured on pages 286-289. Note the quilter's imaginative use of subtle prints and minute variations in color to enhance the designs.

Building up from leaves and vines to foreground flowers, continue to cut out, baste, and carefully stitch each shape to the background square. When all of the pieces are stitched in place, remove the basting stitches and use a damp cloth to clean away any remaining traces of water-soluble marking pen. Press the block lightly on the wrong side.

Add the remaining design details with fine lines of indelible marker, or use tiny straight or stem stitches taken with one or two strands of embroidery floss.

The Gorsuch quilt is backed with muslin and the appliqué designs are outline-quilted, but no batting or filler is used in the quilt. The background is quilted in a fine diamond pattern.

For another way to use these appliqué patterns, see the fire screen on page 163.

1 Square = 1 Inch

1 Square = 1 Inch

1 Square = 1 Inch

vines. Then baste together pieced top, batting, and backing; quilt as desired.

The quilt pictured was embellished with diagonal bands of dense quilting. For a similar effect on your own coverlet, work bands of three closely spaced rows of stitches, leaving about 1 inch of unworked fabric between the three-row bands.

❖

EIGHT-PETAL FLOWER QUILT
PAGE 290
Finished size is 88x88 inches

Materials
5¼ yards of muslin for background
2 yards *each* of red and olive green fabrics for appliqués
5 yards of fabric for backing
Batting
Water-soluble marker

Instructions
Each finished block is 17½ inches square. Eight appliquéd blocks alternate with eight quilted muslin blocks across the face of the quilt.

To make one block: Enlarge the pattern, *opposite above,* to size, and transfer to brown paper. Trace the pattern onto an 18½-inch square of muslin, using a water-soluble marker.

Next, trace and cut out paper templates for the main appliqué shapes (pieces A, B, C, and D). For each block, cut one A, eight Bs, and four Ds from red; cut four Cs from green. Also, cut 28 red and 24 green 1-inch circles for the berries, and cut four ½x10-inch bias strips of green fabric to use as stems for the berry clusters. Press under ⅛-inch seam allowances on stems. Baste under seam allowances on all other appliqué pieces.

First, appliqué blossoms (D), petals (B), stems, and berries. Then, stitch the center circle (A) and the green leaves (C) in place,

❖

ROSE TREE QUILT
PAGE 290
Finished size is 86x84 inches

Materials
10½ yards of muslin for background and backing
2½ yards of green, 1½ yards of red, and 1 yard of pink cotton fabric for appliqués
Batting
Water-soluble marking pen

Instructions
Each finished block is 24 inches square. The quilt is composed of eight Rose Tree blocks facing in toward a center block that consists of four branches with blossoms radiating from an open rose. Combine elements from the pattern for the Rose Tree motif, *above,* to create a pattern for the center block.

To make one Rose Tree block: Enlarge pattern to size and transfer to brown paper to make a master pattern. Trace the design onto a 25-inch square of muslin, using a water-soluble marker.

Then, following the master pattern, trace and cut out appliqué shapes for flowers, leaves, and tree trunk. For the berries, cut eight 1-inch-diameter circles from red fabric. Baste under ⅛-inch seam allowances on all pieces.

For the curved branches, cut 1-inch-wide strips of green fabric on the bias. Press under (but do *not* baste) ⅛-inch seam allowances on each side of strip. Pin, baste, and slip-stitch all appliqué pieces in place. Complete the block, remove basting stitches, and clean away traces of water-soluble marker with a damp cloth or a cotton swab dipped in water.

To make a quilt similar to the one pictured on page 290, appliqué a total of eight Rose Tree blocks and one center block, as described above. Add a 7-inch-wide border appliquéd with a design of oak leaves, berries, and concealing raw edges and trimming away excess fabric where shapes overlap.

Complete appliquéd squares; remove basting stitches and remaining traces of marking pen. Piece appliquéd blocks together with plain muslin squares and add a 9-inch-wide border appliquéd with vines and berries.

Baste top together with batting and backing, and quilt as desired.

❖

COXCOMB, OR LOTUS FLOWER, QUILT
PAGE 291
Finished size is 88x74 inches

Materials
5 yards of muslin for background
2 yards *each* of red and green
  fabrics for appliqués
5 yards of fabric for backing
Batting
Water-soluble marker

Instructions
Each finished block is 16 inches square, and measures approximately 22½ inches from corner to corner. Squares are set together on the diagonal and joined with 3½-inch-wide muslin sashings. Triangular pieces (half-blocks) that complete the pattern are embellished with a single appliquéd blossom, stem, and two leaves (see photograph).

Adjust the number of blocks and the size of the sashing strips to create a quilt of the desired dimensions. (The Coxcomb Quilt pictured on page 291 does not include a border, but you may add one to lengthen or widen the quilt, if desired.)

To make one block: Enlarge the pattern, *below right,* to size and transfer to brown paper. Trace the pattern onto a 16½-inch square of muslin, using a water-soluble pen. Next, make templates for each of the five basic appliqué shapes, and trace these shapes onto fabric.

(Continued)

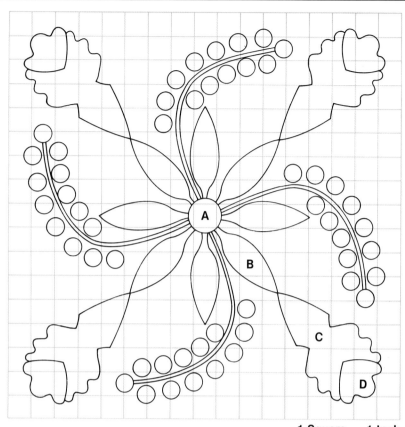

1 Square = 1 Inch

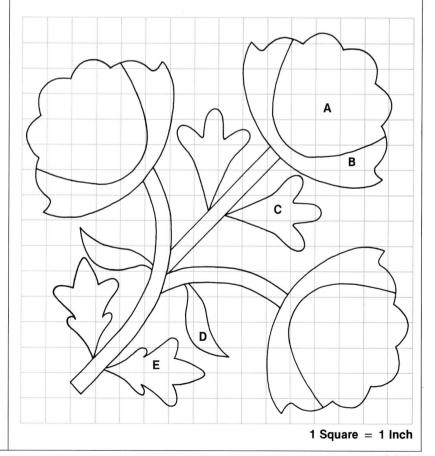

1 Square = 1 Inch

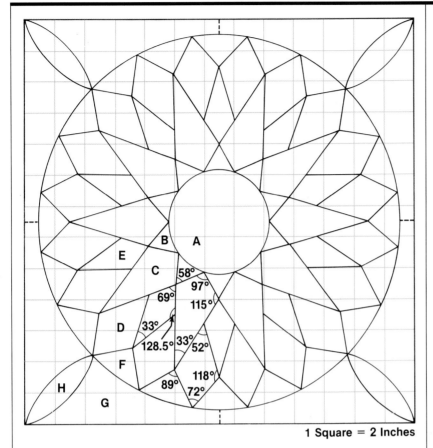

1 Square = 2 Inches

(Continued)

Cut three blossoms (A) from red fabric and cut three B pieces and two each of C, D, and E from green. Baste under ⅛-inch seam allowances on all pieces.

First appliqué the red blossoms (A) in place. Then appliqué the small leaves (pieces C, D, and E) in position. Next cut ¾-inch-wide bias strips of green fabric for the stems. Press ⅛ inch under on each side of the strips; pin and stitch the stems in place.

Finally, appliqué the three B shapes in place to conceal the raw edges of the flower and stem. Remove basting stitches and blue markings used as guidelines for the appliqués.

Complete the desired number of blocks and assemble them with sashing strips into the quilt top. Baste the top, batting, and backing together and quilt as desired.

The quilt pictured on page 291 is embellished with an exceptionally fine overall pattern of simple squares. In addition, an elegant feather pattern is quilted into the sashing strips.

❖

MARINER'S COMPASS QUILT
PAGE 292
Finished size is 78x88 inches.

Materials
9 yards muslin
2¼ yards orange gingham
2⅜ yards green fabric
Quilt batting
Cardboard or plastic lids
Bias tape for binding

Instructions
The quilt consists of nine pieced blocks set in three rows of three blocks each. A 5-inch-wide border edges the top and bottom of the quilt. To piece a larger quilt than the one shown, add another row of blocks to the design or additional borders along the top, bottom, or sides.

You may wish to tint muslin and gingham fabrics using light tan fabric dye to impart an aged appearance to the design. Use high quality dye, follow manufacturer's instructions, and test-dye swatches before coloring fabric to be used for piecing.

Before cutting pieces for the compass, cut from muslin two 45x80-inch strips (backing); set aside. Also cut two 5½x80-inch strips from muslin (borders); set aside.

Next, enlarge the pattern, *left;* cut plastic or cardboard templates for the pattern pieces. *Note:* Careful enlarging and cutting of patterns is essential to the success of this pattern. It's a good idea to use a protractor to check the angles of each of the patterns before cutting templates. Also note that pattern piece D is *not* symmetrical.

Do not add seam allowances to templates. Replace worn templates with new ones so angles are consistent and correct.

To piece one block: Assemble a block to check the accuracy of the patterns. Using a water-erasable pen, trace templates onto wrong side of fabrics, leaving at least ½ inch between pieces to allow for ¼-inch seams. From muslin, cut 1 A, 20 D, and 4 G pieces. From orange gingham, cut 10 *each* of B and E, and 20 of F. From green fabric, cut 10 C and 4 H pieces.

Begin piecing the design in the center. Join pieces by hand or machine, stitching along seam lines *only;* press carefully as you go. When the circular design is complete, join G pieces along the short sides, then set the compass design into the circular opening in the G pieces. Finally, turn under the seam allowance on the H pieces; appliqué them in corners of the block. Make nine blocks.

To assemble the quilt: Join blocks in three rows of three blocks each; sew muslin borders to opposite ends. Cut and appliqué H pieces to border to correspond to pieces on blocks (see photograph).

To finish the quilt, piece muslin backing fabric to size. Layer backing, batting, and pieced top; baste layers together and quilt in closely spaced rows of outline quilting as shown or in the pattern of your choice. Bind edges with bias tape.

FLOWER BASKET QUILT
PAGES 294-295
Finished size is 91x93 inches.

Materials
1 to 1½ yards of solid-color
cottons in each of the following
colors: red, light and dark
pinks, light and dark blues,
lavender and purple, light and
dark browns, light and dark
greens, light and dark oranges,
light and dark yellows, caramel,
gray, and white
8 yards of muslin for pieced top
and borders
7 yards of fabric for backing
Batting

Instructions
Each petit-point pieced block of
the Flower Basket Quilt is 18
inches square and measures approximately 25 inches from corner to corner.

The quilt top is composed of 13
Flower Basket blocks set together
on the diagonal. Corner motifs
have been eliminated from outer
rows of blocks where these blocks
meet borders (see photograph).

The pattern is filled out with
rose motif triangles (not-quite-
half blocks), and framed with a 9-
inch-wide border of pieced vines
and rosebuds.

Each ⅜-inch-square patch of
the design (finished size) is pieced
from two small, right-angle triangles. Because the pieces are so tiny
and the matching of corners and
points is so crucial to the success
of this pattern, it is almost essential that the piecing be done by
hand, rather than by machine.

Before attempting to make an
entire quilt using this intricate and
painstaking method of piecing,
you may wish to practice the petit-point patchwork technique by
piecing a single block of the pattern from larger triangles. For example, using right-angle triangles
that are 1¼ inches long on the
sides adjoining the 90-degree angle and pieced together with ⅛-
inch seams, you can stitch a
48-inch-square block that would

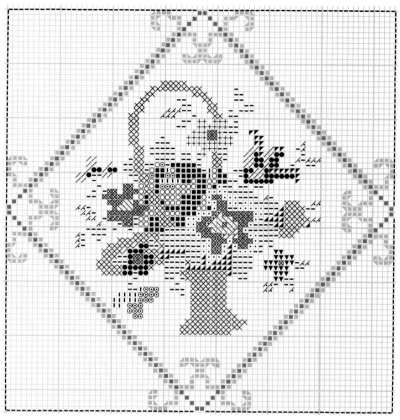

1 Square = 1 Patchwork Square

COLOR KEY
- ◼ **Red/Red**
- ◯ **Pink/Red**
- ◉ **Light Pink/Dark Pink**
- Ⅱ **Light Pink/Light Pink**
- ◪ **Pink/Dark Blue**
- ◩ **Light Blue/Light Blue**
- ◗ **Light Blue/Dark Blue**
- ⊞ **Lavender/Purple**
- ⊡ **White**
- ▦ **Solid Purple**

- ⊠ **Light Brown/Dark Brown**
- ◪ **Dark Brown/Caramel**
- ⊟ **Light Green/Dark Green**
- ◪ **Gray/Light Green**
- ▼ **Light Orange/Dark Orange**
- ◺ **Yellow/Orange**
- ⊠ **Light Yellow/Dark Yellow**
- ◩ **Gray/Yellow**
- ▥ **Solid Light Green**

make a spectacular center medallion for a more conventionally
pieced quilt top. Using smaller triangles or a deeper seam allowance
would result in a smaller square.

To use the pattern: The diagram,
above, is keyed according to each
square (not triangle) in the design.
The color key refers to the two-
color combination used for each
square.

For instance, "Light Brown/
Dark Brown" refers to the squares
that make up the basket, in which

the light brown triangle is on the
upper left and the dark brown on
the lower right. The first color in
each reference is always the upper
left triangle and the second color
is always the lower right. Use solid muslin squares for every block
that is not color keyed.

For the border design between
each block, the darkly shaded
squares are solid purple, and the
lightly shaded squares are light
green. Flop the pattern along dotted lines to complete border motifs for each square.

(Continued)

(Continued)

To make one block: Cut out an ample supply of triangles in the various shades called for in the color key. Then, carefully piece triangles together into squares in color combinations as needed, working row by row, from top to bottom of the pattern. Use ⅛-inch seam allowances throughout.

Stitch each horizontal row of pieced squares together before moving on to the next row. Press seams between triangles toward the darker fabric. Press seams between squares all in one direction, alternating direction from row to row. Press all seams between rows in one direction, either up or down.

Mrs. Snyder's Flower Basket design is quilted only along the diagonals between the blocks (through the purple squares) and around the small square motifs in the corner of each block. Intricate piecing of this sort does not readily lend itself to embellishment with complex quilting patterns.

Once completed, a single Flower Basket block can be incorporated into a quilt top or simply framed. Smaller versions of the design (stitched in needlepoint or embroidery, for example) might be worked into a pillow top, an inset for a piece of clothing (such as the back of a jacket), the front of a tote, or any number of decorative accessories.

❖

FARMYARD QUILT
PAGES 298–300
Finished size is 80x70 inches

Materials
Assorted scraps of wool, silk, cotton, velvet, and brocades in deep, rich colors (about 5 yards total, including at least 2 yards of black wool)
4 yards of lightweight muslin
No. 8 pearl cotton embroidery floss in assorted colors
Hot transfer pencil or dressmaker's carbon paper

Straight Stitch

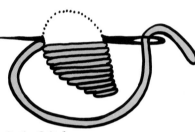

Satin Stitch

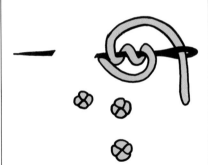

French Knot Stitch

Instructions
Each finished block is 14 inches square and measures approximately 19½ inches from corner to corner.

Mrs. Barrier's design includes 25 elaborately pieced and embroidered blocks set together on the diagonal. The four blocks on either edge of the quilt are shaved to reduce the width of the quilt, and the pattern is filled out with pieced and embroidered triangles (sides) and half-blocks (top and bottom).

All of the blocks are pieced in a random, crazy-quilt pattern, but each block is carefully constructed around a roughly rectangular piece of black wool on which scenes of birds, chickens, bunnies, horses, or other animals are embroidered in soft colors.

To make one block: First, enlarge one of the patterns, *opposite*, to size, and transfer to tracing paper. Use light-colored sewing carbon, a hot transfer pencil, or basting stitches to transfer the basic outlines of the design to the center of a 9x15-inch rectangle of black wool. (For tips on transferring designs, see page 312.)

Embroider the scene in simple straight and satin stitches, using pearl cotton thread. (Refer to stitch diagrams, *left*.) Follow the color scheme suggested by the color photographs of the quilt, or use colors of your choice.
◆ BIRDS IN THE TREE: Use dark brown French knots for the birds' eyes. Work a row of short lazy daisy stitches along the edge of each bird's wings and the tail feathers with a contrasting color. Also work the clusters of buds on the tree in French knots.
◆ HENS AND ROOSTERS: Work the chickens' eyes in brown French knots. Add texture to the fowls' bodies and wings with Mrs. Barrier's inventive woven stitch: First, work the bodies and wings in regular satin stitches. Next, use your needle to weave a double strand of pearl cotton over and under alternating groups of two or three threads on the satin stitching. Repeat the weaving in the opposite direction, working stitches in reverse order under and over sets of threads for a basket-weave effect.

Work the fan-shape tufts of grass at the chickens' feet in straight stitches, using a single strand of pearl cotton.
◆ GAGGLE OF GEESE: Embroider the geese in satin stitches, then embellish the top of each wing with weaving, as described above for the chickens. The geese's eyes are French knots, and

the violetlike flowers are worked in straight stitches.

To turn an embroidered rectangle into a block, trim the rectangle to approximately 8x11 inches, adjusting the size and shape to accommodate the embroidered surface. Baste the trimmed shape to the center of a 15-inch square of lightweight muslin. Piece out the block, using scraps of wool, silk, brocade, medium-weight cottons, and velvets. Study photographs on pages 298 and 300 for piecing and color arrangements. (For more information on constructing a crazy-patch block, see pages 240-241.)

When the block is completely pieced, embellish the seams between each piece of the patch with rows of decorative stitches in various shades of pearl cotton.

Once you've mastered the piecing and stitchery techniques used on Mittie Barrier's farmyard quilt, and completed one or more of the patterns illustrated here, experiment with your own adaptations of other designs pictured in the quilt on page 299. Or, try your hand at sketching your own versions of homey scenes to embellish squares for your quilt.

Piece completed squares into the quilt top, using ½-inch seams for strength. Embellish seams with more decorative stitchery.

Line the pieced top with cotton or a lightweight blanket and tack together the top and backing. (Crazy quilts are rarely quilted beyond the lavish stitchery on the pieced surface, and batting would make the piece too bulky.)

For a contemporary patchwork interpretation of these delightful motifs, turn to page 206.

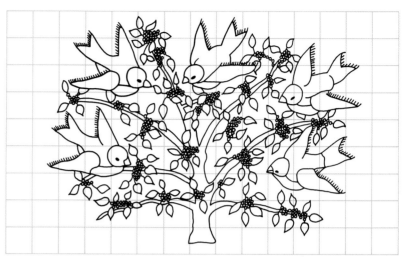

1 Square = 1 Inch

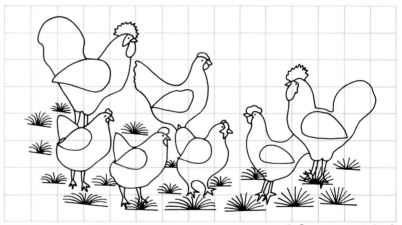

1 Square = 1 Inch

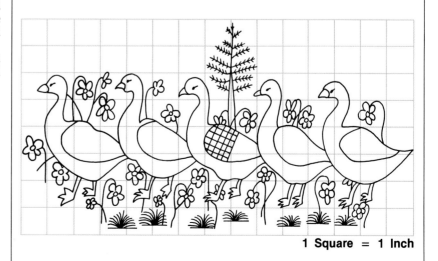

1 Square = 1 Inch

ENLARGING AND TRANSFERRING DESIGNS

Once you've mastered these simple techniques for enlarging and transferring patterns, the design sources for patchwork are limitless. Besides the patterns printed in books and magazines, you'll be able to adapt ideas from snapshots, posters, postcards, art books, kids' books—almost anything.

ENLARGING DESIGNS

Most designs in this book are printed smaller than actual size and must be enlarged before they can serve as workable patterns. For best results, follow the suggestions below.

Patterns with grids

A majority of the patterns in this book are printed on grids—small squares laid over the design. To translate these drawings into working patterns, you must transfer the design onto a larger grid that you have drawn on a piece of paper, using the scale indicated on the pattern as a guide.

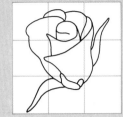

The original design

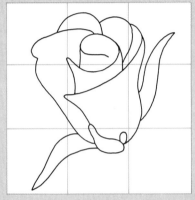

The enlarged design

For example, if the indicated scale is "1 square = 1 inch," draw a series of 1-inch squares on the work sheet and use this grid to enlarge the pattern to size. (To avoid drawing your own scaled grids, purchase graph paper for your work sheets.)

To form a working grid for pattern enlargement, count the number of horizontal and vertical rows on the original pattern. With a ruler, mark off the same number of horizontal and vertical rows on your grid paper.

To enlarge the pattern, locate a square on your working grid that corresponds to one of the squares on the original pattern (lower left-hand corner, for example). Mark your working grid with a dot wherever a design line intersects a grid line on the original pattern.

For best results, visually divide every grid line into fourths to gauge whether the design line cuts the grid at the halfway point or somewhere in between.

To sketch in the new, enlarged pattern on your working grid, simply connect the dots. Sketch lightly, using a soft pencil, until

the new, enlarged pattern duplicates the lines on the original pattern. (See the drawings, *left.*)

To further alter the size of any design printed on a grid, adjust the *scale* of the working grid. For example, if the instructions call for enlarging the pattern onto a grid of 1-inch squares, but you want your finished project to be 25 percent larger than called for in the instructions, simply draw a working grid of 1¼-inch squares.

Similarly, to reduce a pattern, make a working grid with squares that are proportionately *smaller* than the squares on the original grid. Then sketch the new, smaller pattern on the scaled-down grid.

Patterns without grids

Many patterns do not appear with an enlargement grid and scale measurements, such as children's drawings, postcard pictures, and book and magazine illustrations.

To cope with this minor inconvenience, create your own reusable grid from a thin sheet of clear acrylic (available in art supply shops). Use a fine-point, smudge-proof pen to mark off a grid of ½-inch squares on the acrylic. Tape this see-through grid over the design you wish to enlarge or reduce. (You also may wish to make a grid of ¼-inch squares for use with very small designs and another with 1-inch squares for larger designs.)

To determine the scale for your kraft or tissue paper working grid, first decide on the size you want the finished project to be, then draw the working grid accordingly. For example, to transfer a 3-inch-square design to a 12-inch square for a pillow front, the squares on the working grid must be *four times* as large as the ½-inch squares on your acrylic grid. Each square on the acrylic grid will correspond to a 2-inch square on the working grid. Once you have drawn the working grid, enlarge the pattern as described above.

Photographic enlargements

Three methods of enlarging patterns do not require the grid work described above. They do, however, require special equipment or a modest outlay of cash.

One method is to take a photograph of the pattern, using high-contrast black-and-white slide film. Project the slide onto a piece of paper taped to a wall and adjust the image to the desired size, then trace the pattern onto the paper. (A variation of this technique is used for Becky Jerdee's fabric portraits on pages 252-253. For complete instructions, see page 260.)

Another way is to check with local libraries and schools for an opaque projector you can borrow or rent. To use the opaque projector, slip the scaled-down pattern into the projector. Then, use the projector to transfer the pattern image onto a wall. Trace the projected image onto a piece of paper taped to the wall.

A third method is to go to a blueprint or photo reproduction shop and have the pattern enlarged photographically (often while you wait). Ask for a "positive copy" of the design, specifying the finished dimensions. This is the easiest way to enlarge a design, but it may be costly, depending on the percentage of enlargement.

TRANSFERRING DESIGNS

Once you have adapted a design to the desired size, transfer the pattern from paper to fabric, using one of the methods described below. Choose a method that's compatible with the specific materials you're using. All tools described below are available at the notions counter in most fabric stores.

Dressmaker's carbon paper

Dressmaker's carbon (*not* typist's carbon) comes in a range of colors, from yellow to black. Select a color that is as close as possible to the color of the fabric you intend to mark, yet still visible.

Place the carbon facedown between the pattern and fabric, and trace over the design, using a tracing wheel or an empty ballpoint pen. Use just enough pressure to transfer the design to the fabric, without tearing the pattern. Dressmaker's carbon does not always wash out easily, so it is best used to mark cutting lines only, or to mark stitching lines that will be concealed on the finished project.

Hot transfer pencil

Transfer pencils are particularly useful for transferring appliqué designs to fabrics that are too dark or opaque to trace through and for transferring complex designs (embroidery details, for example) to the right side of smooth-surfaced fabrics, such as linens or cottons.

Always keep the transfer pencil sharp so that lines do not blur. Lightly trace the outlines of the design onto the *back* of the paper pattern. Then position the pattern, transfer side down, on the fabric and iron the design in place, being careful not to scorch the fabric. (Check package directions accompanying the pencil for appropriate heat settings.) Strive for a line that is heavy enough to see, but faint enough not to show when your project is complete.

It's a good idea to test your transfer pencil on scrap fabric before you begin a project, because the color deposited on the fabric does not always fade when the article is washed or dry-cleaned.

Washable needlework pen

This is a light blue felt-tip marker especially designed for needlecrafts. Use the pen to draw or trace a design onto light-colored fabrics. Work the design, and when you are finished, simply dampen the fabric and the lines disappear. This pen is ideal for tracing designs on sheer to medium-weight fabrics, or for sketching designs freehand.

Basting

This is an efficient way to transfer design lines to dark, soft, highly textured, stretchy, or sheer fabrics. Use this technique to transfer designs when the methods explained above won't work.

First draw the pattern onto tracing paper and pin the paper pattern to the fabric. Hand- or machine-baste along the design lines, then tear away the paper and proceed with the project. When you've finished with the project, remove the basting stitches (if they are not covered by appliqué or stitchery).

PROTECTING PATTERNS

Once you've enlarged, reduced, traced, and otherwise translated a favorite design into a workable pattern, keep a clean copy or master pattern of the design for possible future use.

If you plan to transfer the pattern using carbon paper, a hot transfer pencil, or the basting method—all of which tend to damage the original pattern sheet—take time to make a second pattern for use in the transfer process. Use your master pattern to record color and fabric notations, mark adjustments, or note areas that presented special difficulties in execution.

Finally, avoid folding patterns whenever possible. Small patterns tuck handily into file folders, manila envelopes, or a loose-leaf binder.

Larger patterns may be rolled around, or tucked into, long cardboard tubes. Use wrapping paper tubes, or purchase a few sturdy mailing tubes from the local art supply shop. For convenience, label each tube with the names of the patchwork patterns enclosed.

Commonly Used Patchwork Terms

ALBUM QUILT—A quilt assembled from individual blocks, each designed and/or executed by a different person. Album blocks are appliquéd or pieced (or both), and frequently stitched into quilts by a group for presentation to a public figure to commemorate a special occasion. Blocks often are signed and dated by the maker in India ink or embroidery. (Also called Presentation Quilt.)

APPLIQUÉ—Derived from the French *appliquer*, meaning "to apply" or "to lay on." Appliquéd patchwork consists of small fabric shapes stitched by hand or machine to a background fabric to form a design. Traditional appliqué designs feature realistic motifs, including birds, flowers, and baskets of fruit, as well as stylized houses, figures, and animals.

AUTOGRAPH QUILT—A form of Album Quilt, in which the central decorative element on each block is a signature—either that of the maker or of a famous person. The individual blocks of an autograph quilt frequently are pieced, rather than appliquéd, and they often feature a center square or rectangle on which a signature is embroidered, quilted, or inscribed in india ink.

In an Autograph Quilt, all of the blocks usually are stitched in the same pattern, although fabrics may vary from block to block.

BACKING—The bottom layer of a quilt or any patchwork project with a front and back or right and wrong sides. The backing fabric generally is pieced to size from solid-color or print fabric that complements but does not compete with the pieced or appliquéd top.

BATTING—The most common term for the filler, or middle layer, inserted between the top and backing of a quilt or other patchwork project. Batting (also called a quilt batt) adds insulation and warmth and lends dimension to the quilted surface.

BIAS—The diagonal line (in contrast to the straight grain) of a woven fabric. Cloth cut on the bias stretches easily, and consequently, bias strips are especially useful for piping, binding, and narrow appliqué shapes (such as flower stems) that will be manipulated into graceful curves and yet lie flat when stitched in place.

BINDING—The method used to finish the raw edges of a quilt or other textile sandwich. Edges may be bound by covering them with strips of bias-cut fabric, by turning the top or backing edges to the opposite side and slip-stitching in place, or by folding both top and bottom edges toward the inside of the sandwich and sewing them together.

BLOCK—One complete unit of a quilt pattern (usually a square), composed of a single patch or several smaller shapes sewn together. (Also called a pattern block.)

BORDERS—Horizontal and vertical strips of fabric stitched onto a quilt top to frame the finished design. Not all old quilts have borders. On many, particularly those with overall repeat designs, the pattern extends to the binding. Amish quilt designs, on the other hand, often feature two or three broad borders in different colors, set one within the other, making an effective frame for a center medallion design.

BRIDAL QUILT—Traditionally, a young woman was expected to complete a dowry of 13 quilts before her wedding day. A girl usually pieced and quilted the first dozen quilts herself, beginning as a child with a simple one-patch design and progressing to more complex patterns as her stitchery skills improved.

But the thirteenth, or Bridal, quilt was supposed to be a masterpiece, and the design and piecing of this often was not begun until the young lady was actually engaged.

In many communities, it was considered unlucky for the bride-to-be to stitch the bridal or wedding quilt herself. So after she had completed the piecing and appliqué work, her friends quilted the finished top to celebrate her betrothal. Many nineteenth-century bridal quilts were either elaborate appliquéd designs or white-on-white masterpieces, featuring intricate quilted patterns stitched in white thread atop a white background. (Also called Marriage or Wedding Quilt.)

COMFORTER—Usually refers to a fairly thick textile sandwich, with 3 to 4 inches of fluffy batting, rather than the $\frac{1}{4}$- to $\frac{3}{4}$-inch-thick filler common to most quilts. Because of the thickness of the filler, which makes stitching through all three layers especially difficult, comforters are usually tufted or tied, rather than quilted.

COVERLET—A small quilt or a quilted throw.

CRAZY QUILT—A form of patchwork popular during the last quarter of the nineteenth and first decade of the twentieth centuries, in which pieces of fabric of various colors and textures, in irregular shapes and sizes, are stitched together in a random pattern. The shapes frequently are outlined and embellished with elaborate embroidery.

FILLER—*(See BATTING.)*

FREEDOM QUILT—A quilt prepared specifically to commemorate a young man's coming of age (his twenty-first birthday) or the completion of an apprenticeship. A popular custom in nineteenth-century pioneer communities, Freedom quilts usually were stitched as a gift by all the women among a young man's family and friends. They often incorporated scraps of the young man's outgrown clothing, as well as scraps of eligible young ladies' prettiest dresses by way of remembrance.

FRIENDSHIP QUILT—Another variation of the Album or Presentation Quilt, but usually stitched for a friend, neighbor, or family member, rather than for a public figure.

GRAIN—The directions in which the warp and woof threads lie in woven fabric. Warp threads are parallel to the selvage; woof threads are perpendicular to warp threads.

Whenever possible, geometric shapes used for patchwork should be cut so that at least one edge runs parallel to the grain of the fabric. (See BIAS.)

LATTICE STRIPS—(See SASHES.)

LOFT—The height, puffiness, and resiliency of a quilt batt or other filler.

MITER—To join two pieces of fabric so that the ends or edges meet to form a perfect right angle (usually refers to sashing or border strips).

PATCHWORK—A generic term referring to the process by which pieces of fabric of various shapes and colors are assembled to form a new textile surface; also refers to the results of that process (includes both piecing and appliqué techniques).

PIECED WORK—A form of patchwork in which pieces of fabric—usually straight-edge, geometric shapes (squares, rectangles, triangles, or diamonds)—are sewn together to form a design.

QUILT—The process of joining together a fabric sandwich (consisting of a top, bottom, and filler) with rows or patterns of hand or machine stitches. Quilting stitches always are taken through all three layers of material.

The term "quilt" also designates the result of this process: a fabric sandwich that has either been quilted with a pattern of small running stitches or tufted with lengths of floss or yarn.

QUILTING FRAME—A large, usually rectangular frame on which a quilt top, filling, and backing are assembled and stretched taut for quilting. Traditionally, the frame is assembled from long strips of wood or young saplings and held together with clamps or pegs at the corners.

Sometimes the frame was suspended by a system of pulleys from a cabin ceiling, and sometimes it rested upon log legs or sawhorses, but in either case it generally was large enough for at least six and sometimes as many as a dozen or more women to sit around it and stitch on a stretched-out quilt during an old-fashioned quilting bee.

Although such frames were a staple of pioneer households, modern homes rarely have space to accommodate a full-size quilting frame. Compact frames are available, but today many quilters prefer to use a quilting hoop (a large, circular embroidery hoop), or they adopt the quilt-as-you-go, or lap-quilting method, in which each block of the design is quilted (with filler and backing) before the blocks are assembled to form the completed quilt.

SASHES, OR SASHING—Strips of fabric (usually 1 to 4 inches wide) used to join together completed blocks to form a quilt top. Many quilt designs, particularly those with self-contained pattern blocks, need sashing strips to set off each patchwork block. Others, particularly overall patterns such as Ocean Waves, are best stitched block to block without sashes so the pattern from one block seems to flow into the next.

SET—The arrangement of completed pattern blocks, sashing strips, and borders when they are stitched together to form the quilt top. The process of arranging the blocks is called "setting together."

TEMPLATE—A pattern shape made of paper, plastic, cardboard, or metal; used to trace shapes for appliqué or piecing and to ensure consistency in repeat shapes.

Templates are of two sorts—with and without seam allowances. Experienced patchworkers may prefer to trace the actual stitching lines for each pattern piece and to estimate the seam allowance when cutting out each shape. Novices may prefer to use a double set of templates, first tracing the outlines of a larger shape that includes seam allowances, and then positioning and tracing a smaller shape inside to mark stitching lines.

TOP—A completed patchwork design that is intended for use as the top or right side of a quilt, but that has not yet been joined to filler and backing. (Also called pieced top or quilt top.)

TUFTING—This is one of the simplest ways of attaching the three layers of a quilt (top, filler, and backing) together. Several strands of thread, floss, or yarn are drawn two or three times through all three layers of the quilt and knotted or tied off. These tufts are repeated at regular intervals across the surface of the quilt to keep the layers from shifting or bunching. (Also called "tying," as in "tied quilt.")

WHOLE CLOTH QUILT—A quilt or coverlet of which the top layer consists of a single piece of fabric or a surface pieced entirely from the same fabric, usually white or a solid color. The surface pattern on a whole cloth quilt is achieved entirely with intricate quilting.

All-white whole cloth quilts often were made as bridal quilts or marriage gifts.

CREDITS

We would like to express our gratitude and appreciation to the many people who helped us with this book. Our heartfelt thanks go to each of the artists and artisans who enthusiastically contributed designs, ideas, and projects. Thanks, also, to the photographers whose creative talents and technical skills added much to the book.

In addition, we are happy to acknowledge our indebtedness to the companies, collectors, needlecrafters, and others who generously shared their patchwork pieces with us, stitched projects, or in some other way contributed to the book.

DESIGNERS

Donna Barnett—wall hanging, 13

Taresia Boernke—bear, 98; lion, bear, and tiger toys, 110–111; alphabet, 112–113

Gary Boling—quilt, 200; coverlet and pillows, 208–209

Jackie Curry—quilt, 134

Ruth DeCook—star quilt, 145

Barbara Dotze—pictures, 115

Duncan Enterprises—ceramics, 66

Linda Emmerson—floorcloth, 63; stencil, 68

Mary Engelbreit—quilt design, 110–111

Debbie Felton—frames, 43–45; tablecloth and napkins, 66; boxes, 87

Diane Gilman—skirt, 275

Arlette Gosieski—appliqué paintings, 14–17.

Carol Vanderpool Hall—floor-cloth and pillows, 220

Diane Hayes—bunny, house, teddy bear, clown, and bead designs for quilt, 96–97

Judith Wasserman Hearst—wall hanging, 184

Laura Holtorf Collins—cross-stitch inserts, 43–45; table and cross-stitch shutters, 49; sheets and pillowcase, 64; apron insert, 66; footstool, 71; pictures, 128–129; headboard, 141; wall hanging, 232; pillows, 234; pillow, 241; jacket, 270; lapel embroidery, 274

Madge Huntington—collage, 251

Rebecca Jerdee—pillows, 23; pillows and curtain, 34; wooden trivets, 46; boxes, place mats, and candle holders, 60–61; doll stroller, 63; chair, 64; pillows, 68; mirror frame and curtains, 71; screen, 88; tablecloth, 89; quilt, 151; all projects, 252–259

Carolee Knutson—quilts, 6–9

Carol Maguire—paint-and-stitch projects, 18–21; wall hanging, 95; baby quilt, 99; fan quilt, 166; wall hanging, 187; pinwheel quilt and headboard, 198–199

Janet McCaffrey—Mother Goose quilt, 100–101; rose designs, 204–205

Barbara O'Connor—heart quilt, 60–61; wall quilt, 84

Mary Ostlund—firescreen, 163 and 170

Jan Peterson—clown, 101

Bette Prighoff—pillows, 216–217

Robin Rice—doll, 50

Mimi Shimmin—felt appliqués, 268–269

Margaret Sindelar—slipcover, 29

Ciba Vaughan—place mats, 24; tablecloth and chair cushions, 26; blanket and pillows, 35; child's dress, 50; sweater, 125; album cover, 173; wall hanging, 219; hutch motifs, 221; wall hanging, 222; clothing, 272–273 and 276–277

Jim Woland—straight furrow quilt, 80–81; pictures, 81; table mat, 82; table runner, 90

Ruth Wrightam—quilt, 218

PHOTOGRAPHERS

Darwin D. Bearley—152–153

Peter Bosch—188

Ross Chapple—12, 13, 172, 182–183

George de Gennaro—22–23, 230–231

Mike Dieter—13, 96–97, 98, 100, 101, 110–111, 112, 113, 114–115, 134, 151, 163, 170, 173, 186, 208–209, 222, 255, 256, 273

Harry Hartman—202–203, 252–253

Bill Hedrich, Hedrich-Blessing—282–283, 284–285, 286, 287, 288, 289, 290–291, 292, 293, 294, 295, 296, 297, 298, 299, 300

Jim Hedrich, Hedrich-Blessing—18, 19, 20, 21, 28, 95, 99, 166, 187, 198, 204–205, 220, 254, 255, 256, 257, 258, 259, 270, 271

Sandi Hedrich, Hedrich-Blessing—6–7, 40–41, 80–81, 94–95, 124–125, 140–141, 162–163, 180–181, 250–251

Thomas Hooper—Cover, 10, 11, 34, 43, 44–45, 69, 70, 71, 82, 89, 90, 114, 125, 142–143, 146–147, 164, 168, 181, 184, 216–217, 268, 272, 275, 276, 277

Hopkins Associates—25, 27, 41, 49, 68, 81, 83, 85, 91, 127, 131, 133, 135, 165, 167, 169, 171, 190, 206–207, 219, 221, 232, 233, 239, 277

Mike Jensen—23, 24, 31, 50, 51, 60–61, 84, 87

Scott Little, 26, 30, 32, 33, 46, 63, 64, 66, 88, 115, 200

Bruce McAllister—14, 15, 16, 17

Bradley Olman—152–153, 174

Maris/Semel—35

Joseph Standart—150, 185, 189

Perry Struse—7, 9, 29, 47, 48, 62, 65, 67, 86, 126, 128–129, 132, 141, 144, 145, 148–149, 218, 234–235, 236, 237, 238, 240–241, 273

ACKNOWLEDGMENTS

Appalachian Fireside Crafts
Main Street
P.O. Box 319
Berea, KY 40403

Ginger Bassett

Barbara Bergman

Steven B. Coulter

Joan Cravens

Mr. and Mrs. Thomas Delach

Phyllis Dunstan

Kathy Engle

Mr. and Mrs. Marshall Fredericks

Donna Glas

Bryce and Donna Hamilton

Karen Hunter

International Printworks, Inc.
100 Wells Avenue,
Newton, MA 02159

James O. Keene

Susan Knight

Mrs. Bruce Kresge

Nancy Lindemeyer

Locust Grove
561 Blankenbaker Lane
Louisville, KY 40207

Meadow Brook Hall
Oakland University
Rochester, MI 48063

Judy Murphy

Sally and Peter Riffle

Diane Schultz

Becky Senti
Country Sampler Ltd.
Story City, IA 50248

Catherine B. Shoe

Patricia Smith and Alan Alovus
American Quilts and Textiles
Route 1, Box 301
Celina, TN 38551

Nancy Starr

Stearns Technical Textiles Co.
Mountain Mist
Consumer Products
100 Williams Street
Cincinnati, OH 45215

Lois Stulberg

Barbara Wanke
Heronbrook Antiques
1920 North Clark Street
Chicago, IL 60614

Mike Wiggs

Judy Williamson

Jean Wood

Woodlawn Plantation
Mount Vernon, VA 22121

Nellie Yost

W–Z

R–S

T–V